ALONG THE JOURNEY

Mark O. Wilbanks

Praise for *Along the Journey*

Who among us doesn't need a lift each day to face all that life throws at us? And some days are more debilitating than others? For those of us who are always looking for something that will give us that lift, we can turn to the musings of Mark Wilbanks, who in this devotional book provides us with faith stories and examples that remind us we aren't alone in our struggles. There is a Holy Presence that abides with us, and with it the grace that will see us through.

Doug Dortch
Minister, Captiva Chapel by the Sea, Captiva, FL

Dr. Wilbanks is a well-respected pastor, encourager, and writer. His creativity, humor, and common sense always takes the reader to a good place—a little closer to Jesus.

Dr. Jon K. Duncan
Senior Professor of Worship and Music
Southwestern Baptist Theological Seminary, Fort Worth, TX

Dr. Wilbanks has the unique (and somewhat rare) ability to teach deep theological and Biblical truth in a way that is so palpable to any reader or hearer. To dissect the Living Word of God into a daily consumption of life has been a blessing to so many over the course of his life...especially me. Thank you Mark for being a friend and mentor...this book will do the same for you.

Dr. Jeff Duke
University of Central Florida, 3D Institute
Fellowship of Christian Athletes

As a beloved pastor, an illustrative preacher, a seasoned traveler, and an insightful writer, Mark Wilbanks has a knack for sharing stories that bring truth to life in ways that are heart-warming and soul-nurturing. Whether you read it from cover to cover, or you use it as a devotional resource, I have a hunch that this book will bring out the best in you.

Dr. Barry Howard
Senior Pastor, The Church at Wieuca, Atlanta, Georgia

Mark's writings and quick wit have me in tears in one paragraph and laughing in the next. His wisdom expressed through his writings touches the heart, inspires the mind, and results in a greater depth of love for God and grace to others.

Linda Leathers
President, Operation Andrew Group

I have been privileged to call Mark Wilbanks friend for over four decades. In this wonderful collection of essays, stories, devotions, and random musings, Mark displays the wit and wisdom that are the hallmarks of a pastoral and preaching career spanning half a century. His commentary on and insights into life and a flawed humanity are pithy, poignant, and frequently hilarious! He will make you laugh and cry ... sometimes in the same paragraph! But at the heart of all his stories is the reminder that life is a precious gift of God, a journey made more pleasant if we put our faith in Him and treat our fellow sojourners with grace and love.

Cindy Graves
Ministry Assistant to the Pastor
Aspire Church San Marco, Jacksonville, FL

Dedication

Over forty-seven years of ministry, I have had the privilege of serving churches in Kentucky, Florida, Georgia, and Alabama. My wife Kim and I are profoundly grateful for treasured relationships and life-changing moments. This book is a compilation of years of devotionals, weekly columns, sermons, and articles. With the encouragement of family and friends, I dedicate this work to the glory of God.

Mark O. Wilbanks

© 2023 Mark Wilbanks

All rights reserved. No part of this publication may be reproduced, stored in a retrieval system or transmitted in any form or by any means, electronic, mechanical, photocopying, recording or otherwise without the prior permission of the publisher or in accordance with the provisions of the Copyright, Designs and Patents Act 1988 or under the terms of any license permitting limited copying issued by the Copyright Licensing Agency.

ISBN: 979-8-8690-4997-1

Printed in the USA

Table of Contents

Foreword 1
What Are You Going to Do About It? 7
The Power of Grace 8
The Gift of Grace 9
Where to Turn 10
Who's Driving This Car? 11
You Don't Have That Kind of Time 13
A Watched Pot Never Boils 14
Life In the Spirit 15
Aim High 17
Ticktock 18
A Monument Worth Building 19
I'm Glad I'm Not Like That Guy 20
One Man's Junk 21
Wish I'd Thought of That 22
Closer Than You Think 23
Impact 25
There's a Pill for That 26
Opportunity 27
The Folly of Predicting 28
Feel His Pleasure 30
"Why Are You Working in the Dark?" 31
I'm Only Human 32
Eureka! 33
How Tall Are You? 35
Through the Eyes of a Child 36

Live Free!	37
Love Lines	38
Honor Those Who Have Gone Before Us	39
Not Quite Right	40
Hope Springs Eternal	42
It's Worth It	43
Reboot	44
Never Forget	45
Mismatches	46
Rocking Our World	47
It's Not a Sprint	49
Say What You Mean, Mean What You Say	50
Can You Top That?	52
Don't Do That!	53
Missed Opportunities	54
Slow Is Good	55
Salt of the Earth	56
Doing Grace	58
Ups, Not Downs	58
Disappointment	60
Thy Word Have I Hid in My Heart	61
It Seemed Like a Good Idea at the Time	62
Clothes Make the Man?	63
Excuses	65
Serve the Lord With Gladness	66
Making Sense of Suffering	67
Follow the Leader	69
His Eye Is On the Sparrow	70

Believe It or Not	72
I'm Dreaming, Right?	74
Spin	75
Just One Little Letter	76
My Hero	77
Spring Brake	79
Making it personal	81
You Matter	82
He Should've Looked Up	83
Rich!	85
Warning Signs	86
It Can't Happen to Me!	87
Imagine	89
Courage	90
Grave Crisis	91
Failure	93
Awkward	94
No Rain	96
"I'm Old Enough"	97
Leave a Mark	99
Once Upon a Time	100
Perspective	102
Triumph in Tragedy	103
Just for Peanuts	104
Motivation	105
Limits	107
So Close	108
Make Up Your Mind	110

It Used to Be Funny 112
Habits..113
The Power of One 114
Life Happens 115
Name That Tune 117
Just a Sinner Like Me 118
Make No Little Plans 119
For Heaven's Sake...120
Wish I Had Thought of That...122
Views of God..123
Be Where Your Feet Are 125
God Is Faithful; Let's Join Him 126
Sure, I Can See That 127
A Piece of Rock 128
Sacrifice..129
Respect...131
They're Not Dumb, You Know...132
Assuming 133
86,400 135
Another Year, Another Opportunity.....................................136
Signs 137
The Positive Side of "You're Not Good Enough" 139
You Can Count On It 140
Can It Get Darker? 141
Who's Flying This Plane?...143
These Guys Are Good 144
Are We There Yet? 146
Aim High 147

Slow Down	148
Change	150
Transitions	151
What If?	153
Now, Where Did I Put That?	154
On Time	156
You Shall Know the Truth	157
Jesus Loves the Little Children	158
Wishes Come True?	160
What Did You Say?	162
Missed Opportunities	163
Why Not Now?	164
Melting Pot or Fiery Cauldron?	166
Reaching the Bleachers	167
Flopping	169
Making Your Mark	170
Well, What's It Going to Be?	172
Well, You See	173
Weary and Wary of the Storm	174
Humility	175
Just How Old Are You?	176
A Helping Hand	178
The Joys of Childhood	179
What's Up With All These Snakes?	180
Leadership	182
A Great American	183
The Perils of Political Correctness	184
You Gotta Cheer for the Underdog	186

Is That Right?..187

911...188

Okay, God, Please Be You...190

Starting Over 192

A Blast From the Past..193

Crutches...194

God Will See It..195

No, You Don't Have To 196

Beside Myself 198

Things You Shouldn't Say...200

You Can't Get There From Here 202

In Every Frame 203

How Does He Do That? 204

The Lost Art of Waiting 205

Goldmedalitis..207

Coke What? 208

Life In the Lions' Den 210

Lessons Learned?...211

Glad You Noticed 212

Is Jesus There? 213

I Quit! 214

Anything But Cheap 215

Contentment 217

What About Me? 218

Not One of Your Better Days..219

"Slow Church Ahead"..221

The Dash Between the Dates 222

Shallow Places 224

Life Stewardship	225
Body Life	226
Present	227
Joy	229
Transcendent	230
Motivation	231
Put the Device Down	232
Because It's There	234
Here's to You, Mom	235
Run the Play	236
The Real Thing	237
A Godly Man	239
Dreaming Big	240
Strength in Numbers	242
The One You Feed	243
If I Could Ask Him Just One Question	244
Whatcha Makin'?	245
What We Leave Out	247
"I Used To…"	248
The Gracious Hand of God	249
The Butterfly Effect	250
You Think We Have Problems	252
Advanced in Years	253
Measuring the Heart	254
Freedom and Faith	255
Intersections	257
The Value of Inheritance	258
We Are Family	259

Just Google It 260

It's About Time 262

The Perfect Family 263

Maybe, Maybe Not 264

Years Gone By 266

Stylish Bomb Shelters 267

Who Would You Rather Be? 268

Thumbs Up! 269

Windows to the World 270

I Got Nothin' 271

Better Together 273

Who's On First? 274

Make Me a Fire 275

Healthy Ego 277

Crackpots 278

Time Change 279

Acting Like the Rest of Us 280

Who Are You Supposed to Be? 281

The Cup of Wonder 282

It Sounded Like a Good Idea at the Time 283

Tapestry 285

In My Seat 286

For the Bible Tells Me So 287

"You're Not Wearing That?" 289

And Jesus Had Compassion 290

When Is It Over? 292

Amazing Grace 293

Of Course I Pray 295

Whoops!	296
The Empty Chair	297
Where Is the Body?	298
Won't You Be My Neighbor?	300
Live This Day	301
Heavens to Betsy!	302
It Used to Be a Church	303
Rise Up, O Church of God!	304
A Walk in the Dark	305
Press On	307
Unstoppable	308
Expanding My World	309
Stick the Landing	310
Blessed	311
"And Another Thing…"	313
Gotcha!	314
Who's in Charge Here?	315
If It's Up to Me…	317
"I'm So Glad You Came"	318
Any Color You Want	320
Please Get It Right	321
Changing Lives	323
Freedom	324
What Do You Need?	325
Living the Dream	326
The Right Thing, the Godly Thing	328
A Gatekeeper in the House of the Lord	329
Dumb Things You Say…or Do…or Think	330

There's an App for That	332
"You're Not the One I Wanted."	333
Give Him the Glory	335
April 15	336
Point Guard	338
Halftime	339
Win At All Cost?	341
Every Life is Precious	342
MRE's	344
Remembering	345
Remember Memorial Day	346
D-Day Remembered	347
America	348
A Day That Changed History	349
A Soldier's Story	351
Labor Day	352
"Almost" Isn't There	353
Veteran's Day	355
Sacrifice	356
Freedom	357
I Pledge Allegiance	358
Vacation Bible School	360
What Will They Say Next?	361
You Gotta Go	363
Growing Up	363
Through the Eyes of a Child	365
All You Need is Love	366
The Silly Season	367

Hidden Treasures	368
A Gift for Mom	370
Don't Forget Thanksgiving	371
Silence	372
Give Thanks	374
Extra! Extra! Read All About It!	375
Give Thanks	376
I Want, I Want	378
I'm So Busy!	378
Thank Him	380
What's It Worth to You?	381
Look What I Found!	382
Time and Eternity	383
Show Up	384
The Word Became Flesh	386
A Story Worth Telling	387
Hope For the Bad Guys	387
Almost Forgotten	389
CHRISTmas	390
A Man of Many Names	391
A Tribute to the Grieving	393
The Journey that Changed the World	393
Almost Made It	395
A Love Story	396
The Best Christmas Ever	397
Light Out of Darkness	399
Reflections on Christmas	400
Roses for Mom	401

Whaddya Get?..402
Now What?...403
Have You Got the Time?..404
Things I Learned from My Dad 407
Respect Dads...409
The Perfect Father 411
A Reason for Honor 411
Father's Day 414
Notes and Reflections..415

Foreword

In the heart of Florence, Alabama nestled beneath the shade of towering oak trees stood an old beautiful two-story house that held the keys to my fondest childhood memories. 518 North Cherry Street, a place where time seemed to slow down, and the world felt so peaceful and tranquil all the time. It was our grandmother's house, and it was a haven of nostalgia and comfort, an embodiment of southern charm that etched itself into my soul from an early age. With its old red brick siding and a welcoming front porch adorned with a metal glider and wooden rockers, it exuded a timeless grace that drew me then, as it does even today, like a magnet. It was a house that had witnessed the passage of time with much grace and dignity.

Surrounded by a tree lined neighborhood, our grandmother's house was a sanctuary of serenity with sidewalks that beckoned us to explore the surrounding historic district, where stories of the past seemed to linger in the very air we breathed. The streets and sidewalks were perfect for riding our bikes, our childish imaginations fueled by the stories we imagined of a few mysterious houses we were certain inhabited ghosts.

In just a stone's throw away, the city high school loomed as what seemed like a massive structure. We would hear the school bell chime, and on Friday nights we could hear the crowds at the football games, a reminder of the world beyond our grandmother's house, but we felt content and safe within the cocoon of our ideal surroundings.

Venturing a little further, we could stroll or ride our bikes into the heart of the downtown shopping district. Here, quaint store shops lined the streets, our favorite being the historic and still standing Trowbridge's Ice Cream and Soda Fountain. We moved around carelessly as it was a place where time and tradition coexisted, harmoniously with the old, historic building.

But the true magic lay within the walls of 518 North Cherry Street. It was a place where my two brothers and three cousins would gather as often as the holiday seasons would allow, and time seemed to stretch into infinity as we played for hours and days. In the loving embrace of that old house, we forged deep bonds that would last a lifetime, our laughter echoed through the rooms creating a symphony of joy.

As I reflect on those cherished memories, I realize that our grandmother's house was more than just another building; it was a repository of love, laughter, and the magic of childhood. It was a place where the world felt perfect, and every moment was a treasure waiting to be discovered. It is with a heart full of gratitude that I look back now and see that God was shaping something that was beyond our imagination.

The cousins were not only close in our relationships, but in our ages. David, a name taken from the great king of Israel, was the oldest, and he reminded us constantly of his senior position. James, a name that drew reminders of the brother of Jesus. He was number two, the quieter one, oftentimes leaving us with the sense he was the deep thinker in the group. The youngest two, John, the great apostle and Stephen, the great martyr were limited in their ability to give us "older boys" input, so they frequently just tagged along obediently. And then there were the two cousins in the middle of it all. The ones that were credited with any of the problems, mistakes, jokes and always the ones having the most fun. Mark, another Biblical namesake, and reminder of the great evangelist, and then there was me, number three in line to the throne.... I was Kenny. I often wondered what happened……it was noticeable that I was the only one not named for any great Bible figure, not Paul, not Timothy, not Luke, any of which would have sufficed, no I was just Kenny.

How did my cousins get these grand names? I know my parents did not just run out of Bible names. I can only assume that they wisely contemplated I was going to be the loudest and perhaps the one who created the most trouble and most challenges when the six of us were together? I was number three, born in June of 1951 and 15 days later came what was to be my closest friend, my cousin Mark. From the early days Mark and I were inseparable. We spent as much time together, did as many things together, and played as often as we could. Although we grew up in different cities, we maintained a close friendship throughout our lives. It was during those childhood days that God was doing something that while mysterious to us at the time, looking back with years of perspective has become so clear.

Our grandfather was 14 years older than our grandmother and had early onset of what was then called "hardening of the arteries" (now known as Alzheimer's) and so our early memories of him were that he was noticeably quiet and loving yet did not communicate very often. Our grandmother, Erma Howell, known to all as Ms. Erma, struck a stately figure, highly respected by all, she was a wise, prominent, well-educated, and deeply faithful woman. As we all knew, she was the matriarch of the family, when grandmother spoke, we all listened. It was there in her home at 518 North Cherry, we would listen and learn from her constant reminders to do the right thing, be the right kind of young men, it was here that we were introduced to what a Christ centered life would mean. I remember she would often pray for us, specifically and collectively, and she would always tell us that God had a plan for us, and we should strive to be young men who sought after the Lord in everything we did.

Each of us came to accept Christ at an early age and as we moved into our twenty's we each pursued our own individual business careers. Mark was different, I recognized that Mark, even as a young boy, the fourth of the six boys, seemed to have a wisdom about him that was greater than his age. He had an easy laughter about him. He was athletic. I admired him. I looked up to him, but I reminded him constantly that I was much older, and he should listen more to me. Thankfully, he did not in most cases. True to that nature and character I observed in that young boy, God had a plan for Mark.... a special calling. As the years collected behind us God's plan for Mark was revealed, and he committed his life to the study of Scripture and to the teaching and pastoring of a flock. Like his father before him, he wanted to be a pastor. God had uniquely gifted him for that purpose. Dr. Mark Oliver Wilbanks pastored faithfully and lovingly for over 40 years.

In the realm of spiritual exploration and guidance, there exists a unique and cherished perspective that only a seasoned pastor can offer. *Along the Journey* is a remarkable collection of stories, wisdom and profound insights gathered over four decades of Mark's pastoral service. He is a marvelous storyteller. As you delve into the pages of his book, you will be reminded of the ancient adage that "life is a journey," and within these stories, you will find the essence of that journey reflected in the most meaningful and transformative ways.

Mark has been a steadfast beacon of hope for me and countless souls traversing the often-tumultuous path of life. With an unwavering dedication, compassion, and a deep reservoir of spiritual knowledge, he has been a guiding presence, offering solace in times of despair, wisdom in moments of confusion, and unwavering support in the face of adversity of so many. Along the Journey is a testament to the power of faith and resilience of the human spirit.

Within these pages you will encounter stories that will move you to tears, moments of profound revelation, lots of laughter and lessons that will stay with you long after you have turned the last page. Whether you are a devoted follower of Christ, or on a journey to seek truth, Mark has written a book, full of insights that will resonate with your heart and soul. In this collection of stories, Mark shares the tapestry of those experiences, unveiling the wisdom, humor, joys, and challenges of a pastoral life. From stories that celebrate love's enduring power to those that offer comfort in the face of loss, these stories provide unique clips into the sacred moments that define a life dedicated to service. They also delve into the complexities of human nature, exploring the depths of forgiveness, the healing power of compassion.

What makes *Along the Journey* truly exceptional to me is not just the marvelous storytelling, but the authenticity and vulnerability with which these stories are shared. Mark touches our heart and soul, allowing us to witness the power of faith in the profound impact of his ministry and the lives of others. As you embark on this journey, I encourage you to approach each story with an open heart and a curious spirit for within these narratives you will find deep truths that transcend boundaries and speak to the very essence of our shared humanity. Mark reminds me that regardless of our individual paths, we are all fellow travelers on the extraordinary journey of life. So, dear friend, I invite you to join Dr. Mark Oliver Wilbanks on this inspiring voyage through *Along the Journey*. May his stories illuminate your own path as they have mine for many years, offering guidance, solace, and a deeper understanding of the beauty and complexity of the human experience and God's design. As you turn the pages, may you find inspiration to continue your own journey with faith, love, and unwavering belief that no matter what challenges arise, there is always hope, redemption and grace along the way. Our grandmother Erma would be so proud.

Ken Edmundson #3
Founder, CEO of The Edmundson Group

Author of
Navigating the Nexus
Next Level Leadership
ShortTrack CEO
Listen, You're Trying to Tell You Something
Teamwork

What Are You Going to Do About It?

There are just some things that cannot be allowed to stand:

- A middle-schooler watches as a new guy becomes the target of verbal and physical abuse.
- An employee witnesses unethical behavior in her company that affects the bottom line.
- A college student learns that answers to a crucial exam are being passed around.
- A guy finds out his best friend is cheating on his unsuspecting wife.
- A homeless veteran wanders city streets.
- A single mom can't keep up financially and loses her home.
- A child dies every few seconds somewhere in our world from preventable causes.

We all know these things happen. But once we know, we are faced with a decision: What are we going to do?

There are plenty of places in our lives and in our world where we could be aroused by what some have called "holy discontent." Others might use the term "righteous indignation." What bothers us enough that we are willing to do something about it? What moves us beyond unsettling discomfort to determined action?

We can be overwhelmed by all the challenges and problems, or we can start where we are. To paraphrase: Just because you cannot do everything doesn't mean you can't do something.

An old story drives home this principle. A man walks along a beach near sunset. In the fading light, he sees another man in the distance. He watches as the man keeps stooping, picking up something, and casting it into the ocean. The man repeats the action again and again. Then the first guy looks at what lay on the sand near the water's edge. Thousands and thousands of starfish are washed up on shore. He realizes what's going on. He approaches the second man and, with a bit of a smirk, says, "You know you can't save them all. Do you really think you're making a difference?" The man holds a starfish in his hand and casts it into the surf before responding, "I made a difference to that one."

We'll never meet a person God doesn't love. He loves each of us like He loves all of us. Oh, you've heard that before? What are you—what are we—going to do about it?

The Power of Grace

Will D. Campbell was born into a farming family in Mississippi in the shadow of the Ku Klux Klan. Ordained at 17 in his Baptist church, he began to sense God asking him to take a difficult, controversial direction in life.

As a white man, supporting and working for civil rights in the deep South was dangerous. He received death threats and was warned to stay away from his hometown. He did, except on one occasion. His 12-year-old nephew had been struck and killed riding the bicycle his Uncle Will had given him, and he had to return. Following a long-held tradition called "sitting up with the dead," Will Campbell sat at the funeral home late into the night.

Around 3:00 that morning, someone approached in the dim light and handed Will a cup of coffee. It was Will's uncle, a man he hadn't seen in many years—a man who vehemently disagreed with Will's activism. Looking back on that experience, Campbell wrote, "Until the dawn, I sat in the redemptive company of a racist Jesus." [1]

I think I know what he meant. Grace wins. When we try to make sense of the racial divide that still exists in our country, we need grace more than ever.

[1] Will D. Campbell. *Race and the Renewal of the Church*. Louisville: Westminster Press, 1962.

The Gift of Grace

Grace. It's a word we hear a great deal. We use it to describe a ballet dancer. It defines a difficult situation handled well. It's a common term used at mealtime: "Would you say 'grace'?" Many of us know someone with the namesake.

Years ago, R. Lofton Hudson wrote the book, *Grace is Not a Blue-Eyed Blond*, in which he wrestled with the idea of grace. He admitted it was hard to define: "It is not possible to define grace because it is always primarily a movement, an attitude, or a sentiment." [2]

He also noted that a definition of the word does not exist in the Bible. We see it most notably in action and as an illustration in the life of Christ. John's Gospel tells us that by coming into the world as He did, Jesus demonstrated the grace of His Father. In fact, John wrote that Jesus was "full of grace." (John 1:14)

So, what exactly is grace? By its nature, grace is never earned or deserved. When God looks at me, He sees a sinner. But His love is greater than my sin. Jesus did not defeat the power of sin and death because of my merit. Paul wrote that if we could earn our salvation, we would just boast about it in Ephesians 2:9. God made the unworthy worthy through His Son's redemptive work.

Once you have accepted His unearned favor, you have a choice to make. If grace is worth experiencing, it has to be worth sharing! Now it is up to each of us.

[2] R. Lofton Hudson. *Grace Is Not a Blue-Eyed Blond*. Waco: Word Books, 1972.

Where to Turn

In 2013, the woman who wrote the advice column Dear Abby died. For more than 40 years, Pauline Esther Friedman Philips responded to curious, discouraged, desperate, and quirky readers chosen for her columns. In syndication her readership topped 110 million people in some 1,400 newspapers. At the height of her popularity, she received 10,000 letters a week.

What many do not know is that her twin sister, Esther Pauline Friedman Lederer, was the first advice columnist in the family. She took over the Ann Landers column for the *Chicago Sun Times* in 1955. Pauline helped her sister at first and then decided to write her own. Her first Dear Abby column appeared on January 9, 1956. An awkward rift developed between the sisters that kept them estranged for a number of years.

Perhaps they needed some advice.

We all do. We need someone to turn to. Anyone who claims to know all the answers is someone to avoid. Thankfully, we have Someone who doesn't need to claim to have all knowledge. He really does know it all—the what, when, how, and why. He asks us to follow His lead while trusting His love, wisdom, and grace. From Proverbs: "Don't lean on your own understanding. In all your ways acknowledge Him and He will direct your paths. Don't be impressed with your own wisdom. Instead, revere the Lord and turn your back on evil. Then you will gain renewed health and vitality." (3:5–8)

In Peter Lord's classic work, *Hearing God*, he quotes this writing of Louis Eberly:

> "God hasn't ceased being Revelation any more than He has ceased being Love. He enjoys expressing Himself. Since He's Love, He must give Himself, share His secrets, communicate with us, and reveal Himself to any who wants to listen."

And therein is the problem. Remember when your mother told you that you had two ears and only one mouth for a reason? Why then do we think we are supposed to talk and God is supposed to listen? What could we be missing because we refuse to hear His voice? I recommend two books on this subject, both entitled *Hearing God*, written by two exceptional men: Peter Lord and Dallas Willard. They knew Who to turn to for knowledge, understanding, and wisdom.

Who's Driving This Car?

We like being in control, don't we? One of life's great challenges is to surrender or submit our will to God. It started in the Garden when the first humans decided their way was better than God's. We may think we know best, but too often our lives ends up in the ditch or traveling down the wrong road.

Recently, I referenced a prayer written by poet Glen Martin. His words are timely:

> "Lord Jesus, I have been in control of my life, but I now want Your Spirit to be the One who runs my life. I am giving You all my rights. Please take control of every area of my life. Whenever I am tempted to take back control, please point that out to me and help me to have the courage and strength to resist successfully the temptation or desire to do so. Show me how to live on top of my circumstances and not under them. Help me to keep my eyes on You instead of my problems. Let me see You, Father, as the One who can and will meet every need in my life. Let me be sufficient in You and not in my abilities and strengths. Help me to have the right balance between living in Your control and exercising diligence as I respond to every facet of my life. Whenever pressures come that have been unbearable or debilitating, show me Your perspective—anything I've been doing wrong or thinking improperly. Then show me how to correct my faulty actions and thoughts so that I can continue to walk in Your Spirit's control. Thank You that You want to see these things in my life even more than I do. Remind me of that when my faith gets weak."

What could our lives be like if we would truly seek the Kingdom of God and His righteousness, if we would trust Him with all our hearts, if we would lean on His understanding instead of our own? What kind of power could be unleashed if we sincerely devoted ourselves to living under His control? What direction could our lives take if we really let Him take the wheel?

You Don't Have That Kind of Time

It's amazing what people can be bothered by:

- "I dislike having to drive four hours to our vacation home."

- "The restaurant gave me cold butter, and my bread ripped when I tried to spread it."

- "Just had my praline spread confiscated by TSA at Dulles. As far as I am concerned, the terrorists have won."

We all can be guilty of majoring on the minors. Author Anne Lamott was interviewed for an article in *Clarity* magazine. She said she was raised to present herself to others in a way that would make people either envious or approving. Keeping up that façade required a great deal of energy. One day she was visiting her friend, Pammy, who was in the midst of a battle with cancer. Lamott asked her friend if the dress she was wearing made her look fat. Pammy responded, "Annie, you just don't have that kind of time."

That moment seared Lamott's soul. Her reaction is worth our attention: "You don't have time to live a lie. You don't have time to get the world to approve of you. You only have time to become the person you dream of being. You only have time to accept yourself as you are and start getting a little bit healthier so you can be who God needs you to be."

I confess I focus on things that just don't matter. I need to step back and seek a longer view. From his prison cell, the apostle Paul wrote to the Philippians that he had learned how to be content, regardless of the circumstances. Like Paul, my joy doesn't come from warm butter on my toast. The joy that sustains us lifts our eyes and encourages our souls. Knowing that we are children of the King, knowing that the Good Shepherd cares for His sheep always, provides the peace of His presence. The time I have is measured in the moments He grants. I can live with that.

A Watched Pot Never Boils

We're not good at waiting, are we? We like to get stuff fast. *The Boston Globe* published an article by Christopher Muther in February 2013 entitled "Instant Gratification is making us perpetually impatient." Evidently there is a price for our hurried, impatient ways. Who knew?

Same-day grocery delivery, high-speed Internet, on-demand streaming, fast-food meals, short sermons (how did that get in there?), and amusement park GO FAST Pass, FastPass, FastPass+, and MaxPass programs represent just some of the ways companies have responded to our unwillingness to wait.

Muther pointed out, "The Pew Research Center's Internet and American Life Project sums up a recent study about people under the age of 35 and the dangers of their hyper connected lives with what sounds like a prescription drug warning–'Negative effects include a need for instant gratification and loss of patience.'"

In reality, few people under 35 have time to read a Facebook post. They have found other platforms to be far faster. So, I guess this column is for all us dinosaurs. Our pace is too rushed, too, though. Regardless of age, we have problems waiting.

The truth we're trying to avoid is that some things just take time. Building a friendship, growing in your faith, working on your marriage, raising children, honing a craft, gaining wisdom, learning to listen and contemplate … if you'll take time to think about it, you can probably add your own items to my list.

Time is too precious to waste, but it's also too precious to rush through. You can't always microwave life.

Jesus told a story about a landowner who grew impatient because a tree he had planted wasn't bearing fruit as quickly as he wanted. The landowner's gardener wisely told the man that waiting for good fruit was worth it (Luke 13:6–9). We too need to be careful not to demand instant gratification when delaying it brings rich rewards.

Take a deep breath. Whatever it is, it's worth the wait.

Life In the Spirit

In his classic work, *The Spirit of Christ*, Andrew Murray quoted a young Christian: "I think I understand the work of the Father and the Son, and rejoice in them, but I hardly see the place the Spirit has."

The third Person of the Trinity has been misunderstood by many. We don't know quite how to take Him. Is He wind… the force… a ghost? How are we to relate to Him?

Murray offered help: "God created man's heart for His dwelling. Sin entered and defiled it. God's Spirit worked to regain possession for four thousand years. Finally, the redemption was accomplished, and the Kingdom of God was established through Christ. The Spirit of Christ Himself is to be within us as the power of our lives. I have God Himself—a living Person—to dwell with me. And so, the Spirit becomes to me what He was to Jesus, the very life of my personality." [3]

The Spirit of God is not a portion of God; He is fully God, present in the life of the believer. Christ promised the presence of the Advocate, the Comforter, the One who would guide and teach and empower those who put their faith in Him. Jesus promised He would never abandon His own. The Spirit is the fulfillment of that promise.

As followers of Christ, we can certainly agree that we would choose power-full lives over power-less lives. Sadly, we cannot appropriate the power of God until we acknowledge the person of the Spirit.

What does Scripture teach about Him?

- He teaches us truth.
- He consoles and comforts us.
- He intercedes for us in prayer.
- He endows each believer with gifts for the edification of the Church.
- He kindles hope within our hearts.
- He reminds us of how much we are loved.

Life in the Spirit is opportunity, not obligation. It is a deepening relationship with our Creator, Redeemer, and Sustainer.

"Spirit of the living God, fall fresh on me. Spirit of the living God, fall fresh on me. Break me, melt me, mold me, fill me. Spirit of the living God, fall fresh on me."

[3] Andrew Murray. *The Spirit of Christ*. Public Domain, 1888.

Aim High

Who wants to be average? I doubt you have ever seen this bumper sticker: My child is a C student. The old adage applies here: Why flock with turkeys when you can soar with eagles?

Through the years, one of my favorite authors has been Charles Swindoll. Of his books, the one that has meant the most to me is *Living Above the Level of Mediocrity*. In it he discussed how to raise the bar in life through personal commitment and extravagant love. He challenged readers to refocus their priorities and refuse to settle for "good enough." He gave advice about conquering stagnation and selfishness with conscious, deliberate expressions of passionate joy.

James Russell Lowell penned these words:

> "Life is a leaf of paper white
> Whereon each one of us may write his word or two,
> and then comes night.
> Greatly begin! Though thou have time but for line,
> be that sublime.
> Not failure, but low aim, is crime."

In Isaiah 43:18–19, we find these words from the Lord: "It is nothing compared to what I am going to do. Look, I am about to do a new thing. It has already begun. Do you not see it?"

The most memorable people in my life—parents, teachers, coaches, ministers—were those who challenged me to do better, to be better. Joyce Landorf Heatherly called those people "balcony people." They pull for us, cheer for us, believe in us, hold us accountable, love us, and encourage us to aim high. I hope to be on the balcony for others.

Ticktock

Two men contemplate the passage of time in a scene from Indiana Jones and the Kingdom of the Crystal Skull. The older says to the younger "We've reached the age when life stops giving us things and starts taking them away."

Cynical, right? I don't think so. I've thought about that more as life moves on. In my profession, I have experienced many moments of outrageous joy and deep satisfaction. I've also known moments of heart-wrenching and tear-stained grief and pain Many of those have been in hospital rooms by death beds and in homes where bad news arrived: infants delivered stillborn, teenagers taken by accident, disease, or suicide, young adults victimized by cancer, retirees whose plans were dashed by a heart attack, dear family and friends who left us far too soon. I know loss is inevitable, but it still hurts when life "starts taking them away."

If someone who actually knew promised to tell me the future, I would say, "No, thanks." I'd rather make the most of right now without being weighed down by what might be. In the Sermon on the Mount, Jesus spoke about the danger and damage of anxiety: "Seek the Kingdom of God above all else, and live righteously, and He will give you everything you need. So don't worry about tomorrow, for tomorrow brings its own worries. Today's trouble is enough for today." (Matthew 6:33–34 NLT)

A popular paraphrase of a song lyric is often used but never out of date: "I don't know what the future holds, but I do know Who holds the future." God alone is the One who promises to be with us, to care for us, to hold us close to His heart, to love us forever.

Nobody can take that away.

A Monument Worth Building

The Taj Mahal is one of the world's most beautiful and admired architectural masterpieces. The man who had it built was Mughal emperor Shah Jahan. He conceived the structure as both mausoleum and monument to his third wife, the beloved Mumtaz Mahal, who died in giving birth to the shah's 14th child. He became so obsessed with the details of the project that he dedicated himself to overseeing the construction personally.

Started around 1632, it was completed in 1653. As the months dragged into years, the emperor visited the site daily. He wanted every detail to proclaim his love for his dead wife. He turned his grief into a lavish and extravagant tribute.

Legend has it that one day as he toured the construction site, he noticed a scarred and battered box. Mistaking it for construction debris, he had it removed and destroyed. It wasn't debris; it was the coffin containing his wife's remains. The one for whom the magnificent edifice was being built.

We are all engaged in construction projects of one kind or another. Building a home, a family, a business, a reputation, a career. Along the way, it is important to remember why. We must be careful not to discard the important but remember the reasons we started building.

Two friends were discussing the difficulty of making it in today's competitive market. One said to the other, "But what would happen to me if I should undertake to do business with the principles Christ teaches? Why, it might mean financial ruin for me!" The response: "And what will happen to you if you don't carry on your business the way Jesus taught? What kind of ruin do you want?"

I'm Glad I'm Not Like That Guy

Jesus told a hard-hitting story about spiritual pride that is recorded in Luke 18:9–14. Since He went to the Temple on a number of occasions, He might have witnessed this telling episode.

Two men enter to pray. One was a Pharisee. Pharisees were not bad people. In fact, they prided themselves in being good. This Pharisee saw himself one way and everyone else another. "The proud Pharisee stood by himself and prayed this prayer in a loud voice: 'I thank You, God, that I am not a sinner like everyone else, especially that tax collector over there!'" The man went on to list all the reasons why he could stand by himself and inform God what a treasure he was. If you have ever been called "pharisaical," you should know it is not a compliment. This guy was living proof.

The other man did not stand with his face lifted heavenward. His voice did not boom. He was overcome with grief and guilt. His prayer was a cry of despair: "O God, be merciful to me, the sinner." In his view, there could not be anyone lower than him. He describes himself as "the sinner," his humility in stark contrast with the pride of the Pharisee. Jesus certainly noticed.

Prayer should always begin with humility. The posture of prayer for the Hebrews was arms lifted, hands empty in recognition that God alone was their shelter, their provider, their hope. The Pharisee's prayer was an exercise in arrogance. The tax collector flung himself on the mercy of God. We must follow his example.

We will never be able to tell God something He doesn't already know. He is never taken by surprise. So why do we pray? Perhaps prayer helps us align ourselves with God. Perhaps it enables us to be honest with ourselves. Perhaps it opens a channel that leads to deeper intimacy.

Jesus spent a great deal of His time in prayer with His Father. If prayer was important to the Son of God, don't you think it should be important to us?

One Man's Junk

Found in the 2018 winter edition of *Biblical Archaeology Review*: "Garbage is among humanity's prodigious physical legacies to those who are not yet born."

Profound, huh? This quote was placed at the beginning of an article entitled, "Jerusalem and the Holy Land(fill)." Five thousand years of trash have accumulated in and around the Holy City. Mostly found on the slopes of the Kidron Valley, the garbage is now being excavated and studied in order to discover how people lived.

I wonder what our descendants will learn about us from sifting through our trash. One thing is for certain: they will find plenty of Styrofoam.

We live in a throwaway society. Despite our larger closets, storage units, and secondhand (or my favorite, "gently used") stores, we still have plenty to cast off. Dumpsters behind restaurants and grocery stores fill daily with uneaten food. Clothes are discarded when they no longer fit or aren't in style. Technology quickly becomes obsolete. Cars, appliances, furniture … the list goes on. We could clothe, feed, and house a lot of people with the stuff we throw away.

Speaking of that, the worst tragedies involve thrown away people. We don't like to be reminded of these cast-offs. Like car junkyards, we like to hide them, abandon them, ignore them, or forget them.

As people of faith, we believe every person is made in the image of God. We will never meet a person God doesn't love. I heard a phrase this past week I haven't heard in years: "God don't make no junk." Do we?

Perhaps history won't judge us so much by what we threw away as who we threw away. Oh, God, may we treat others as we wish to be treated!

Wish I'd Thought of That

They say everyone has one really good idea inside them. I don't know who "they" are, but could it be true? Who would have thought what started out as joke would make millions for a guy named Gary Dahl? He came up with the Pet Rock. At $3.95 each, rocks purchased for a penny from a beach in Mexico became a sensation in 1975. With some creative packaging and instructions, the rocks were sold in cardboard carrying cases punctured with holes and lined with straw. Dahl was amazed: "You might say we packaged a sense of humor," he said in an interview.

Then there was the toy company, Wham-O, who took advantage of the UFO craze in the fifties. They designed a plastic disc based on the Frisbie Pie Company pie tins made in their factory in Bridgeport, Connecticut. College students would take the tins and toss them to each other. The Frisbee was born in 1957 when the company improved on the tin plate with plastic.

What's the point? Our creative God has instilled imagination in His people, giving us the ability to dream big dreams, try new things, reach beyond the ordinary, and explore new horizons. I have had this plaque in my office for years. It reminds me of the opportunity imagination presents:

> Take time to…
> work, it is the price of success.
> play, it is the secret of perpetual youth.
> think, it is the source of power.
> read, it is the fountain of wisdom.
> pray, it is conversation with God.
> laugh, it is the music of the soul.
> listen, it is the pathway to understanding.
> dream, it is hitching your wagon to a star.
> worship, it is the highway of reverence.
> love and be loved;
> it is the gift of God.

Closer Than You Think

The relational God. The invitational God. How close is He? Jesus responded to the inquiry of the soon-to-be disciples with this invitation: "Come and see." (John 1:39) To the dispirited and confused, He said, "Come to Me, all of you who are weary and carry heavy burdens, and I will give you rest." (Matthew 11:28)

In his impactful book, *God is Closer Than You Think*, John Ortberg quotes Frederick Buechner: "There is no event so commonplace but that God is present within it, always hiddenly, always leaving you room to recognize Him or not … because in the last analysis all moments are key moments, and life itself is grace."

The waiting God. The beckoning God. The gracious God. How close has God come? Ortberg writes: "So close that your heart will be beating with life because Someone is walking around in there. God is closer than you think."

All of us have known times when God seemed distant. You may have entertained thoughts like these: Perhaps He is too busy. Perhaps I'm not important enough. Perhaps He cannot love me after what I have done. Perhaps He doesn't care. Perhaps He cares but chooses not to act.

My dad told me this story about how relationships change. An elderly couple was riding together down a country road. The man was driving. The woman was leaning against the passenger door. They had been quiet for some time when she glanced over at him. "Fred, do you remember when we used to sit close and cuddle in this old car?" He paused for a moment before muttering, "I ain't moved."

In those times when God feels distant, I have to admit I'm the one who gets distracted, who overschedules myself, and who becomes complacent. The relational, invitational, waiting, beckoning, and gracious God hasn't moved.

Nicholas Herman was unhappy with his life. He felt disconnected from God and wanted to change. He decided to make his life an experiment in what he called a "habitual, silent, secret conversation of the soul with God." He joined a monastic order and was given a new name, Brother Lawrence. After he died, friends gathered his writing and produced *Practicing the Presence of God*, a book that has been widely read for four centuries. One friend noted, "The good brother found God everywhere, as much while he was repairing as while he was praying with the community."

Perhaps we're not looking like we should. One thing seems certain: God is indeed closer than we think.

Impact

Jackie Robinson, the man credited with breaking the color barrier for African Americans in baseball, was quoted late in his life as saying, "A life is not important except in the impact it has on other lives." He paved the way for many others who just needed an opportunity. On April 15th during the 2007 Major League Baseball season, evidence of his impact was apparent in every ballpark in the country when 150 Black players wore his uniform number, 42, to honor his contribution to America's pastime.

Robinson also said, "Life is not a spectator sport. If you're going to spend your whole life in the grandstand just watching what goes on, in my opinion you're wasting your life." At some point, each of us has to decide to get in the game. Although few of us could earn our way onto a major league field, every person has unique ways to impact the people in our circles of influence.

You might be surprised to realize whose eyes are on you, who is watching how you live. The impression we make begins in our most intimate relationships. Our family members and friends see us at our best and our worst. Some of our most impactful moments come when we are knocked down. How would our behavior change if we knew others could be changed by whether we get back up, blame someone else for our woes, or just quit? Jackie Robinson had plenty of moments when he was flat on his back. He kept getting up.

As Christians, we are given many opportunities to impact our world. In these days of division and strife, it is time for believers to speak the truth in love and live out our convictions based on God's Word. This "playing field" is full of divine appointments where the grace of God becomes our incentive to demonstrate His love. Too many Christians have justified the world's opinion that we are judgmental, insulated, uncaring, and rigid. The authors of Growing Young spoke of "myopic spirituality," a dangerous complacency that can rob us of vitality and relevance in a cynical world. [4] You and I can open our hearts and minds to those moments that allow us to live out the grace and compassion of Christ.

We may not have the notoriety of Jackie Robinson, but we all have impact. I hope mine is positive; there is enough negative to go around!

[4] Kara Powell, Jake Mulder, Brad Griffin. *Growing Young: Six Essential Strategies to Help Young People Discover and Love Your Church*. Ada: Baker Books, 2016.

There's a Pill for That

Have you noticed the content of drug ads these days? You may not, because you either tune it out or mute the sound. In a typical 30- or 60-second commercial, about 10 to 15 percent of the time is spent listing the wonderful benefits of the drug. The rest focuses on the side effects, which could easily convince you that you will die a horrible death if you take the product.

The opioid crisis is no joke. Pain medication abuse is responsible for a tragic upswing in addiction and death. We are an overmedicated society. Overweight? Take a pill. Can't sleep? Take a pill. Losing your virility? Take a bunch of pills. Want to spice up your love life? First, get two bathtubs, set them facing the sunset, sit in one while your partner sits in the other, take a pill, and voilà! (Sorry, I don't get the two tubs.)

Modern science enables us to deal with serious physical, mental, and emotional issues with the proper use of medication. Many of us who experience depression, anxiety, and other challenges benefit from taking the right prescriptions.

I don't think we were created to fill our bodies with chemicals, though. I think we were designed to function quite well if we eat well, exercise, get enough sleep, and avoid stress. Unfortunately, often I don't get past "eat well."

I think we have a deeper problem. Pills won't make our prayer lives more significant. Pills won't help us be more compassionate and loving. Pills won't convince us that our relationship with God can be so much more meaningful than it is. We won't find the life Jesus came to give us, which He described as "to the full," in a pill bottle.

Perhaps we need to accept His invitation. Read the words our Savior spoke two thousand years ago and see if they don't apply today to all who are hurting, lonely, stressed, and needy: "Come to Me, all of you who are weary and carry heavy burdens, and I will give you rest." (John 10:10) Sounds like the right prescription to me.

Opportunity

The following quotes represent a few interesting perspectives on opportunity:

> "The secret of success in life is for a man to be ready for his opportunity when it comes." –Benjamin Disraeli

"I am an ordinary person who is blessed with extraordinary opportunities and experiences. Today is one of those experiences." –Sonia Sotomayor

"If opportunity doesn't knock, build a door." – Milton Berle

"A pessimist is one who makes difficulties out of opportunities, and an optimist is one who makes opportunities out of difficulties." –Harry Truman

"If you want to walk on water, you've got to get out of the boat." –John Ortberg

I believe in opportunities. I believe in divine appointments. I believe we travel in the circles we do because God wants us to be available to respond to His promptings and urgings. I call these nudges "glory moments," times when we have the opportunity to partner with God in ministering and serving. The words we speak and the acts of service we perform can bear witness for Christ. Record your glory moments and share them with your family and circles of influence. Seize the opportunities God grants.

No one likes to live with regret—the conversation we didn't have, the action we never took, the love we withheld. Each day offers something new. Carpe diem!

The Folly of Predicting

From the (fictional) Contemporary Dictionary: meteorologist (aka weatherman, weatherwoman, weatherperson): a vocation where the person holding the position is mostly wrong yet can keep his/her job. These experts can often be seen on our televisions during the latest weather event offering such scintillating and fascinating commentary as:

- "It's really windy here."

- "If you look over my shoulder, you can see that there is a storm."

- "This handy poncho is really getting wet."

The predicting business can be problematic. Radio preacher Harold Camping convinced his followers that the world was coming to an end on May 21, 2011. His proof text of Scripture led him to declare Judgment Day would occur that May evening. When the Apocalypse didn't occur, Camping revised his forecast to October 21. His explanation (my paraphrase): "My bad." Yeah, it was particularly so for the gullible who had divested themselves of their worldly possessions in preparation for the end of days.

Truth is, we don't know when the end will come. Jesus told His disciples that only the Father knows the end of history. The way the world is going, it certainly seems the day is drawing near! Instead of being distracted by prognostications, we would be better off spending our time doing what the Lord told us to do. One Sunday morning, I was at the door of my son's fifth grade class. One of his friends saw me and whispered loudly, "Look, there's the pastor. Do something religious!"

That's not what I mean. We are called to bring hope to the despairing, compassion to the marginalized, love to the unloved, and peace to the troubled—all in the name of Christ. Instead of watching the skies, let's be living for Him.

Feel His Pleasure

"When I run, I feel God's pleasure." Those words were spoken by Scottish runner Eric Liddell. In 1924, he won a gold medal at the VIII Olympic Games in Paris. With an unusual running style and fierce competitive spirit, the Flying Scotsman, son of missionaries with the London Missionary Society, was also known for his religious convictions. Those beliefs cost him a chance to compete for a gold medal in his best event, the 100 meters. The heat was scheduled for a Sunday and he refused to run on the Sabbath. Liddell had known about the schedule for the months leading up to the Olympics and endured a great deal of pressure to run for his country. Remaining steadfast, Liddell trained at the greater distance and prepared to compete with the highly-favored American runners Jackson Scholz and Charles Paddock.

Just before the race began, a member of the American Olympic team slipped a piece of paper into Liddell's hand with an inscription from 1 Samuel 2:30: "Those who honor Me I will honor."

The runners strained, trying to gain some advantage over the distance. Liddell held on to his slim lead to finish first, breaking the existing Olympic and world records with a time of 47.6 seconds. The 1981 film Chariots of Fire depicted Liddell's Olympic quest.

Born in China, Liddell returned there to serve as a missionary from 1925 to 1943. In 1945, five months before liberation, Eric Liddell died in a Japanese internment camp on February 21. He had refused to be involved in a prisoner exchange months before his death so a pregnant Chinese woman could be released. What do you pursue that allows you to feel God's pleasure?

"Why Are You Working in the Dark?"

Since 2010, ads for Allstate have featured a guy who causes mayhem. One of his targets is the DIY crowd. We know who they are. They want to prove they can save money by doing something themselves. Once they've had a turn, it might cost even more to fix what they broke and do the job right.

The Family Handyman website has a section entitled "10 Marriages Almost Destroyed by DIY Projects." Here are two samples from the world of ceiling fans:

1. A man decides to replace a ceiling light/fan fixture. Knowing he should have cut off the power at the box, he turns off the light switch. The day was growing dark with a passing storm overhead, but the man thought he had enough light to finish. His wife came in to see if she could help. He asked her to pass her some tools. Looking around in the dim space, she said, "Why are you working in the dark?" and switched on the light. They were treated to an impromptu light show as sparks flew from his screwdriver. Luckily no one was hurt. What are the lessons to be learned, kids?

2. They had been renovating the great room. New hardwood floor had been installed. New furniture had been purchased. Now it was time for the expensive ceiling fan. No problem. Been there, done that. The man laid the instructions aside and got busy. He noticed this one red tag but was hurrying to finish the project. Adding the extra bracing for the fan, the man finished the installation and called his wife to show her his handiwork. He flicked on the switch and watched in horror as the fan unscrewed itself from its support pipe and crashed to the new floor, leaving deep scratches in the hardwood and pieces of fan

all over the room. His wife began to speak words he didn't know she knew. In the pile of rubble was that red tag, which he finally picked up and read: "Once the support pipe is installed, use the locking screw to secure the pipe to the main support."

Paul wrote to the Galatians: "Be honest in your estimate of yourselves. . .." I'm not sure he meant DIY projects, but who knows? I envy people who complete DIY projects successfully with fingers and toes and pride and marriages intact. Personally, after more than 40 years of wedded bliss, I've learned to pick up the phone before I pick up a tool. Happy wife, happy life.

I'm Only Human

This week you've probably heard someone say, "I'm only human." Ever wondered what your other choices are?

- Animal
- Vegetable
- Mineral
- Robot

Some might suggest we represent all four plus more.

God didn't create automatons. His amazing gift of life carried with it an enormous risk. He gave humans alone the privilege and responsibility of living with free will. There was always the possibility, the probability—okay, the certainty—that we would make bad choices and try to live life on our own terms.

Is being "only human" a bad thing? Flaws are evident, even in the most respectable persons of high integrity, because in living we experience fear, failure, disappointment, and betrayal. Scripture makes it plain: "For everyone has sinned; we all fall short of God's glorious standard." (Romans 3:23)

We're not perfect. We stumble, we fall. Sometimes we wallow in our misdeeds and mistakes. But being "only human" isn't a curse; it's an opportunity. Brené Brown, one of my favorite authors, said this about our humanity: "To become fully human means learning to turn my gratitude for being alive into some concrete common good. It means growing gentler toward human weakness. It means practicing forgiveness of my and everyone else's hourly failures to live up to divine standards. It means learning to forget myself on a regular basis in order to attend to the other selves in my vicinity. It means living so that 'I'm only human' does not become an excuse for anything. It means receiving the human condition as blessing and not curse, in all its achingly frail and redemptive reality."[5]

Could today be a celebration of being "only human"?

[5] Brené Brown. *I Thought It Was Just Me.* New York City: Avery Books, 2007.

Eureka!

In his book, *Handbook of God's Promises*, Dr. Ken Boa used this illustration: "Archimedes, a Greek mathematician, engineer, and physicist, was trying to figure out how to measure the volume of an irregular solid object and thereby determine the purity of a gold object. When he finally arrived at the solution, he supposedly exclaimed, 'Eureka!' – or, 'I found it!'

More frequently in my life when I am trying to find something I have misplaced, like my phone, keys, wallet, glasses, I think I'm losing my mind. (I can't find that either.) I have exclaimed "Eureka" or something close to it on many occasions, since I am having more and more of these kinds of occasions.

Boa continued: "What do you do when you find something for which you have been looking? Two things can be measured by your response: the value of the object of your search, and the gratitude you feel upon its discovery."

Frankly, the value of the missing object might be closely related to how late you are. Inevitably, someone will ask (usually with a measure of condescension), "Where was the last place you were when you had it?" If I knew that, I would have already gone there and retrieved the missing item!

"Eureka" is a grand exclamation that should be applied to that which is of utmost value to us. Value shouldn't be defined by discovering things. Value in life has been and always will be exemplified by relationships.

Perhaps there is a relationship you've neglected, a person you've taken for granted, a priority you've misplaced. Perhaps you've allowed your love for the people who matter most to grow cool. In Luke 15, Jesus told three stories about lost things: a sheep, a coin, and a son. In each case, there was a "eureka" moment. The most important involved the recovery of a prodigal who had come home. Look at the celebrations that ensued when the lost was found, when the relationship was restored. All of heaven rejoiced. I think Jesus was illustrating how God feels about each of us. The last thing He wants for any of His children to be lost. Eureka!

How Tall Are You?

Do you think tall people love to be asked about their height? Do you think they really enjoy comments like, "How's the weather up there?" or "You played basketball, right?"

The tallest man in history was Robert Pershing Wadlow. He was born in Illinois on February 22, 1918. When last measured, he stood 8 feet, 11.1 inches. We can only imagine how he was treated in his brief life.

On the other end of the spectrum was Chandra Bahadur Dangi, a Nepalese man who was a primordial dwarf. He was 21.5 inches tall and weighed just over 30 pounds. He lived 75 years, well beyond what was expected for someone with his condition.

How do you measure a person? In 1 Samuel 16, the prophet is sent on a critical errand to find a new king to replace Saul. Samuel journeys to Bethlehem to meet with Jesse, the village elder. Jesse's seven sons are paraded before Samuel. None passes muster. In fact, God tells the prophet as he's assessing Eliab: "Don't judge by his appearance or height, for I have rejected him. The Lord doesn't make decisions the way you do. People judge by outward appearance, but the Lord looks at a person's heart." (1 Samuel 16:7) There is one more son, the shepherd boy David, the person later described as "a man after God's own heart."

Saul had looked the kingly, standing a head taller than his contemporaries. But he lacked kingly character. Billy Graham once said, "When wealth is lost, nothing is lost. When health is lost, something is lost. When character is lost, all is lost." David was far from perfect, but when God examined his heart, He found what mattered. What does God see when He looks at our hearts?

Through the Eyes of a Child

Have you ever noticed how often Jesus was surrounded by children? They wanted to touch Him, be near Him, and listen to Him. Even when His well-meaning disciples tried to keep them away, Jesus rebuked the adults and welcomed the kids.

Children should feel safe, like Nora did when she wrote: "Dear God, I don't feel alone since I found out about You." Children should feel hopeful and be honest, like Frank who wrote: "Dear God, I'm doing the best I can." [6]

Even at my age, I still remember the men and women who cared for me, taught me, and served as role models for me at church. I can recall the names of those who worked in the nursery or taught me during Sunday School, Missions, or Training Union. I even remember the woman who would sit behind us in worship and pop us on the ear if we moved or spoke at the wrong time.

You can learn a lot hanging around kids. One of my favorite stories is of a third grade Sunday School teacher who leaned over Johnny's shoulder while he is intently working on a drawing and asked, "What are you drawing, Johnny?" Too busy to look up, he responded: "I'm drawing a picture of God." The teacher gently remarked, "But no one knows what God looks like." Still working too hard to look up, he said, "They will when I finish this picture."

[6] Stuart E. Hample. *Children's Letters to God*. New York City: Workman Publishing Company, 1991.

Live Free!

Have you ever done something you knew would embarrass your kids? Oh, yes, you have. My wife Kim and I know that, no matter how old our guys are, they still turn their heads and make faces if they see us kiss. To be honest, I did the same thing when I was growing up. You'd think I would have been glad (to a point) to see my parents show each other love and affection.

I know another surefire way to gross 'em out. Start dancing. There is nothing as unappealing as seeing an old white guy bust some moves. Well, "busting" may have more to do with the potential for physical harm. The grandkids start laughing; the sons start hurling.I looked up the definition of embarrass: to cause to feel self-conscious, confused, and ill at ease; to disconcert and fluster. It sounds like my state of mind most of the time!

We live in a world of many uncertainties that may leave you feeling ill at ease or flustered. The ground beneath our feet seems to be shaking. There are plenty of reasons to be disconcerted, if not absolutely terrified. Commercials on television market medicines that address my many challenges of aging. The first 15 seconds describe the wonderful benefits. The rest of the ad warns how that particular product could cripple or kill you. Certainly adds to my peace of mind.

The truth is we don't have to live with fear and anxiety. The psalmist wrote, "Give thanks to the Lord, for He is good! His faithful love endures forever. ... The Lord is for me, so I will have no fear. What can mere people do to me? ... Yes, the Lord is for me; He will help me. ... The Lord is my strength and my song; He has given me victory." (Psalm 118:1, 6, 7, and 14)

That gives me joy and the freedom to keep embarrassing my kids while there's still time. I don't even mind when one of my sons says to me, "Dad, don't ever do that in public again."

Love Lines

Have you ever written a love letter to God? Here are some that were compiled in *Children's Love Letters to God*:

> "Dear God, I love you. How are you? Fine? I'm fine. My mother has five girls and one boy. I am one of them." Nancy, age 6

> "Dear God, I think about you sometimes even when I'm not praying." Elliott

> "Dear God, I do not think anybody could be a better God. Well, I just want you to know but I am not saying that because you are God." Charles (Smart kid.)

> "Dear God, I bet it is very hard to love all of everybody in the world. There are only 4 people in our family and I can never do it." Nan [7] (Nod your head if you relate to Nan.)

Love is hard sometimes. It may seem that the Bible is a long story of the difficulty of loving and being loved. For example, the Old Testament prophet Hosea was married to a woman who was unfaithful. Gomer left her home and marriage and prostituted herself. God told heartbroken, embarrassed Hosea to reclaim his wife. "Go and get your wife again. Bring her back to you and love her." (Hosea 3:1) Understandably, Hosea was stunned that God would ask such a thing of him. The prophet had to learn that love is hard sometimes.

There was a larger story in Hosea's book. God was saying to His prophet, "Now you know how I feel. Israel has rejected My love and sought other gods. They have turned from My ways to seek their own path—a path that will lead to devastation."

You may have known the pain of rejection, of seeing someone you love take a wrong turn that leads to trouble. Love is hard sometimes.

The third parable in Luke 15 is the familiar story of two wayward sons: one leaves home and drags the family name through the mud while one stays home and hardens his heart in self-righteousness. The real story is about the Loving Father who welcomes the prodigal home and urges his older brother to do the same. Haven't we been both in our lifetimes and experienced God's unconditional love, nonetheless? Love is hard sometimes ... but it beats any alternative!

[7] Stuart E. Hample. *Children's Letters to God*. New York City: Workman Publishing Company, 1991.

Honor Those Who Have Gone Before Us

You want to learn something new? Talk with someone who is old. Although that is relative for me as the days continue to race by, I know this: spending time with people who are older than you can be an enriching experience.

We can be overwhelmed by life's circumstances, driven to our knees by discouragement. Many are. But there are those who make the best of it, even while realizing they're not as young or as strong as they once were. One lady in her nineties put it this way:

"I used to race my engine quite a bit, but now I think my idle's stuck."

People in their golden years have obtained great insight and hard-won wisdom. One man who was just shy of 100 passed on this keen observation: "When I was a boy, you weren't." I got it. He's probably forgotten more than I will ever know.

In many cultures, the elderly continue to hold prominent places in families and communities. They are not forgotten or abandoned. The young are taught to honor them, learn from them, and take care of them.

Many of our older friends and family members are rich—not in material things, but in experience, perspective, and faith. They have seen great change in their world. They have encountered the good and the bad.

You may believe the expression "You can't teach an old dog new tricks," but some of the most engaged, energetic people I know make it a priority to keep learning and growing. On the other hand, perhaps younger dogs can learn from old tricks. One of my 95-year-old friends told me recently: "Been there, done that."

Do yourself a favor. Listen and learn.

Not Quite Right

Have you ever missed by just a little? It happens in sports all the time. It can also happen in relationships. Just ask the guy who believed his wife when she told him she didn't want anything for Valentine's Day.

In a Church of England publication a few years ago, there was a list of "not-quite-right" answers offered by children (and perhaps a few adults). The collection included the following:

- Noah's wife was called Joan of Ark.
- The four Gospel writers were John, Paul, George, and Ringo.
- The fifth commandment is "Humor your father and mother."
- Abraham begat Isaac, and Isaac begat Jacob, and Jacob begat 12 partridges.
- The first commandment was when Eve told Adam to eat the apple.

If we're honest with ourselves, we experience plenty of "not-quite-right" moments in life. We don't do what is right. We choose what is wrong. We make plenty of mistakes. I believe that's where grace comes in. The Bible says, "While we were yet sinners, Christ died for us." (Romans 5:8 KJV)

God gives grace. It is His nature to do so. Our holy, just God extends grace to the undeserving (and often ungrateful). Every day we live, there are fresh mercies headed our way (Lamentations 3:22–25). God is as compassionate as He is faithful. He knows we need all the help we can get. That is why He sent His Son to pay a penalty we couldn't.

But grace isn't intended to pass only from God to us. He wants it to pass through us as well. If we truly grasp grace, we know others are just as desperate for it as we are. We share grace because we have received grace. The only One who got it right every time called us to treat others as we would like to be treated (Matthew 7:12).

Grace isn't just a word for a season. It's a lifestyle for every day.

Hope Springs Eternal

The popular idiom that is the title of this piece originated in 1732 in Alexander Pope's An Essay on Man. Here is the rest of it:

> "Hope springs eternal in the human breast;
> Man never is, but always to be blessed;
> The soul, uneasy and confined from home,
> Rests and expatiates in a life to come."

I had to look up "expatiate" to understand Pope's point. The word means "to roam or wander freely." Hope does liberate; it allows the soul to break free from the fears of this life—from despair, from defeat. Hope isn't rose-colored glasses; it isn't an unrealistic perspective that ignores the height of the mountain or the depth of the valley. Hope enables us to climb the slope and encourages us when we have to descend into the shadows. We can live without many things, but we weren't created to live without hope. Take away a person's hope, and the soul shrivels.

Theologian Peter J. Gomes wrote: "Hope does not deny the circumstances of the present, and hope doesn't help us get out of our difficulties. Hope doesn't get us out, it does get us through."[8]

On Ash Wednesday each year, we come face to face with the awful cost of salvation. The darkness and devastation of our sin can all but overwhelm us. The Lenten season takes us on a journey of reflection, repentance, and remembrance. On Easter morning, hope indeed springs eternal! Those whose souls belong to Him break free because of the empty cross and empty tomb.

[8] Peter J. Gomes. *The Good Book: Reading the Bible with Mind and Heart*. New York City: HarperCollins, 1996.

It's Worth It

In 2011, businessman Charlie Whittington of Plano, Texas, came up with an idea. As the owner-operator of a Kwik Kar Lube and Service franchise, he decided to offer a discount to customers who could quote John 3:16. He printed coupons offering the discounted price of $19.99 to anyone who could recite the verse accurately.

You can imagine the range of reactions. Some applauded his efforts to open conversations with people about his faith. Others cried discrimination, particularly when refusal to quote the verse resulted in a charge of $46.

I know it might be hard to conceive, but lawyers got involved. A Dallas attorney named Andy Siegel offered his opinion that, since the station was a private business, the use of a Bible-based discount was technically not against the law. He did add, "The study of the Bible has many rewards. I'm not sure that God intended a lube discount to be among its many riches."

In today's climate, Whittington might have a harder time with his promotion, but he was right about one thing. Applying the Word of God leads to life. According to Paul, the purposes of the Bible are clear: "All Scripture is inspired by God and is useful to teach us what is true and to make us realize what is wrong in our lives. It straightens us out and teaches us to do what is right. It is God's way of preparing us in every way, fully equipped for every good thing God wants us to do." (2 Timothy 3:16–17)

The Bible is a love story, a 66-book revelation of God's desire to draw us to Himself. It is brutally honest about the devastation of evil, sin, and death and the consequences of our rebellion and disobedience. It is full of stories of flawed people like us. There are moments of heartbreaking and confusing events and actions. But there are also those glimpses of a loving Father who just wants His children safe and secure in His arms. The end of the story foretells the destruction of all that shouldn't be and the redemption of all that should. The last words of the last verse of the last chapter of the last book tell us: Love wins.

TLB: The whole Bible was given to us by inspiration from God and is useful to teach us what is true and to make us realize what is wrong in our lives; it straightens us out and helps us do what is right. [9] It is God's way of making us well prepared at every point, fully equipped to do good to everyone.

NLT: All Scripture is inspired by God and is useful to teach us what is true and to make us realize what is wrong in our lives. It corrects us when we are wrong and teaches us to do what is right. [9] God uses it to prepare and equip his people to do every good work.

Reboot

One day, a mechanical engineer, electrical engineer, chemical engineer, and computer engineer were riding together on their way to lunch. Suddenly, the car sputtered to a stop.

- The mechanical engineer: "I think it threw a rod."
- The electrical engineer: "It has to be the alternator."
- The chemical engineer: "It must to be a clog in the fuel line."
- The computer engineer: "I think we should all get out and get back in. It will be fine."

Sometimes we would like life to reboot.

- "Let's start this day over."
- "Let's end this day differently."
- "I should have turned left instead of right."
- "I'd like to take back what I just thought, said, did."

We all have had those moments we wished we could reclaim. A little-used reserve on a college basketball team was summoned by his coach to get in the game. He was so excited that he forgot something. He forgot that his uniform pants had gotten torn in the laundry. He was only wearing his warm-ups. He jumped to his feet and took off his warm-up pants and raced to the scorer's table sans britches. Boy was he a hit that night!

Aren't you glad we have a God who shows us mercy and grace? We stumble, we fall, He picks us up. We sin, He forgives. He is the God of second chances. The Shepherd loves His sheep, knowing full well they will stray. He lays down His life, knowing full well our lives hang in the balance.

Thank You, God, for loving us no matter what.

Never Forget

Once you see one, you never forget it. She was a vivacious lady, full of laughter and song. You would never know what she had been through if she hadn't shown it to you. She lifted her sleeve and there it was. She got it in Auschwitz - a tattoo with a six-digit number. Auschwitz numbers ran from 1 to over 202,000. Those selected for death were not registered in the camp and did not receive numbers.

Most of her family didn't get numbers. She did. If you asked her about it, she wouldn't say much ... but the look in her eyes let you know there was still pain and grief harbored in her soul.

Eugen Schoenfeld, a much-loved professor, retired from teaching at Georgia State University, can speak from his own tale of horror and loss. He knew what it meant to survive the Warsaw Ghetto, Dachau, and Auschwitz while losing many of his family – brother, sister, and mother.

Recently an Egyptian political minister offered the asinine opinion that the six million Jews who perished at the hands of Adolph Hitler and his Nazis didn't really die. They were transported to the United State during World War II. The Holocaust was nothing more than propaganda by Israel and her Western allies.

Dr. Schoenfeld lived the nightmare as a boy in his teens. You can see his appearance at a local middle school – http://www.youtube/watch?v=81X-izB4ETM. We must never forget the horror of the Holocaust.

Mismatches

Udonis Haslem has had quite a career. While a senior at Miami Senior High School, he led his team to two state titles. He played at the University of Florida where he was a significant part of four UF tournament teams. After a year of professional ball in France, he signed with the Miami Heat of the NBA. The Heat have won three NBA titles while Udonis has played for them. He has played fifteen years with the team, a remarkable achievement in a not-for-long league.

Before moving to Miami to finish high school, Udonis attended Wolfson High School in Jacksonville. He was a formidable presence in a really good high school basketball program. My oldest son and my nephew were on those teams. Together, they also played on a youth church league team when rules allowed such things.

So, use your imagination. Think of your average youth church league basketball team and envision one of those kids dribbling down the court to face a 6'8" guy waiting for him in the paint. David and Goliath come to mind ... only every time David shot, Goliath swatted the ball into the bleachers. What a mismatch!

The classic story of the shepherd boy against the giant of Gath is known by almost everyone. What a mismatch! Goliath never had a chance. David didn't just come to the battle armed with a sling and 5 stones; he came in the power of the God he represented.

Sometimes we can be overwhelmingly intimidated by our opposition. We may feel we have no chance for success. Who wants to go into challenge with no confidence of a positive outcome?

The David and Goliath story reminds us of a great truth. You plus God makes a majority, no matter who or what is standing in your way. When Paul wrote, "I can do all things through Christ who strengthens me" he wasn't relying on his own might. He knew better. I hope we do, too.

Rocking Our World

I hope you were prepared. A mountain-size asteroid zoomed by Earth last Monday. Affectionately known as Asteroid 2004 BL86, the hurtling mass is about 1,800 feet wide. The massive rock is roughly twice the size of the Rose Bowl. Not until 2027 will something this large pass by our planet again. Flying by at 35,000 mph, it never got closer than 745,000 miles so we were never in any danger. You would have had to some significant equipment to see it last Monday night.

They tell us that all kind of stuff is flying at us from outer space. We have also learned that thousands of pieces of space junk orbit the planet. Most of it burns up when it enters the atmosphere, but it's getting crowded up there.

If you listen to the dooms-day folks, sooner or later one of those big rocks won't miss. It will come close enough to cause a cataclysmic event. It might be a direct hit, a global killer. As if we didn't have enough to worry about.

There is a great deal of things wrong in our world. Threats abound – terrorism, environmental disasters, epidemics, wars, and more. We can live in fear if we choose. A lot of things can rock our world.

An old hymn comes to mind – "This is My Father's World." [10] The last verse seems particularly appropriate: "This is my Father's world, O let me ne'er forget that though the wrong seems oft so strong, God is the ruler yet. This is my Father's world, the battle is not done. Jesus who died shall be satisfied, and earth and heaven be one."

In 1 John 4:18, we find this encouragement: "Such love has no fear because perfect love expels all fear."

What love? When the Bible defines love, it is profoundly simple: "God is love" (1 John 4:8) I love the old saying: "I don't know what the future holds, but I do know Who holds the future."

[10] Maltbie Davenport Babcock, *This is My Father's World*, published in 1901

It's Not a Sprint

Years ago, I chose the title for weekly blogs. "Along the Journey" suggests the reality of the twists and turns of life, the moments when we soar and the moments when we stumble. The road isn't straight, the way not easy. There are times when we feel it's all up hill. There are other times when we can coast. Life is more marathon than sprint.

After the author presented the hall of faith in the letter of Hebrews (chapter 11), he or she gave us one of the most impressive word pictures we can find in the Bible. We can understand the image because we have seen it in person or on the screen – a stadium full of people cheering on their favorite teams. We have witnessed the compelling sights of the world's best athletes competing in international events like the Olympics.

As chapter 12 opens, individual runners are surrounded by a cheering throng. The noise begins to swell as the participants stretch, strip down to their uniforms, and find their place at the starting line. On the huge video board, a single runner is pictured – a Champion who finished the greatest race of His life, achieving a record never to be broken. His victory becomes the inspiration for every runner about to begin his own race.

The athletes have trained for this moment. They know there will be moments when they have to push through fatigue, cramping, depleted oxygen, and soreness. They somehow find a second wind, and then another and another. Their eyes are fixed on the journey ahead, knowing there is a finish line. The temptation to slow up or even quit is resisted. You cannot win if you don't keep running.

The writer knows all this. The roll call of those who also struggled to finish serves as motivating encouragement. Your eyes lift to the video board again and see the lone figure who battled all the tests and trials runners face. He has mounted the victory stand as the crowd roars. You dig deeper and stretch your stride. His example calls you to greater effort. Their encouragement gives you a surge of determination.

No one can run your race for you, but you do have the example of Christ and you do have a crowd of witnesses who cheer you on. It might not be easy, but it is worth it. Run on!

Say What You Mean, Mean What You Say

Here are a few "Classifieds" that could have used a little editing:

- We will oil your sewing machine and adjust tension in your home – wow, who wouldn't pay for that second skill even if you didn't have a sewing machine!

- We do not tear your clothing with machinery; we do it carefully by hand – at least they're honest when your clothes are ripped to shreds.

- Have several very old dresses from grandmother in beautiful condition – I'm sure she is comforted by their assessment

- Pony for sale, looks like small horse – I see what you did there.

- Army vehicle missing, presumed stolen. Vehicle is worth $100,000 and was recently painted with camouflage – Perhaps they need to look harder.

- Lost white male cat, fixed, yellowish-green eyes, deaf. Answers to Spike – I guess there is feline sign language involved.

- For sale: one slightly used set of dentures, only two teeth missing – I don't want to know anything else.

Words matter. Sticks and stones will hurt your bones ... and words can break your heart. James wrote: "We all make many mistakes, but those who can control their tongues can also control themselves in every other way ... the tongue is a small thing, but what enormous damage it can do ... blessing and cursing can come pouring out of the same mouth" (James 3:1-12).

He was right on so many levels. All of us have said things we shouldn't and not said things we should. We have this amazing capacity of using words to tear down or build up. Words become weapons or tools in relationships, both intimate and casual.

James had otherwise words of counsel: "Be quick to listen, slow to speak, and slow to get angry" (1:19). If we followed his advice more consistently, think of the regrets we wouldn't have and the apologies we would never make!

Today's goal: lift up, encourage, bless with your words; bite back the sharp retort or criticism; and please read your classified ad before printing.

Can You Top That?

Kim and I went to see illusionist David Copperfield years ago. In a career that has spanned over 40 years, his illusions have included making a Learjet disappear, escaping from Alcatraz, levitating over the Grand Canyon, and making the Statue of Liberty vanish. He is the best-known and most commercially successful magician in history. He even owns a chain of islands in the Bahamas!

The challenge for people like Copperfield is that the next illusion must be better than the last one. He must be more sensational. He must cause consternation at higher levels than ever before. He wants to go beyond "How did he do that?"

Our featured song this week was written by George Beverly Shea, the man best known for his singing at Billy Graham crusades for many years. The text for the worship service is Psalm 8. Both Scripture and song extol the magnificence of the Creator – the One who brought the universe into being and breathed life into humans.

> "There's the wonder of sunset at evening, the wonder of sunrise I see; But the wonder of wonders that thrills my soul is the wonder that God loves me." "O Lord, our Lord, Your majestic name fills the earth!"

The songwriter and the psalmist knew that God didn't have to top anything. He didn't have to come up with a new trick. As our knowledge of the universe expands, we realize more and more that there is no end to the wonder of God's creation. As we grow deeper in our relationship with the Lord, we realize we will never fully explore the depths of His love for us.

Oh, the wonder of it all!

Don't Do That!

You had to see it to believe it. Georgia and Mississippi State were tied 67 apiece last Wednesday night. A State player was at the foul line, trying to win the game with .5 seconds to go. As Quinndary Weatherspoon missed the free throw, a stuffed animal was tossed on to the court behind him. In the video you can see a referee stare at the toy as the Mississippi State bench jumped to their feet, pointing and shouting. Georgia was assessed a technical foul. Witherspoon sank one of the two shots. State won.

What possessed some cranium-challenged idiot to toss the stuffed animal at all much less at such a critical time? I'm sure that someone will figure out who the offending fan is. I'm certain he or she will be punished. I have a few ideas that should be considered:

- Find a chalkboard and have the fan write 10,000 times – "I'm an idiot"

- Make the fan sweep the gym floor before every practice and game next season with a brisk broom

- Apologize to every player, coach, and fellow fan who was present and give each a stuffed UGA bulldog

- Must listen to every broadcast ever recorded with Dick Vitale commentary (OK, that would be cruel and unusual)

Why do we do stupid things? The Apostle Paul wrote in Romans 7: "I don't really understand myself, for I want to do what is right, but I don't do it. I want to do what is good, but I don't. I don't want to what is wrong, but I do it anyway."

I can relate, can't you? I'm so glad that God is still working on me. I am listening right now to a song by Daywind that really speaks to my heart. The title is "Life is hard, but God is good."[12] When I get in my own way, I need His goodness, His faithfulness, His correction, His grace. Thank You, Lord ... and help me to keep from taking stuffed animals to sporting events.

[12] Pam Thum, *Life Is Hard But God is Good*" Daywind, 2007.

Missed Opportunities

People write letters to advice columnists that can be heart-breaking, confusing, heart-warming, or ... stupid:

> "Dear Abby, while I was eating lunch the other day, I saw the image of Abraham Lincoln on one of my potato chips. I got so excited, thinking about how I might be able to share this wonderful news (and how much money I could make), I popped the chip in my mouth before I could stop myself and ate it. Is there anything I can do about this?"

I don't know how the columnist answered, but I've tried to come up with several appropriate responses but none seem very dignified:

- Buy more chips, maybe there's a presidential series.
- Quit eating chips, there's too much salt and it may be affecting your brain
- Have your stomach pumped and have some glue nearby
- Sift through your .... No, that's gross
- It's too late so move on
- Have someone take all of your electronic devices away so you cannot communicate again ... ever

When I think of missed opportunities, this bozo is not what I had in mind. I think of those moments when I could have said the right word ... or when I did say the wrong word; when I did the right thing or when I did the wrong thing. I think of that moment when I could have noticed God at work but was too busy, distracted, or clueless. I think of when the prompting of the Holy Spirit was ignored and a divine appointment was missed.

It is wondrous when we pay attention, when we actively listen, when we slow down and open our eyes and ears and hearts. Today you and I will have opportunities. I hope we don't miss them!

Hey, look at that cloud. Doesn't that look just like Abraham Linc... Sorry.

Slow Is Good

In 1989, Carlo Petrini launched a global, grassroots organization "dedicated to preventing the disappearance of local food cultures and traditions, counteracting the rise of fast life and combating people's dwindling interest in the food they eat, where it comes from, and how our food choices affect world around us." Slow food ... they have a chapter in Atlanta and involve people in 160 countries around the world.

Slow is good, right? In a hurried world, it makes sense to do more than just take your time eating well. We were not designed to live at this pace. The price tag for our mile-a-minute lifestyles is staggering. Suffering from information overload, we find it increasingly difficult to process what we need to know when we need to know it. The ravages of stress and pressure take their toll, and that's just with our kids! 72% of adults say they feel stressed most of the time.

Here's a test: Complete this statement – "I don't have time to ......"

Often the answer has to do with sleep, exercise, choosing and eating food, time alone, time with friends or family, time to focus on spiritual matters.

Fatigue is not our friend. The physical, emotional, mental, and spiritual strain wears us out. We are more susceptible to depression. The lack of motivation for needed change leaves us feeling sad and hopeless. Our brain function is impaired. Feelings of guilt, resentment, and agitation grow.

I'm no psychiatrist and I haven't spent a night at a Holiday Inn, but I do know we don't have to live on this treadmill all our lives. The psalmist urged us to cease striving, be silent and remember who God is (Psalm 46). Why is that important? Because "God is our refuge and strength, always ready to help in times of trouble" (Psalm 46:1). Because Jesus invited us: "Come to Me, all of you who are weary and carry heavy burdens, and I will give you rest" (Matthew 11:28). Because Paul wrote to the Philippians: "My God shall supply all your needs according to His riches in glory in Christ Jesus" (Philippians 4:19).

It makes sense. The One who made us knows exactly what we need.

Salt of the Earth

It was dated March 6, 1975. He wrote a devotional for the state Baptist paper. I found it in a notebook he gave me years ago:

"The speaker at an agricultural meeting used the cliché: You can lead a horse to water, but you cannot make him drink." Immediately a farmer at the back of the room shouted: 'Salt him.'"

In the light of today's word, both individual and collective, there seems to be no cure for the infection of sin, but there is.

"Long ago Jesus said to His followers, 'You are the salt of the earth' – not bread, or water, but salt. The Christian has the function of preserving, flavoring, and curing the community.

"In II Kings 2:19-22, Elisha purified or 'healed' water that was impure and not fit to use by putting salt into it. This Old Testament story reminds us that salt is almost always something that is added.

"Our world needs the salt of Christian living desperately today. Also, we need to remember that the addition of salt is disproportionate to the extent of the crisis. Even one Christian totally committed to Christ can change conditions. Yes, even you or I can accomplish much if we really function as 'the salt of the earth.

"One of the most evident characteristics of salt is that it makes a person thirsty. This is the needed ingredient in the Christian life that is often missing. If we truly function as the salt of the earth, our lives will make people thirsty for the living water, the water of life, Jesus Christ. Our function is not to draw people to ourselves but to our Savior and Lord."

What was true in 1975 is still true to this day. Well said, Dad. [13]

[13] Oliver Wilbanks, *"The Christian Index,"* 1975

Doing Grace

I heard we had a grumbler ... not so unusual in a church. It was reported that he said he wasn't going to 'do grace.' I knew what he meant. He wasn't going to participate in the Bible study on grace that our congregation was beginning. But I must tell you it sounded wrong whatever he meant. "I'm not going to do grace." Wow, what if God had said that? What kind of trouble would we be facing?

"For all have sinned and fallen short of the glory of God." (Romans 3:23)

"For the wages of sin is death, but the free gift of God is eternal life in Christ Jesus." (Romans 6:23)

"For by grace you have been saved through faith; and that not of yourselves, it is the gift of God." (Ephesians 2:8)

Every day you and I have a wonderful opportunity to help people around us to more fully understand how much God loves them and desires a relationship with them. We get to choose to get personally involved in sharing our faith and serving others.

Grace didn't come our way because we deserve it or have earned it. It's a gift, a gift meant to be given ... from a loving God to each of us and from each of us to everyone whom God loves.

Ups, Not Downs

One of my favorite comedians has been John Pinette. Because of his large size, he would joke about his attempts at diet and exercise. In his routine, he would declare he was not an "up" person – sit ups, push ups, chin ups, jump up, speed up, etc.; he was a "down" person – lie down, slow down, tone it down, etc.

Are you an "up" person or a "down" person? Usually we think of an up person as one who is positive, a glass is half-full attitude, and a down person as negative, glass is half-empty attitude.

Let me give you some encouragement to do "ups" ...

- Next time you're at a restaurant, greet your server with a smile. Ask them how their day is going. Ask them to tell you their name and use it.

- Begin and end your day with a prayer of thanksgiving. It's hard to be a grouch with a grateful spirit.

- Contact an old friend you haven't seen for a while. I cannot count the times that someone has come to mind. When that happens, act on it.

- Have a conversation with a neighbor. Too often we're too busy to do more than wave at each other.

- Contact your preacher, not with a complaint but with a word of encouragement. I promise it will be well received!

- Thank a first responder at the next opportunity.

- Perform an intentional, not random, act of kindness.

- Conduct a blessing check. Make a list of those things that cause you to be grateful. If you find that hard to do, dig deeper. We are all blessed more than we deserve.

Disappointment

If you are fan of the University of Alabama and/or the Atlanta Falcons, 2017 didn't start off very well. A last second loss at the national championship game and the Super Bowl melt-down could wreck your day, mess with your mind, rip out your heart, force you to look for someone to blame, or cause you to say words your mom wouldn't like.

Perhaps disappointment is too mild a word. AAARRGGGHHH might be better. You can always try: "We'll get 'em next time" or "Wait til next year" or "We wuz robbed!"

The mild-mannered, sensible, "what's the big deal?" crowd will say things like: "It's only a game" or "grow up" or "why don't you care about something really important?"

AAAAAAARRRRRRRRGGGGGGGGGGGHHHHHHHHHH!

I get it. Disappointment isn't fatal – it just seems that way. I know what 'fan' stands for – fanatic. We do get worked up about things that get more attention than they should … maybe.

Webster's defines disappointment: "To leave unsatisfied; to fail to meet hopes or expectations."

We all experience disappointment. It hurts. It hurts when our favorite team doesn't win but it really hurts when a relationship goes south, or when we feel unwanted, abandoned, taken for granted, or when life becomes cruel and unjust.

Paul wrote to Christians in Rome when the heat was on. It was tough to live out your faith when there was so much at stake. The trophy he talked about was far more significant. Try these out:

"If God is for us, who can be against us?"

"Can anything separate us from the love of Christ?"

"We are more than conquerors through Him who loved us."

Sometimes it helps to remember what team really matters.

Thy Word Have I Hid in My Heart

She woke up, assailed by an unpleasant burning smell. Groggily, she asked the attending nurse, "What is that odor?" The nurse responded, "That's you, dear. We had to use the paddles to bring you back." Her heart had stopped on the operating table. The medical team had used the defibrillator paddles to save her life.

The nurse went about her duties, making my mother more comfortable as she lay in the recovery room. After a few minutes, mom was more alert and full of questions. Another few minutes went by and the nurse said, "I have a question for you. I'm used to hearing all kinds of things in this recovery room as people are emerging from anesthesia, but I can't remember too many people who woke up quoting Scripture. How do you explain that?"

Still a little woozy, mom was able to tell her about the importance of the Bible in her life. She talked about reading God's Word every day, teaching Sunday School for years, attending seminary, leading devotionals at home, church, and other places. As a final word, she told the nurse: "I have tried to hide the Word of God in my heart so that it comes easily to my mind and mouth." The nurse smiled, "Well, it certainly worked."

I challenge me to hide the Word of God in our hearts for some significant reasons:

- It can guard us from sin (Psalm 119:11)
- It can teach us truth and prepare us for purposeful living (2 Timothy 3:16)
- It can guide us in making good decisions and taking good steps (Psalm 119:105)
- It opens the door for blessing in and through our lives (John 15:7,8)

Let's try something: Memorize one verse each day (you can only use John 11:35 once). Keep an account of the Scripture you have dedicated to memory. Share a verse with a family member or friend. Use that verse to explain to someone who needs to hear a word from God what the verse means to you. There is power in the timeless words of Scripture. Unleash it in your life.

It Seemed Like a Good Idea at the Time

Have you ever had a dream that contained what seemed like a brilliant idea at the time, then you woke up and wondered if you had lost your mind? Perhaps, but you're not admitting it, right? These guys tried to turn their idea into reality:

- In 1950, a man created the Venetian Blind Sunglasses – glasses with little slats that you could close when the sun was too bright. Just what you need – glasses that render you sightless.
- Near the same time, a man thought a tiny umbrella that you could fit onto your cigarette or cigar was a great idea. You could smoke in the rain!

- There was a guy who thought it important to know if tomatoes felt pain. His conclusion was that they screamed when sliced.

- Patent # GB2272154 was registered for the "Incy-Wincy Spider Liberator" – a tiny ladder to enable spiders to climb out of a bathtub before it fills up with water. When you see a spider, do you (a) automatically think "How can I help this poor fellow escape?" or (b) reach for a shoe or some other object. Liberating spiders may not be high on your list.

Not all ideas are wacky and witless, particularly when it comes to considering how God might inspire us to serve Him and others. Some of the most exciting and effective ideas come from those who are open to the prompting of God and the passion to make a difference.

One of the greatest gifts God has bestowed on us is the gift of imagination. If you don't believe it, hang around some children and listen and watch. I know these days you are more likely to see kids staring at their tablets, but they can still teach us about how to play, dream, imagine.

You might come up with an invention that will change the world, but you can let God open your mind and heart to new possibilities. Who knows? You might come up with next Pet Rock.

Clothes Make the Man?

She had found it online. She needed an evening dress. It was perfect but it cost a great deal. Her husband was taking her to the annual dinner, and it was a formal affair. She would have to save for months. The date was circled on the calendar and she was so excited. The dress was beautiful, and it fitted her just right. When she walked down the stairs that evening, her husband was impressed. At least, that's what she gathered when his jaw dropped to the floor. She was a vision – hair, nails, jewelry, shoes – everything was just right.

When they arrived at the ballroom, the energy in the crowd added sparkle to the event. Strolling through the lobby, they smiled at friends as they headed toward the tables. And then she stopped abruptly. There, not ten feet in front of her, was a woman wearing her dress, the same dress! The woman was wearing the same dress! Her husband, seeing the look on his wife's face, asked one of those clueless-husband questions, "What's wrong, dear?" How would you have answered?

I wonder what would have happened during the red-carpet silliness at the Oscars if two of those women had walked up wearing the same outfit ... or falling out of the same outfit. Mark Twain once said, "Clothes make the man. Naked people have little or no influence on society." I don't think we should experiment to see if that is really true. I'll take Twain's word.

Paul wrote in Colossians 3 what Christians should and should not wear. He wasn't referring to articles of clothing; he was talking about characteristics and qualities. If we are truly new creatures in Christ, Paul noted, our lives should display the difference the Spirit of God is making in our lives. Because life is a marathon, not a sprint, there will be 'wardrobe malfunctions' along the journey. There are times when we aren't merciful, kind, humble, gentle, patient, and loving. I'm glad God keeps working on us, helping us when we fall down (or up) the stairs.

I need all the help I can get. "Hey, honey, does this go with that?"

Excuses

Creativity is a wonderful thing. We see it everywhere. It shows up in some interesting places … like when parents come up with excuses for their kids:

> "Please excuse Josh for being absent. I forgot to wake him up and I did not find him until I started making the beds -- by then it was too late for him to go to school."

> "John didn't come to school yesterday because he was feeling like he was going to be sick. Thankfully, he wasn't!"

> "Please excuse Janet's absence from school. It was Take Your Daughter to Work Day. Since I don't have a job, I made her stay home and do housework."

> "Please excuse Ricky from school yesterday. He spilled gasoline on his stomach and I was afraid he might explode."

> "Please excuse Mary for missing school yesterday. We forgot to get the Sunday paper off the porch and when we found it on Monday, we thought it was Sunday."

Excuse is defined as an attempt to lessen the blame attaching to (a fault or offense); to seek to defend or justify.

We've all done it. We have tried to excuse ourselves for something we have or haven't done. We would like to justify ourselves or simply get off the hook in an embarrassing or an uncomfortable situation.

Eve had an excuse: It was the serpent's fault. Adam had an excuse: It was Eve's fault.

Somebody has to take the fall (pun intended). One of the marks of maturity is when we own our thoughts, words, and deeds. We live in a shaming/blaming society where it seems to get easier to point to someone or something else.

My mom, and probably yours, used to say that when you point your finger at someone else, you still have four fingers pointed back to you. Lord, help us to take responsibility for our own lives!

Serve the Lord With Gladness

I knew a man named Ernie. He died twenty five years ago this month. Ernie was the kind of man you hope to meet at church. He had a great heart for ministry and loved his church. Through the years, he had led a Sunday School department, taught a Bible class, and served in other capacities. He was named Deacon Emeritus by his church family. He had an exuberant spirit and was willing to help wherever he was needed.

It had not always been that way for Ernie. He met a young lady named Sarah in Atlanta. As they got to know each other and interest grew, she invited him to attend her church, the Baptist Tabernacle. At first, he declined, so she kept asking. He wasn't used to going to church, especially a Baptist church. It wasn't church attendance that he was interested in.

There was a catch, a delicious one it turns out. Sarah's invitation included lunch with her family after the service. On a couple of occasions, Ernie would offer one lame excuse or another – he had to miss the service but could make the lunch.

One Sunday Sarah invited another young man to come to church and join the family for lunch. That was the last Sunday Ernie missed.

Sarah wasn't the only one Ernie met in Atlanta. Due to Sarah's gentle encouragement and the prompting of the Holy Spirit, Ernie met God in Atlanta. One night, Sarah and Ernie were sitting on the back row during a Sunday evening at Tabernacle. Sarah had been praying for Ernie since they met. She wanted Ernie to make a decision for Christ, but she wanted him to do so for the right reasons. Usually they liked to sit closer but, on this occasion, Ernie had his sister and her young child with him.

He had told Sarah more than once that he didn't like the idea of 'walking the aisle' – it made him uncomfortable. Imagine Sarah's surprise that evening when Ernie handed her the hymnal during the invitation and told her, "Here, take it. I'm going." The next thing she knew Ernie was running down the aisle to meet the preacher. I guess he wasn't kidding – he'd rather run than walk the aisle! Pumping the hand of the pastor, Ernie's joy at coming to Christ marked his life with the Lord from that day forward. Serving the Lord with gladness just seemed to come naturally to him.

How would you complete the phrase for yourself? Serve the Lord with _____. Ernie set a great example. How are we doing?

Making Sense of Suffering

First of all, making sense of suffering is an almost impossible task. The tragedies that the author of *It is Well with My Soul* experienced, a hymn that has comforted countless grief-stricken, heart-broken people, are almost incalculable. Horatio Spafford lost so much in a short span of time that it would have been quite understandable if he had given in to bitterness and fury. How did he cling to faith in the midst of such pain?

Most of us have known the wrenching devastation of grief and suffering. Platitudes don't help. It would be better if those who try to explain our misery would just remain silent. When there are no answers, we don't need someone to try to give them to us.

Where do we turn? Where is the God who promises protection and provision for His children? How can God claim that "never again will you fear any harm" and be "mighty to save" (Zephaniah 3:15, 17)? How can a loving God allow so much suffering?

Scotty Smith, founding pastor of Christ Community Church in Franklin, Tennessee, wrote a wonderful book, *Objects of His Affection*.[14] In the eighth chapter of the book, he offered his thoughts on the love of suffering. The love of suffering? Whose love? Can we really believe that God can love us through suffering? Can't He just take our suffering away or keep it from happening altogether? Can there possibly be a purpose in our suffering?

We draw close to Holy Week, the week of the passion of Jesus. Smith noted that God has responded to the suffering of His world through His Son. Jesus Himself spoke of His purpose in coming into our world. After His encounter with Zacchaeus, Jesus said, "The Son of Man has come to seek and save those like him who are lost" (Luke 19:10). Mark's gospel recorded these words of the Lord: "For the Son of Man came not to be served but to serve others and to give His life as a ransom for many" (Mark 10:45).

Smith wrote: "To desire the saving of many lives over the preservation of one's own life is the way of the cross. It is the saving of many lives that defines the suffering of Jesus." It is ultimately the suffering of Jesus that can help us gain a better perspective. "It is the suffering of Jesus that answers our cry for justice in the face of evil, suffering, and injustice. And it is the suffering Jesus who knows how to console us until the promised day of vindication and consummation of our redemption."

"The Way of the Cross Leads Home" is not just some trite religiosity. It is a life view. It is a way of facing the tragedy and pain with hope that sin, evil, and death are not the end of the trail. The cross is our symbol of what we mean to the Father. The cross is His statement that nothing would prevent the ultimate destruction of that which seeks to destroy us. Even through a veil of tears, we continue to be a people of faith, trust, and love.

[14] Scotty Smith, *"Objects of His Affection: Coming Alive to the Compelling Love of God"* Howard Books, 2010

Follow the Leader

A young woman was stuck in a snowstorm when she remembered her dad's advice: "If you ever get stuck in a snowstorm, wait until a snowplow drives by and then follow it." Eventually she saw a snowplow, so she followed it along in her car. After 30 minutes, the snowplow driver stopped, got out, and walked up to the woman's car asking, "Lady, why are you following me?" She explained what her father had told her, and the driver said, "Well I'm done with the Walmart parking lot now. Do you want to follow me to Best Buy?"

We must be careful who we follow. If you don't think you're following someone or something, you might rethink that. We all are subject to those who influence our lives, for good or ill. What voices do we listen to? Are they trustworthy? If you're a Christian, you know whose voice you should be heeding … you know, the One who said, "Follow Me."

There is another way to look at this. Who are you leading? Who is watching you, learning from you, paying attention to your attitude or words or behavior? Since we're using a snow theme, here's an old story: a father had just returned from a trip to the shed. The snow was deep, and every step left a large footprint. He happened to look out and see his 6-year-old attempting to match dad's footsteps. The boy would leap from one deep impression to the other. Dad realized his boy was just trying to be like him. He thought to himself, "I had better watch where I walk. He's going to follow my steps."

Throughout my ministry, I've heard people say that they weren't leaders. Not true, if you have influence over one life, you're leading someone. We better watch where and how we walk. Somebody's paying attention.

His Eye Is On the Sparrow

"What is the price of two sparrows – one copper coin? But not a single sparrow can fall to the ground without your Father knowing it. And the very hairs on your head are numbered. So don't be afraid; you are more valuable to God than a whole flock of sparrows" (Matthew 120:29,30)

Mrs. Civilla Martin, author of the gospel hymn text, tells of a visit in 1904 to a bedridden Christian friend. [15] Mrs. Martin asked the woman if she ever got discouraged because of her physical condition. Her friend responded quickly: "Mrs. Martin, how can I be discouraged when my heavenly Father watches over each little sparrow and I know He loves and cares for me."

What song would you write about your response to the circumstances of your life? With much to complain about or to grieve over or to be terrified by, it might seem that our lyrics might display our disenchantment or disgust or anxiety. Or we could live in trust and faith…

God said to Joshua: "Be strong and very courageous! Do not be afraid or discouraged. For the Lord your God is with you wherever you go." (Joshua 1:9)

David said to Goliath: "You come to me with sword, spear, and javelin, but I come to you in the name of the Lord of Heaven's Armies – the God of Israel. This is the Lord's battle and He will give you to us!" (1 Samuel 17:45-47)

Paul said to the church at Rome: "And I am convinced that nothing can ever separate us from God's love. Neither death nor life, neither angels nor demons, neither our fears for today nor our worries about tomorrow – not even the powers of hell can separate us from God's love. No power in the sky about or in the earth below – indeed nothing in all creation will ever be able to separate us from the love of God that is revealed in Christ Jesus our Lord." (Romans 8:38,39)

Jesus said to His disciples: "I am leaving you with a gift – peace of mind and heart. And the peace I give you is a gift the world cannot give. So don't be troubled or afraid." (John 14:27)

John Henry Howett wrote: "Let us sing even when we do not feel like it, for in this way we give wings to heavy feet and turn weariness into strength."

Civilla Martin wrote: "His eye is on the sparrow and I know He's watches me." What song will you sing?

15 Civilla Martin, *"His Eye is on the Sparrow"* published in 1905.

Believe It or Not

Around this time of year, you can count on media attention on the person and story of Jesus. A few years ago, an article appeared in Newsweek magazine where the religion editor explained that "Easter is a celebration of the final act of the Passion, in which Jesus rose from his tomb in his body three days after his execution. The Gospels insist on the veracity of this supernatural event. Jesus died and rose again so that all his followers could, eventually, do the same. This story has strained the credulity of even the most devoted believer. For truly, it's unbelievable." [16]

Unbelievable? The apostle Paul wrote to the Corinthians, "And if we have hope in Christ only for this life, we the most miserable people in the world" (1 Corinthians 15:19). Is it all fanciful? Has the story of the itinerant preacher who walked the earth two thousand years ago been transformed by mythical proportions? Can we really believe what the Bible has to say about Jesus of Nazareth?

In his marvelous book, *King's Cross*, Timothy Keller offered "a meditation on the historical Christian premise that Jesus' life, death, and resurrection form the central event of cosmic and human history as well as the central organizing principle of our own lives. Said another way, the whole story of the world – and how we fit into it – is most clearly understood through a careful, direct look at the story of Jesus."

So this is not a debate about one of many historical figures who shaped the way we think or live. It is far more important. There is no list. He has no peers. There is no one like Jesus.

As we enter Holy Week, much of the world will shift its attention to the improbable story of God entering His creation, becoming human, suffering an ignoble death, and stirring a following that exists to this day. In Christian symbol, the Lion of Judah became the Lamb of God. The altar of sacrifice was a crude Roman cross where one innocent man died for the sake of every human. Isaiah called Him a man of sorrows who carried the burden of every sinner and every sin.

We don't expect gods to act that way. He came into the world in the most primitive way possible. His abode was not a palace. He had no human-devised credential. He was a common man who came from an obscure village in the hill country of Palestine.

As the week began, He rode into Jerusalem at the beginning of the festival where great crowds had gathered. But He didn't ride on a war horse as a conquering king might have done. Keller described His triumphal entrance this way: "Here was Jesus Christ, the King of authoritative, miraculous power, riding into town on a steed fit for a child or a hobbit."

Jesus did a lot of things in unexpected ways. He focused His attention on the outcasts and the downtrodden. He refused to cater to the powerful. He comforted the afflicted and afflicted the comfortable. He who knew no sin became sin so that humanity be freed from the punishment we deserved.

As we experience this most important week in the entire year, I pray we remember what Jesus determined each of us is worth... whatever it took.

[16] Kenneth Woodward, "Rethinking the Resurrection," *Newsweek Magazine*, April, 1996.

I'm Dreaming, Right?

Michael Licona coauthored the 2004 book, *The Case for the Resurrection of Jesus*. [17] He addressed objections to the resurrection. One of them has been that people hallucinated the risen Christ. They wanted to see Him so badly that they did. Licona lived in Virginia Beach for a number of years. During that time, he got to know several Navy SEALs stationed there. He knew that few applicants made it through the intense, strenuous training. These guys were normally tight-lipped about their experiences, but Licona had heard enough to realize the stress these men had gone through. One of the infamous components of their qualification process was "Hell Week" – sleep deprivation, constant and vigorous exercise, verbal assault, team-building challenges, and much more. Some of the SEALs told Licona that 80% of the men experience hallucinations – but not the same hallucinations. One guy told him: "Hallucinations aren't contagious. They're personal. They are like dreams. I couldn't wake my wife in the middle of the night and say 'Honey, I'm dreaming of being in Hawaii. Quick, go back to sleep, join me in my dream, and we'll have a free vacation.'"

Did people hallucinate the risen Lord? Even though Jesus had announced on at least three occasions the events that would take place in Jerusalem (Including "But on the third day, I will be raised from the dead."), none of His followers would make sense of His warning until after the fact. They weren't expecting to see Him. Those who went to His tomb weren't thinking they would encounter anything other than a dead body.

The tomb couldn't hold Him. What He promised really happened. My life was changed by what took place two thousand years ago.

One day, perhaps soon, He will return. That won't be a hallucination either!

[17] Gary Habermas and Michael R. Licona, *The Case for the Resurrection of Jesus*, Kregel Publications, 2004.

Spin

Spin. It has become a part of public dialogue. Someone has defined it as propaganda or a creative interpretation of events or deflection from potentially controversial topics or playing loosely with the truth or crafted bias.

Here's an example: "If you put aside this Macondo incident, 2009 was the best year we'd had, and 2010 was also heading in that direction." Those were the words of BP CEO Bob Dudley used to describe the trajectory of his company. Macondo was the well that dumped 210 million gallons of oil in the Gulf of Mexico, creating an environmental and economic catastrophe that affected millions of lives and cost billions of dollars. 11 people who worked on the Deep Horizon rig were never found.

"So, other than that, how did you like the play, Mrs. Lincoln?"

I guess we can all be guilty of spin. There are times when we try to cover a mistake, exaggerate a story, make excuses, or try to make ourselves look better. Our personal histories can get a bit clouded, like the guy who admitted, "The older I get, the better I was."

History is full of spin, usually told through the eyes of the victor, the more powerful, the one writing. Christians have been accused of spin through the centuries. To some, the Bible is just a collection of

66 books full of spin. The story of Jesus has often been assaulted as history's greatest spin.

Think about it. It couldn't have happened the way the Gospels spin it. Let's review some of the criticism: (1) There was no such historical figure as Jesus; (2) Jesus was a simple man, a teacher, perhaps a prophet, but nothing more: (3) The miracle stories were concocted to make Jesus look bigger, better; (4) Jesus did not die on the cross – he swooned, he recovered, they used a substitute; (5) The disciples stole his body and hid it, then told fantastic stories about a resurrection; (6) The appearances post-death can be attributed to mass hallucinations.

There are plenty more. To sum it up, I think men like C.S. Lewis and Josh McDowell had it right. Jesus was either liar, lunatic, or Lord. No spin. A great deal rides on the answer people choose.

Just One Little Letter

They sound the same. They are spelled the same ... except for one little letter.

Mourning and morning. Mourning is about grief, about the recognition of loss. You cannot love without loss. That's where the one little letter comes in. "U" stands for each of us because each of us has known and will know what it means to lose something that or someone who matters. The "u" can also refer to us. Grief can drive us apart or bring us together. We may mourn privately but our healing usually comes in community. We can be overwhelmed by our personal sadness, but we can also be surrounded by those who will bear our griefs with us.

And yet there is more. How does mourning turn to morning? We are approaching Holy Week. In order to arrive at Easter, we must pass by the cross. The blackest day in history calls us not to pass by, but to linger and mourn – mourn the death, mourn the devastation of sin, mourn our responsibility. But we cannot linger long because Sunday's coming.

On the morning of the third day, the power of sin and death and evil was broken. In the morning the stone was rolled away. In the morning the perfect sacrifice who suffered a cruel death left the grim reaper in the dust. In the morning He turned mourning to joy.

Within the span of a few days, the deaths of two remarkable women named Debbie have given us reason to mourn. Our hearts are broken for the families who have suffered loss. But we are people of hope as they were women of faith. Our mourning will turn to joy because of that morning two thousand years ago. One little letter … For God so loved "u" that He gave His only Son. Mourning turned to morning.

My Hero

Hero: a person admired for courage, nobility, exploits, ideal qualities, and achievements.

Do you know anyone like that? Most people who are heroic never consider themselves in that light. Someone who claims to be a hero is normally dismissed as arrogant or delusional.

I always thought the term "unsung hero" was interesting. I'll give you an example:

Have you ever heard the name, Benjamin Clark? Out of the horror of 9/11, a number of people emerged into public consciousness because of their actions. Benjamin Clark was one of those, but few know his story. He wasn't a firefighter or a police officer, one of the numerous first responders who acted so bravely on that terrible day. Benjamin Clark was a chef.

He worked for Fiduciary Trust, preparing meals for the company. On that fateful Tuesday morning, he acted quickly to begin urging people on the 96th floor offices in the South Tower to get out of the building. First clearing his department, he went around the floor telling people to leave. A Fiduciary official credited Clark with saving hundreds of lives that day.

On his way down, he encountered a woman in a wheelchair. He wasn't going to abandon her. His mother said of him, "My son was a Marine, so you know he wasn't going to leave anybody behind."

Like so many others, Benjamin Clark died that day. A chef known for his fabulous meatloaf, for remembering peoples' names, for noting favorite meals, he sacrificed his life to help others.

As Michael Daly wrote of this unsung hero, "The enormity of Benjamin Clark's sacrifice is made apparent by the photos of his own five children hanging in his mother's home. He had been happily married to a wonderful woman, LaShawn Clark, and he had been the happiest of dads." [18]

More than 1,200 people attended the memorial service for Benjamin Clark. Many in the crowd that day were alive because of his heroic efforts.

Perhaps the heroes in your life haven't performed in such dramatic fashion, but we all have them. There are people in your life who might escape your notice if you don't take the time to pay attention.

Make a list, pick up the phone, craft a message to someone who has been heroic for you. It might surprise them to know you feel that way about them.

On Good Friday, a man was standing in the crowd watching a procession of condemned men on their way to the cross. The last man in the pitiful line stumbled and fell. The execution detail knew that the man was so weak from the torture he had endured and the blood he had lost that he couldn't make it without help. They picked that man, Simon the Cyrene, out of the crowd to carry the cross beam the rest of the way. Some might say he was forced to do it. I believe he was willing to do it. And he did.

People don't get up in the morning and decide to be heroic. Circumstances present themselves; opportunities are available. Simon made the most of the moment. So did Benjamin Clark.

Thank you, Lord, for people who seize the moment and do things that matter.

[18] Michael Daly, "The Story of an Unsung 9/11 Hero," *Daily Beast*, September 11, 2013.

Spring Brake

No, I didn't spell it wrong. During this time of year, people need a brake. Kari Myers wrote an article entitled "Being good when you feel bad." Here are some of her thoughts.

"Sickness, stress, and sleep deprivation are three things that can really do a number on a person's disposition. Don't ask me how I know this. I just do. Maybe you know it, too. When we feel bad, physically or emotionally, we tend not to handle things as well as we would on a good day. Bad days can tempt us to focus inward. If they persist, we can fall into self-pity or become obsessed with improving our situation. We can be self-absorbed, self-serving, or just plain selfish. But it does not have to be so. Jesus showed us another way. At the moment of His betrayal to an angry mob who would take Him to a cruel death, He healed the servant of His enemy. On the worst of days, as He was unjustly arrested and threatened, He responded with compassion. In the midst of His own pain, He took notice of and tended to the pain of another. Jesus loved in good times and bad."

We need a brake. We need to stop striving so much. We need to inventory our busy-ness. We need to honor Sabbath keeping. We cannot run on empty without damage to us and others.

He had been neglecting his young daughter. He knew it, but what could he do? Work was crazy. Meeting one deadline after the next required immense investments of time and energy. His wife had reminded him often that he was missing a lot at home, with her and with their 3-year-old little girl. He promised he would come home early and spend time with her. He left work only to bring work home. But he could take a few minutes. "What would you like to do with your dad?" he asked her while glancing at his watch. "I wanna take a walk." Simple enough. How long could that take? One quick turn around the block. Only it wasn't one quick turn around the block. Every few steps, she stopped, bent over to examine a bug or a flower or a crack in the sidewalk and exclaim, "Lookit!" His exasperation was evident. Passing them by was an elderly neighbor. The old man whispered to the dad, "You're missing it." Trying to be polite, the father responded, "I've seen a bug. I've seen a flower." The neighbor stopped and said, "That's not what you're missing."

Apply the brake. Don't miss life. "Lookit!"

Making It Personal

What do you take personally? Often that refers to things which might offend, anger, or annoy us. Here's a few:

- The guy who cuts you off in traffic
- The woman who is wearing the same dress you have on
- The obviously-undeserving associate awarded the promotion you sought
- The group that suddenly gets quiet as you approach
- The person who accepts unwarranted praise and deflects deserved criticism at your expense

We could list more, perhaps many more, but let's shift our attention to things that we should take personally:

- Do you take your life personally? One of the signs of maturing, developing people is that they take responsibility for their lives. How you were raised, what you endured, the disadvantages you suffered, the breaks you didn't get ... at some point we have to live in the now. Until they invent a time machine, we cannot return to the past to right the wrongs or make better choices. This one and only life I have been given is my responsibility. I should take it personally.

- Do you take your faith personally? No one can walk your spiritual journey for you. We need a Paul, a Barnabas and a Timothy in our lives, but we have to work out our faith for ourselves. This week I will preach on the 8 "I am" statements of Jesus recorded in John's gospel. I will be encouraging our people to make each of the statements personal. Is Jesus your "way, truth, and life?" Is He your light, your bread, your resurrection, your life? I should take my faith seriously.

- Do you take your stewardship personally? No, I'm not just talking about financial matters, but I'm not excluding them either. Each of us has been entrusted with time, talent, and treasure. Where does God fit into how you express these gifts? If He doesn't get the best and the first, can you truly say that you take your stewardship seriously?

- Do you take your church personally? The Bible describes the assembly of believers as a body with individual parts – each part essential to the whole. Most churches operate at about 8-10% capacity. A human body that only has the use of 8-10% of its functions doesn't function very well.

Worship-Connect-Serve, words that should be familiar to believers. They help us identify who we should be and what we should do as a fellowship of disciples. They represent a multi-directional approach to the Christian life. The vertical relationship is primary. The worship of God is our highest privilege and greatest responsibility. The horizontal relationships we share with each other strengthens and unifies the body; grows deeper connections that help us live life together. The outward expression of serving connects us to the world we are called to serve.

You Matter

Name the twelve disciples. No googling. Perhaps you start off strong – Peter, James, John, Thomas, Andrew, Judas … no, take Judas off since he betrayed Christ …

Having witnessed a few minutes of the red-carpet celebrity strut of the Academy Awards, it still amazes me who seems to matter and what some people will actually wear in public. There will always be headliners who get more than their share of attention, but what happens to the stars if the "little people" don't do their jobs?

You may not know the full list of the disciples, but Jesus did. He called each of them. They mattered. One of the wonderful things about belonging to Him is that each of us matters. He doesn't love some of us more than He loves all of us.

I love the passage in Isaiah 43 – "I have called you by name; you are Mine." He calls each of us. We all matter.

Some people live out their calling without much fanfare. The spotlight doesn't fall on them. They are like the guy who was escorting some starlet to a movie premiere. The media was pushing and shoving to get a picture or an interview, the fans were frantic to see who was in the next limo. This guy steps out and a reporter with microphone and big hair yells to him, "Are you anybody?"

Jesus call us all. The way we employ our time, talent, and treasure illustrates our response. You matter!

He Should've Looked Up

When my dad was a student at Southwestern Baptist Theological Seminary in Fort Worth, he had a friend who was asked to officiate at his first funeral. The young pastor was understandably nervous and sought help and advice from his more seasoned colleagues. One particularly helpful classmate lent him his minister's manual that contained suggested readings and comments for such an occasion. The service at the church went well. After arriving at the cemetery, the young minister took the customary position at the back of the hearse and began leading the procession toward the grave. He was so intent on reading the right words in the right tone of voice that he forgot something. "Ashes to ashes, dust to dust …" then he walked into the hole. He should've looked up.

Are there times when we are so focused on things that we don't pay attention as we should? Distracted driving is a huge and sometimes tragic problem. I've seen people so absorbed in their phones that they walk into wall or poles or other people. They should've looked up.

We can find ourselves so consumed by the minutia of life that we give in to worries and cares that rob us of the vitality God desires for us. The psalmist spoke about this: "I will lift up my eyes to the mountains; from where does my help come? My help comes from the Lord, who made heaven and earth. He will not allow your foot to slip; He who keeps you will not slumber."

Here are a few takeaways:

- We could all use some help from time to time
- The Person to whom we can turn is the One who created all of life, including our own
- He promises to protect us
- He is paying attention
- We should look up

Rich!

We're rich! Can you believe it? We just got this very personal letter from a guy in Nigeria, who I am sure is destined to be a really good friend. He wants to give us $3 million. $3 million! He is doing this out of the goodness of his heart because he wants us to be happy. I can be happy with $3 million, can't you? The details are a bit fuzzy ... something about needing our financial information so that the transfer can be handled without any problems. I am so excited just thinking about all the things we can buy with that money!

Oh, you've heard from him too. He must have lots of friends and lots of money. What a guy!

Somebody must have taken the bait. Somebody has had his/her bank account drained by this scam. I hope they catch the guy and all the rest just like him...but they won't.

I only know one get-rich scheme that works. There was this other guy who sent me a letter. He spoke about treasure and inheritance and abundant life. He wasn't trying to get into my bank account; He was trying to get into my heart. He promised me something money couldn't buy, and I couldn't earn. It was worth far more than any earthly wealth could acquire.

His letter wasn't a scam letter; it was a love letter. He didn't just address it to me. He wanted everybody to read it. He wanted everybody to know it was meant for each of us.

I am rich. I am a joint heir with the King of kings and the Lord of lords. I hope you are, too.

Warning Signs

Warning signs are everywhere – Stop, Yield, 55 MPH, Men at Work, School Zone. Our food and medicine all have labels. Someone is always telling us what will happen if we don't pay attention. These signs are a little unusual:

- "NOTICE! Thank you for noticing this new notice. Your noticing has been noted and will be reported to the authorities." Whew! I feel better now that I have been noticed noticing.

- "Please do not walk, mosey, saunter, stroll, toddle, tread, traipse, troop, ambulate, prance, dance, tramp, skip, lumber, plod, slog, stride, trudge, run, scurry, beat feet, scamper, scoot, crawl, creep or step on plants." I didn't know reading a sign was so tiring.

- "DO NOT PARK HERE! The wrath of the ancients will fall upon your head. Your shoelaces will not stay tied. Rabid squirrels will invade your home. Food in your refrigerator will mysteriously spoil. Your vehicle will start making that expensive knocking sound again and no one will talk to you at parties." I'll just look for another place.

What does it take to get our attention? Jerry Seinfeld said that the only warning label people take seriously is DRY CLEAN ONLY! There are plenty of other warnings we should heed. Most of them are for our own good – they keep us safe, out of danger, healthier.

Perhaps there could be others that would help us stay focused:

- Warning! Your spiritual energy is being drained. Open the Word, pray with a friend, share your faith, and spend some time thanking and praising God.

- Warning! There is a friend who needs your encouragement, support, accountability, patience, presence.

- Warning! Your family could use a little more attention right now. I know business is stressful and demanding but family comes first.

- Warning! Your stewardship of time, talent, and treasure is slipping, Rediscover the joy of serving in His name.

There are some other signs you might not have seen in a while:

- Hey, I'm proud of you. Keep up the good work.

- I've never had a friend as loyal as you.

- I am glad you're my dad. I've got the best mom in the world.

- My grace is sufficient for you.

Here's another sign I'd like you to see: "I'm glad we're in this together."

It Can't Happen to Me!

"I cannot conceive of any vital disaster happening to this vessel. Modern shipbuilding has gone beyond that."

You probably know who said that. Even if you don't know his name, you might know it must be related to the disaster of April 15, 1912.

Several years before the "unsinkable" Titanic sank, Captain Edward Smith made that pronouncement. "It can't happen to me!"

The ship went down in the frigid waters of the North Atlantic after striking an iceberg. The toll was horrific – 1,517 men, women, and children lost their lives. "It can't happen to me!"

When they boarded the ship on April 8, 1912, in Southampton, they could not have anticipated what awaited. The reputation of the pride of the White Star line was trumpeted by media sources which marveled at the advanced technology and superior engineering. The line had never made such a boast, but they didn't discourage the "unsinkable" claim.

One writer, on the 100th anniversary of the event, noted: "The sinking ship continues to be a morality play about what happens when humans buy their own hype. If the Titanic teaches us anything, it's that we are all, indeed, sinkable. "It can happen to me."

Is it arrogance? Is it ignorance? What makes us think we are invulnerable? No one wants to dwell on the possibility of tragedy. We simply cannot go through life untouched by misery and heartbreak. We know that ... we just don't want to think too much about it.

As Titanic steamed full speed ahead, it received warnings of hazardous ice flows. She never slowed down. There were problems below decks that were never addressed, a faulty rudder that had not been upgraded, and lifeboats that could hold only 52% of those on board.

There are certainly times when we cannot avoid trouble, but there are also times when we need to pay attention to areas of our lives that need addressing. Perhaps we should start by looking "below decks". The book of Proverbs contains some applicable insight: "Above all else, guard your heart, for it affects everything you do" (Proverbs 4:23).

Imagine

It was the best-selling single of his career, a career shortened by an assassin's bullet in 1980. Written and performed by John Lennon, the song soared up the charts to critical acclaim. Many agreed with this assessment: "Its lyrics encourage the listener to imagine a world at peace without the barriers of borders or the divisiveness of religions and nationalities, and to consider the possibility that the focus of humanity should be living a life unattached to material possessions."

> "Imagine there's no heaven; it's easy if you try.
> No hell below us; above us only sky.
> Imagine all the people living for today ...
> Imagine there's no countries; it isn't hard to do.
> Nothing to kill or die for, and no religion, too
> Living life in peace ...
> You may say I'm a dreamer, but I'm not the only one.
> I hope someday you'll join us, and the world will be as one."

There is more to the song. It suggests a world without greed or hunger or pain. It's a dream.

One day the dream will come true, John. Probably not how you imagined it. We humans have made a mess of things because we're sinners. And that's where you missed the point. We cannot fix it by ourselves.

We featured an old hymn in worship yesterday: *"This is My Father's World."* In the last verse are these words: "O let me ne'er forget that though the wrong seems oft so strong, God is the ruler yet. The battle is not done; Jesus who died shall be satisfied, and earth and heaven be one."

What you wished for, John, is possible because of what Christ did for you, and me, and all the world you sang about.

More people know your song than the one Maltbie Babcock wrote. His lyrics were published in 1901 after his death at age 42. His original text concluded with: "This is my Father's world, why should my heart be sad? The Lord is King; let the heavens ring! God reigns; let the earth be glad!"

Yes, John, there is much wrong in this world. But there is something more powerful than all the pain and misery and inequity and prejudice because there is Someone more powerful than sin and evil and death. I think you know that now.

Courage

Paul Harvey, loved for his heartwarming tales and unique style, told this story: "One summer morning as Ray Blankenship was preparing his breakfast, he gazed out the window, and saw a small girl being swept along in the rain-flooded drainage ditch beside his Andover, Ohio, home. Blankenship knew that farther downstream, the ditch disappeared with a roar underneath a road and then emptied into the main culvert. Ray dashed out the door and raced along the ditch, trying to get ahead of the floundering child. Then he hurled himself into the deep, churning water. Blankenship surfaced and was able to grab the child's arm. They tumbled end over end. Within about three feet of the yawning culvert, Ray's free hand felt something hard; possibly a rock protruding from one bank. He clung desperately, but the tremendous force of the water tried to tear him and the child away. 'If I can just hang on until help comes,' he thought. He did better than that. By the time fire-department rescuers arrived, Blankenship had pulled the girl to safety. Both were treated for shock. On April 12, 1989, Ray Blankenship was awarded the Coast Guard's Silver Lifesaving Medal. The award is fitting, for this selfless person was at even greater risk to himself than most people knew. Ray Blankenship can't swim."

This Sunday, the featured hymn was written by Lydia Baxter, a woman who was invalid for much of her life. "Take the Name of Jesus with You" is a testimony of courage in the face of suffering and difficulty. During the great Moody-Sankey evangelistic campaigns in the late 19th century, the song with lyrics by Lydia Baxter and tune by William Doane was popular with the great crowds.

The human condition is often one that affords us opportunity to rise above our circumstances. Paul wrote, "I can do everything through Christ, who gives me strength." The key is found in those two words: through Christ. The One who displayed the greatest courage in history offers His presence and power to us daily. When we appropriate what Christ gives, we can indeed take the name of Jesus wherever we go.

Grave Crisis

They are running out of room. At cemeteries around the world, space for burials has been a real problem. In New Orleans, the additional problem of a high water table has made it difficult to keep up with the number of graves needed. In Arlington National Cemetery, more plots are needed to honor America's fallen. In London, a newly instituted practice called grave sharing has been implemented. Graves are opened, caskets are removed, a deeper hole is dug, the first casket is reinterred, and the second casket is placed on top. Many countries have been dealing with this problem for over 200 years.

2000 years ago, a new tomb was needed. A wealthy man in Jerusalem owned a family plot. Someone needed a grave. A man had come to a violent end, another victim of the barbaric Roman form of execution – crucifixion. On many occasions, bodies nailed to a cross were just left there as a grim reminder to anyone who dared oppose the Empire. Sometimes the dead were thrown into the city dump, a place called Gehenna, to make room for the next condemned to die. But on this occasion, the wealthy man appealed to Roman governor Pilate. He had an unused tomb. Could he have permission to bury the battered body in his family tomb? Permission granted.

A borrowed tomb. Jesus was buried in a borrowed tomb. It was temporary loan. When you borrow something, it is expected that you return it. He wouldn't need it for long.

From The Message: "Death swallowed by triumphant Life! Who got the last word, oh, Death? Oh, Death, who's afraid of you now?" (1 Corinthians 15:55)

Failure

The headlines are brutal:

> "Epic Fail"
> "Historic Collapse"
> "Spieth Splats"
> "Worst Collapse in History"
> "A Choke to Remember"

Does it matter that he finished tied for second or that he won $888,000 for the tournament? Do we really need to feel sorry for a guy who plays golf for a living? It might also help to remember that Jordan Spieth was only 22.

After all that, he failed. At the press conference, it was obvious that he was devastated by his failure to finish well. Unlike some other pro athletes, he handled his media grilling with humility and class. He had his moments when cameras were stuck in his face, but he didn't try to hide from his poor performance when it mattered most.

How's your Monday going? How do you think his was going?

All of us have failed. Very few of us have failed on that large a stage. How do you think you would have handled that moment? As crushing as the loss must have been, having to hold the green jacket for Dan Willett must have been incredibly painful. Look at his face as he helped Willett put it on.

You failed. I failed. Now what?

Clichés are abundant:

> "Don't let a stumble on the road be the end of the journey."

> "Failure doesn't come from falling down; failure comes from not getting up."
>
> "What defines us is how well we rise after falling."
>
> "There is no education like adversity."
>
> "If you have not experienced excruciating failure, you may never experience exhilarating success."

Do you think Jordan Spieth wanted to hear any of these? Probably not. What helps you most after you have failed? Consider what we could learn:

- Don't allow one failure to define you.
- While you are accepting responsibility for yourself, don't forget give yourself grace.
- Don't move on too quickly – we typically learn more from our misses than our makes.
- We serve a God who specializes in new beginnings.

I was pulling for him to win. Now I'm pulling for him dust himself off and get back in the game. I hope he has more encouragers than detractors.

Awkward

We've all had awkward moments:

- In 8th grade, I threw up a beautiful shot ... in the wrong basket.

- I was asked to officiate at a funeral for a person I did not know. The funeral director gave me the wrong name that I promptly used throughout the service.

- In my first wedding, I solemnly switched a key phrase – Instead of "What God has joined together …" I began with "What God has torn asunder."

You've had them, too.

- Perhaps you burst out laughing at a funeral.

- Perhaps you began to sing loudly when no one else had started.

- Perhaps the person you asked out for a date thought you were kidding.

- Perhaps your boss sent you a friend request on Facebook.

- Perhaps you're Steve Harvey and you announce the wrong winner at the Miss Universe pageant.

- Perhaps you're Brooke Shields in a public announcement spot: "Smoking kills. If you're killed, you've lost a very important part of your life."

- Perhaps you're Dan Quayle, who began a speech at NASA: "My fellow astronauts …"

Awkward, embarrassing, hard-to-recover-from moments of life happen. You hope people around you are kind, understanding, and compassionate … or not. When I returned to school after my goof at the basketball game, one of my coaches was waiting to christen me with a new nickname – "Wrong Way Wilbanks." Tough for a 13-year-old boy to handle.

We should strive to show more grace in the awkward moments. You won't meet a person who hasn't stumbled or blown it or messed up. Jesus had a way of dealing with such things: "Treat others as you wish to be treated."

A sign of a maturing person – if everybody's laughing, you might as well join in. It may lessen the sting a bit.

No Rain

A Native American was invited by a friend to hear a revival preacher at a meeting in a church in the Midwest. After the service, the man's friend commented, "Boy, he sure preached up a storm, didn't he?" The man thought for a moment then responded: "High wind, big thunder, no rain."

Too many times at church there is a lot of wind, perhaps a good bit of thunder, but not enough rain. Our people deserve better than that. Our people need more than that. At the same time, James wrote we are to be doers of the Word, not hearers only. For both messenger and audience, it would certainly help if we put into practice what we say and hear.

I can trot out clichés:

- People don't care how much you know but they do know how much you care.

- Walk the talk.

- Practice what you preach.

- If you don't really believe it, how do you expect people to really receive it?

Preachers usually know if they have swung and missed. There are times when the best approach would be to read a passage of Scripture, pray, and go home. On that particular day, you just didn't have your best stuff.

After one such Sunday, the custodian was cleaning around the pulpit and happened to notice the sermon notes lying on the pulpit. Out of curiosity, he looked at the several pages and saw on one that the preacher had scribbled some notes in the margin. Looking closer he read, "Argument weak here. Yell like hell."

Another preacher was delivering a rather dry sermon and he noticed one of his key leaders slumped over, sleeping in the first row. The preacher leaned over and whispered to the man's wife, "Wake him up!" She quickly retorted, "You put him to sleep; you wake him up."

Speaking of rain ... did you hear about the country church who decided to have a prayer meeting to ask God to end the drought and send the rain? The church was full that day. The preacher stood up and announced that the service had been cancelled. Shouts of protest rang out. The pastor waited for quiet then said, "The reason we won't have this service is obvious. Not one person brought an umbrella."

"I'm Old Enough"

"I'm old enough" isn't a complete sentence. There are always qualifiers:

- "I'm old enough to tie my shoes."
- "I'm old enough to sleep without the light on."

- "I'm old enough to drive a car."
- "I'm old enough to make my own decisions."

Sometimes the sentence changes – "You're old enough."

- "You're old enough to sit there and be quiet."
- "You're old enough to mow the grass."
- "You're old enough to stop acting like a baby."
- "You're old enough to know better."
- "You're old enough to do this yourself."

It seems like there are two notions to "old enough." The first is on the way up as you develop, grow, and develop. As you move through childhood and adolescence toward adulthood, you learn lessons, achieve milestones, and become your own person.

Then there is that second. You are not going up anymore; heck, you're heading downhill and you notice you are picking up speed!

- "You're old enough not to try to do that anymore."
- "You're old enough to not be able to do that anymore."
- "You're old enough to know that there are a lot of things you don't know."
- "You're old enough to talk about events and people from the distant past."
- "You're old enough to appreciate things you used to take for granted."

- "You're old enough to understand there are more years behind you than in front of you."
- "You're old enough to treasure relationships and cherish time with people you love."

I know I'm old enough to be grateful for blessings. In a week, Kim and I will celebrate our 37th wedding anniversary. We've had the privilege of raising two fine sons who have become really good men. We've become grandparents to three amazing kids. I was called into the ministry as a senior in high school at a church camp. For over 40 years, I have had the privilege to serve with some of the most dedicated Christians around. I'm old enough to know the road can get rocky and life can be painful, but I'm also old enough to believe that God goes before me, stands beside me, follows after me, and loves me always. I'm old enough.

Leave a Mark

We had lunch together. I was introduced to him through a couple of friends who work with Fellowship of Christian Athletes. He was a regional director with FCA, a former coach who held a total of eight state championships in five different sports, a guy who loved high school kids and the people who coach them. He was a family man - husband of Lee for almost thirty years, a father, and a grandfather. But what defined Mark Tidwell best is his faith.

When the doctor told him about his cancer, it hit him and his family like you would expect. No one wants to hear the "c" word. With a great deal of prayer and thought as well as the encouragement of family and friends, Mark decided to use some "I" words – impact, influence, intentional – instead of dwelling on cancer.

When we met, he didn't launch into his story. He started telling me about the work FCA was doing, the coaches and athletes they were reaching, the churches with whom they were networking ... the lives that were being changed.

My first experience with FCA was in my own home. My older brother was a part of a huddle at North Fulton High School in Atlanta. The huddle met at our house that night and featured a Georgia Tech football player who gave his testimony. Perhaps you've heard of him – Bill Curry.

Mark Tidwell came to our church so our people could hear his story. He may refer to his own battle with colon cancer, but I know he'll ask you to consider what you're doing with the life God has entrusted to you. You can find out more about Mark and his "Leave a Mark" ministry at www.leaveamarknow.com. He has written a book, not just about his circumstances, but a collection of stories of others who have left or who are leaving a mark through their gifts and passions. He has a plan ... to cherish each day and make the most of it. He's been told he's going to die, but he is too busy living: "When I hit the floor in the morning, I praise God for one more day He allows me to be vertical. I challenge you to do the same."

Some might say Mark lost his battle. Cancer took another precious life. But he did leave his mark and continues to do so. He was never living to die; he was dying to live.

Once Upon a Time

When the boys were small, we had a bedtime ritual. Before prayers, we had story time. Sometimes it came from a favorite book; sometimes the boys demanded a creative rendering from their father – I had to make something up. The ridiculous quotient of the story was often measured by how many eye-rolls I got from my lovely wife.

Everybody loves stories. Almost all of us love stories with happy endings. We want the bad guy to lose and the good guy to win. We want justice served and rewards earned.

Life doesn't always have happy endings. Some stories end abruptly. Some fade into oblivion. Sometimes the bad guy defeats the good guy. Sometimes the good guy turns into the bad guy.

If you are familiar with Romans 8:28, you probably have struggled with the implications of Paul's words. Do all things work together for good for those who love God and are called according to His purpose? Paul didn't say that all things are good; he did say that the story comes out for the good in the end.

I believe that. I need to believe that. I believe, as a person of faith, that the story does have a happy ending. I may not understand the twists and turns. I may wish we could be spared some of the pain and suffering. I admit I can't see the end of the journey and don't really want to know what lies in wait around the next bend.

I try to live with two things holding me up – hope and trust. I refuse to believe that evil will win the day. I refuse to accept that life has no purpose or meaning. In this day of cynicism and skepticism, I cling to the promise that the story will come out right. History is His story.

Perspective

Three friends were playing their favorite golf course. One was a minister, one was a doctor, and the other was a time-management expert. The group ahead of them was particularly slow. The time-management guy kept looking at his watch – "What's up with these guys? They have been on this hole for over 30 minutes and they still haven't reached the green." The doctor and minister started grumping, too. A groundskeeper came by in a cart. The minister hailed him and asked, "Why is the foursome ahead of taking so long? Surely we can play through if they're going to be this slow." The keeper responded, "Oh, these guys are firefighters. Three of them were blinded fighting a fire in our clubhouse last year. We let them play for free." The minister apologized for his attitude. The doctor was embarrassed and offered to contact a colleague who was an ophthalmic surgeon to see if he could help the injured men. The time-management expert was silent for a moment, then said, "Why can't they play at night?"

Not very funny. Our perspective in life can be warped by pettiness, by selfishness, or by out-of-control schedules. We can see the outcomes in the traffic snarls in Atlanta or in the local grocery store when the lines don't move fast enough for us. We experience it with total strangers as well as within our closest relationships.

When Paul wrote to the Galatian churches, he spoke of the work of the Holy Spirit in the lives of believers. The fruit of the spirit is a cluster of nine qualities: love, joy, peace, patience, kindness, goodness, faithfulness, gentleness, and self-control (Galatians 5:22,23).

This would be a good time to let the Holy Spirit do His work in us!

Triumph in Tragedy

Monty Williams had just been told his playing days were over. A promising freshman basketball player at Notre Dame, he was devastated by the doctor's diagnosis – a rare cardiovascular condition that could take his life if he continued to play. Disconsolate, he thought about suicide. He had met a young woman named Ingrid Lacy and they were falling in love. When he was at his lowest, she encouraged him to set his sights on new challenges. In the next two years, their relationship blossomed. Friends and family were praying for him. His symptoms vanished and he was able to return to the team and then head to the NBA.

Triumph over tragedy? Monty Williams now coaches with the Oklahoma City Thunder. Life seemed to be on the upswing. He and Ingrid, valued contributors to their church and community, enjoyed a full life. Parenting five children was both daunting but rewarding. On February 9, 2016, Ingrid was driving, accompanied by three of their children when her vehicle was struck by a car traveling at 92 mph. The head-on collision took the lives of Ingrid and the woman driving the other car. The children survived their ordeal.

Triumph over tragedy? On February 18th, more than 900 people gathered for the "celebration of life" service to honor and remember Ingrid Williams. The crowd included NBA and college coaches and players, civic leaders from Oklahoma, media members, and people who just wanted to be there to support the family.

Monty Williams gave the eulogy that day. You can find it easily because the service coverage went viral. The grieving husband acknowledged the family's pain but said, "We didn't lose her. When you lose something, you can't find it. I know exactly where my wife is."

His powerful words spoke of hope in the face of despair, and faith in the presence of heartache. He asked those assembled to pray for the family of the woman who also lost her life. He didn't pretend there was no hole in his heart, but he refused to be defeated.

In our broken world, tragedy happens much too often. How do we make it when it happens to us? There are no easy answers, no simple pathway. Every day is a crisis in faith. But every day is an opportunity to take one step. Bill Gebhardt was the Williams' pastor while Monty coached the New Orleans Pelicans. He said of Monty: "He truly understands that the price of love is grief, and he is deeply grieving. He is facing each day with faith and authenticity."

"God blesses those who mourn, for they will be comforted" (Matthew 5:4). Empty words? Not to Monty Williams.

Just for Peanuts

Martha Berry must have been something. She founded the Berry School for disadvantaged children in Mount Berry, Georgia. In 1932, she was recognized in a national poll as one of the 12 most outstanding women in America. People knew her as a person who could make something out of nothing. She just refused to be defeated.

She once asked Henry Ford, the automobile magnate, to donate $1 million for here school. He sent her a dime. She took the money and bought a bag of peanuts. She sent her mountain schoolboys to a field with those peanuts. The crop that resulted allowed her to plant an even bigger field.

Eventually, Martha Berry set up a roadside stand where she sold peanuts. She wrote a letter to Henry Ford: "Remember that dime?

Well, sir, I invested it in peanuts and we made enough to buy a piano for our music students. How's that for dividends."

It all started with a Sunday School class. She met some boys near her father's farm who were too poor to be able to go to school. She convinced her father to give her some land and she had a small building constructed so she could teach Bible stories to the children in the area.

She was good at convincing. Among her supporters were Theodore Roosevelt, Andrew Carnegie, Ellen Axson Wilson (Woodrow Wilson's wife), Emily Vanderbilt Hammond, and Ford.

She was invited to the Ford home in Detroit where a deeply-impressed industrialist presented that remarkable woman with a check for $1 million. Just for peanuts.

It's amazing what one person can do with so little. Her motto is still the motto of Berry College: "Not to be ministered unto but to minister." She was fond of saying, "Prayer changes things."

I have heard and read about so-called celebrities who are "living large." In their world, that means having the finest in clothes, automobiles, jewelry, and other treasures that Jesus warned would be subject to decay or loss. For Martha Berry, "living large" was a fierce determination to make life better for those who just needed someone to believe in them, to give them a chance.

How large are we living?

Motivation

"I dream of a world where chickens can cross the road without having their motives questioned."

Motive: some inner drive, impulse, intention that causes a person to do something or act in a certain way; incentive or goal." (Webster's Dictionary)

It's really simple – it is the answer to the question "Why do you do what you do?" Sometimes our motivation is driven by fear, anger, vengeance, or selfishness. Sometimes our competitive spirit rises up to respond to a challenge or opportunity. At other times we are moved by compassion or sense of justice. Our actions and attitudes can be shaped by gratitude or empathy.

Why do you do what you do ... or say ... or think? Motivation is necessary in life. Zig Ziglar once wrote: "People often say that motivation doesn't last. Well, neither does bathing - that's why we recommend it daily."

In the Bible, there is a story of two men who each sold a piece of property and donated the proceeds to the Jerusalem church. Barnabas gave all the money from the sale of his land. The other was named Ananias. He and his wife, Sapphira, also sold some land and made a donation to the church. The difference in the two gifts was tragically stark. The latter gift had a false ring to it. The couple pretended that they, too, were giving all the money they received. Peter called them on their deception. Why did they do what they did? Were they trying to impress, were they hoping for praise, were they tainted by greed? (Acts 5:1-11)

It is really hard to determine another person's motives. Have you ever had someone try to define your motive for something? Ultimately, other people cannot peer into your heart or mind and know such things. But, like Ananias and Sapphira, what looks good on the outside might not hold up under scrutiny.

Motivation comes from within. Other factors and issues can influence us, but it comes down to this. We decide what drives us. Jesus was moved with compassion (Matthew 9:36). Paul wrote, "To me, to live is Christ" (Philippians 1:21). Nehemiah was fueled by his determination to rebuild Jerusalem (Nehemiah 1:3,4). Mary anointed Jesus out of her gratitude (John 12:3). David took on Goliath because his God was insulted and his people threatened (1 Samuel 17).

As people of faith, we know the greatest power in the universe. It is the power to transform us. "Being reminded about the incredible power of God's love, and living as He intended, is the most powerful motivation to change." – Rick Warren

Limits

Steve Edington once told a story about a circus bear. Instead of walking on two legs, ride a bicycle, or other tricks, this bear sat and paced in a nine by nine-foot cage. He was a showpiece, a marketing tool to attract crowds to the performances. Day after day, he walked nine feet one way, nine feet the other. For hours he would just lay down.

The circus fell on hard times and went bankrupt. No one was interested in a bear which could do no tricks so he was sold to a zoo. The zoo was rather progressive and provided animals with spaces that would resemble their natural habitats. Moats and rock formation kept the visitors at a safe distance. No bars were needed.

Introduced to his new environment, the bear soon repeated his behavior from his days in the circus cage. Free to wander in his expanded confines, the bear never ventured beyond the area of his old nine-by-nine square.

"The only bars left were the ones in his mind and spirit, which proved to be as real as the ones that had been around him." wrote Edington.

What are the limitations that hem us in? Are they forced upon us from the outside?

- You're no good.
- You'll never amount to anything.
- I don't know why I bother with you.

Or are they self-imposed?

- I'll never be able to accomplish that.
- I'm scared.
- Surely there's somebody better than me.

Where do "I can do all things through Christ who strengthens me" and "Be strong and courageous! Do not be afraid or discouraged. For the Lord your God is with you wherever you go" and "Trust in the Lord with all your heart. Don't lean on your own understanding. Acknowledge Him in all your ways and He will direct your paths" come in? It's time for the bear to quit being a prisoner. How about you?

So Close

Have you ever had one of those days?

- The University of Utah was hosting #4 Oregon in a huge game last November. The Utes had jumped out to a 7-0 lead when wide receiver Kaelin Clay caught a pass and raced for the end zone. It looked like a 79 yard TD and a fourteen point lead early in the game. Except for one thing … on his way to pay dirt, Clay started celebrating a little too early. He dropped the ball at the one yard line. The Utah fans erupted, thinking their team had just scored against the favored Ducks. Oregon's Joe Walker had seen the play, picked up the ball, and took it 99 yards to score a tying touchdown for his team. Whoops!

- At the Pepsi Team Invitational earlier this month featuring runners from Oregon, Washington, and Kentucky, steeplechase runner Tanguy Pepiot had victory in sight. As he approached the finish line, he started waving to the crowd and slowed down. Charging behind him was Washington runner Meron Simon. From the video, Oregon's Pepiot glances over as someone urges him to speed up. Too late. Simon passes him just before the line to win the race. Pepiot lost by 0.10 seconds. He collapsed on the track, snatching defeat from the jaws of victory. Whoops!

Finish. We've been told all our lives: it's not how you start, it's how you finish. History is full of stories about people who begin well. We may start with great intentions, but the challenge is to keep the pace, finish the task. The apostle Paul wrote to a troubled church in Corinth who needed to be reminded to keep running the race: "Don't you realize that in a race everyone runs, but only one person gets the prize? So run to win! All athletes are disciplined in their training. They do it to win a prize that will fade away, but we do it for an eternal prize. So I run with purpose in every step. I am not just shadowboxing. I discipline my body like an athlete, training it to do what it should. Otherwise, I fear that after preaching to others I myself might be disqualified" (1 Corinthians 9:24-27).

The writer of Hebrews encouraged readers to "run with endurance the race God has set before us" (Hebrews 12:1). Nobody can run your race for you. Every race has its challenges. You're the only Christian at your office or on your team? Run your race. You're fighting to maintain your sexual purity? Run your race. You're trying to hold on to your ethics when others around you look for corners to cut? Run your race. You're in a relationship that is rocky and difficult? Run your race. Where does it say that life is easy? Run your race.

Remember that we are not alone. In that passage in Hebrews, the writer pictured stands packed with those who are cheering us on (Hebrews 12:1). Jesus promised, "And remember this: I will be with you always, even to the end of the age" (Matthew 28:20). Paul wrote to the Philippians: "I can do all things through Christ who strengthens me" (Philippians 4:13). Run your race!

Make Up Your Mind

In our postmodern, even post-Christian times, it seems fashionable to deny the possibility of the resurrection. Most arguments against start with a presupposition like that from James Tabor who is chair of the department of religion at the University of North Carolina at Charlotte. According to him, the suggestion of a resurrection could be ruled out from the beginning. He wrote: "Dead bodies don't rise – not if one is clinically dead – as Jesus surely was. So if the tomb was empty the historical conclusion is simple – Jesus' body was moved by someone and likely reinterred in another location." Dr. Tabor has also revealed that Jesus was probably buried in Galilee, outside the city of Tsfat.

Being exposed to such an open mind makes one confident that the religion students at UNC Charlotte have the opportunity for a world-class indoctrination, not education. Tabor is not alone. He has plenty of company who have already decided that Jesus could not possible rise from the dead. Christianity can be simply dismissed.

Concerning such matters, the Apostle Paul agreed to a point: "If Christ has not been raised, your faith is futile" (1 Corinthians 15:17). If the Muslims are right, Jesus never actually died on the cross, much less returned from the dead. A prominent Hindu leader opined: "Jesus was only injured and after treatment returned to India where He actually died.

One Sunday, Kim and I attended a worship service hosted by Rise Again Ministries. Among the speakers was Bishop Roberts from Lynwood Park United Church of God in Christ. He preached with great energy and enthusiasm, underscoring his deep beliefs in the faith he calls his own. One line he spoke remains with me: "Your arms are too short to box with God."

There are plenty of skeptics and cynics. In our country, they are free to express their faith or lack thereof. As Dr. Dale Moody, long-time professor at Southern Seminary, used to say about his good friend and fellow combatant Dr. Frank Stagg over all things theological: "He has every right to be wrong."

Does Christianity rest on a sure foundation? Was Christ really the Son of God who came to earth to defeat the powers that thought they were in charge of the world? Did His death atone for our sin? Did He exit the tomb alive, having defeated our last great enemy? Does He reign supreme? Will He return in glory? Will God redeem and rescue His creation? Does any of this matter?

Make up your mind. Christians around the world will profess their faith this week. They will celebrate Easter – not the end of the story, but the beginning of what God had in mind before creation. Will you join your brothers and sisters to worship and praise the risen Lord? Will you have someone by your side?

It Used To Be Funny

When you are young and know everything, it is easy to make fun of others. We used to have a running joke in the family, usually involving the only female in our tribe of four. She would mention her grandfather or someone we knew who was having trouble hearing. The really mature people (me or the boys) other than her would respond, "Huh?" Yeah, it was hilarious, but you had to be there.

There are plenty of jokes about hearing. Like: "A man is talking to his neighbor, 'I finally broke down and bought a hearing aid. It cost me $4000, but they told me it was state of the art. It's perfect.' His neighbor responds, 'Really? What kind is it?' The man answers, '12:30.'"

Jokes like that lose their funny with the passing of the years.

We take a great deal for granted – our sight, our hearing, our mobility, our mental acuity. But hearing difficulty isn't just a physical issue. I've noticed poor hearing can be a discipline issue, a pay-attention issue.

When our oldest son was a preschooler, he was incredibly active. One day when he was bouncing off the walls, Kim gave him an assignment. She was working in the kitchen, standing at the sink. She came up with a brilliant idea: "Andy, I want you to see how fast you can run around the outside of the house ten times. I'll be watching through the window and counting." She thought he would burn up some of that energy and give her some peace and quiet. I don't know what the neighbors thought, but there he went, a 3 year-old blur.

There were times he was so busy that I had to stop him, place my hands on the side of his head, and say firmly, "Andy, look at me when I am talking to you." Then came the moment when he was having a hard time getting my attention. I was watching a game on TV and he crawled into my lap and placed his hands on my face and said, "Dad, look at me when I'm talking to you."

I wonder sometimes if Christ must want to do the same with us. More than once He told his audience, "Anyone who is willing to hear should listen and understand" (e.g., Matthew 11:15). I've never heard Him out loud, but I know He is speaking, prompting, urging, leading. I pray I am paying attention.

Habits

Habit: a repeated action that becomes automatic

That is one way to define behaviors that become a part of our routine. Habits, both good and bad, are hard to break once established. Some you wish you never started; others you are glad you did.

Growing up, one of the habits we developed had to do with preparing for Sunday. On Saturday night, certain things were just done. Clothes were selected (usually by mom, including dad's) and laid out, offering envelopes were filled, check marks were made in the appropriate boxes, and envelopes were placed in Bibles. Evening prayer always included asking God to bless our church the next day. Early to bed and early to rise. We never had a discussion about whether we were going to church. Since dad served on the church staff, that matter was already settled!

But it became more than habit or obligation. Growing in faith came to mean something more significant. It began to matter. It was good to see friends, to learn lessons, to participate in worship, but there was more. Over time, habit turned into yearning. As years passed, faith became personal and powerful. Coming to know a gracious and generous God touched a deep place inside.

Why do we come? Why do we serve? Why do we give? Our time, talent, and treasure should be given out of joy and opportunity, not habit or duty. "I was glad when they said to me, 'Let us go to the house of the Lord'" (Psalm 122:1).

The Power of One

What difference can one life make? What's important to you as you try to make good decisions? For most of us, we realize that character counts. We need people around us who are dependable, loyal, honest, and consistent, right? We need to be people like that, right?

We don't need to be like this: A gangster was charged with murder. His buddies told him not to worry. They were going to fix things so he could get off. They found a man on the jury who had indicated that he was willing to accept a bribe for his vote. After the closing arguments, the accused sent word through one of his lackeys, thanking the tainted juror for his efforts. Instead of murder one, the charge had been reduced to manslaughter. The crooked man wasn't willing to rest without comment. He sent a message back telling the gangster that it was tough convincing the other jurors: "It was really hard. The others wanted to acquit you, but I held out for manslaughter, just like you wanted."

With friends like that ...

The Prodigal Son in Luke 15 found out how easy it was to buy friends, and how easy it was to lose friends you buy. They say everybody has a price. For Judas, it was thirty pieces of silver, the price of a common slave.

Jesus had a price. Satan thought it was easy to buy Jesus, so he offered Christ enticements thinking Jesus could be bought. Yes, Jesus had a price. He was willing to pay the highest price we could imagine for one sinner, for all sinners. What a deal! He accepted sin with all its devastation and horror in exchange for something He considered priceless – your soul and mine. "Greater love has no one than this, that a man lay down his life for His friends" (John 15:13). He said those words, then He went out and did it.

Life Happens

Lightning never strikes twice, right? I ran across this story in Homiletics magazine:

British officer Major Summerford was serving in the army in February 1918 in the fields of Flanders when he was knocked off his horse by a flash of lightning, paralyzing him from the waist down. After retiring, he moved to Vancouver. While fishing one summer day in 1924, he was injured again when lightning struck the tree he was resting against. In 1930, recovered from his paralysis, he was taking a walk in the countryside when lightning found him again. He finally succumbed to his injuries two years later – a victim of three lightning strikes. But lightning sought him out one last time. In 1934, a bolt of lightning destroyed a tombstone in a cemetery. Guess whose tombstone.

What are we to take away from this man's unfortunate experiences? First, don't hang around with anyone named Summerford. Second, we're headed into summer and need to pay attention to weather alerts and warnings. Third, life happens.

The third one demonstrates that we don't have control over much. We don't like that truth. In a broken and fallen world, people get sick ... misfortune strikes ... pain attacks ... fear threatens ... death comes.

On a beautiful Friday morning, Greg Byrd was flying his small plane, accompanied by two of his sons, Phillip and Christopher, and Christopher's fiancée, Jackie Kulzer. They had left Asheville early and touched down in Atlanta to top off the fuel in his Piper Saratoga. They were headed to Oxford, Mississippi to celebrate the graduation of Greg's youngest son, Robert, from Ole Miss. About a mile from the airport, things went horribly wrong. While attempting an emergency landing on I-285, the plane clipped a truck and crashed. All aboard were killed.

For some in Atlanta, the whole thing was terribly inconvenient. Traffic, always heavy on the perimeter, just stalled. People were stuck or had to find alternate routes. Many had no idea what had happened. When the tragic news broke, sympathy and grief replaced frustration and annoyance.

People of faith are not immune to the suffering of this life. We believe in a God who somehow draws even nearer in those times that hurt or confuse us. If we cannot live in hope and trust, our faith must seem empty or in vain. There will come a day when darkness will be no more. Until then ..."Lord, my heart Is not proud; my eyes are not haughty. Instead, I have calmed and quieted myself. O Israel, put your hope in the Lord, now and always" (From Psalm 131).

Name That Tune

Did your graduating class have a commencement song? Was it "Climb Every Mountain" or "To Dream the Impossible Dream"? I'm dating myself, I know. We want our graduates to be inspired, to be ready for the next challenge, to rise to new heights, to soar on wings of eagles, to go where no man has gone before ... okay, I'll stop.

Great music does lift us. Great lives do, too. I have noticed that 'great' can be defined in interesting ways. Young people need role models, they need heroes. Where will they find them these days? The current crop of political types? The entertainment world? Sports stars?

I think they find them where we most likely did. Parents don't raise their children perfectly, but they invest time and energy and resources and, most of all, love. There are teachers who have demanded more, seen something worth challenging. There are coaches, mentors, leaders who have pushed and trained and encouraged. There are people who will never make the headlines, never gain celebrity, or never seek credit who make the difference in life after life.

During this season of milestones, we celebrate with our young men and women who wear the cap and gown. But we also recognize and honor those who will be looking on, who helped to make the day possible, and who formed the chorus of cheers and lessons.

What song should you choose to express gratitude and blessing for the people who believed in you, who cherished you, who loved you enough to say 'no' ... who held you close or held you accountable ... who prayed over you and asked God to keep you safe?

Name that tune. Then sing it to the people who matter so much in your life.

Just a Sinner Like Me

It hit me again the other day. It wasn't an original thought (I'm not sure there are any original thoughts anymore). In this age of division, lack of civil discourse, enmity, and vitriol, we seem to be known for how we're different ... not how we're the same.

Frankly, I'm tired of it. We cannot agree to disagree. We have to go on the attack. We have to belittle someone who doesn't see it our way. We're all guilty of it. The most intolerant people I know claim to be tolerant.

What if we quit focusing on the things that divide us? What if we could agree about the things we have in common? Impossible? Probably. It may not work for you but I think I'll give a try.

What we have in common:

- Every person I will ever meet or know is made in the image of God. Every person. Every person created by design, with a purpose.

- Every person I will ever meet or know is loved by God. Every person. God loves each of us like He loves all of us.

- Every person I will ever meet or know is a sinner. They say it only takes one to make you a sinner – I passed one a while back, how about you? Paul wrote, "For all have sinned and fallen short of the glory of God." Every person is a member of this unfortunate club.

- Every person I will ever meet or know needs to be rescued. Every person. We can't fix what is broken. We can't save ourselves. The good news is that rescue is possible. The bad news is that there are people who don't believe it, want it, or think they need it.

So, from now on I going to try to look at every person the same way. I didn't say it was easy, but for me it's necessary. I get frustrated with myself when I classify people. I grow weary of this "us against them" mindset. I need to remember the words of Jesus when He was talking to Nicodemus: "For God so loved the world ..."

If I understand what He meant, I believe He was talking about all of us. Every person. Here goes: "Lord. I could use some help!"

Make No Little Plans

Ray Ortlund wrote a blog by that name in tribute to David Burnham, an architect who designed the master plans for some of America's largest cities. He was also the chief designer and planner for buildings in New York and Washington, D.C.

During the height of his career, he gave a speech that included these words: "Make no little plans. They have no magic to stir men's blood and probably themselves will not be realized. Make big plans. Aim high in hope and work, remembering that a noble, logical diagram once recorded will never die, but long after we are gone will be a living thing, asserting itself with ever-growing insistency. Remember that those who follow us are going to do things that would stagger us!"

This the season when graduating classes will hear songs of inspiration and challenge. In my long-ago era it would have been "Climb Every Mountain" or "To Dream the Impossible Dream."

From time to time, we need to step up our game. Perhaps this will help ... or not:

- From a new graduate: "I would like to thank Google, Wikipedia, and whoever invented copy and paste."

- Unknown: "I would like to thank my arms for always being by my side; my legs for always standing up for me; and my fingers because I can always count on them."

- From John Wayne: "Life is hard; it's harder if you're stupid."

- From a grad: "I didn't graduate Magna Cum Laude or Summa Cum Laude or Cum Laude; I graduated, thank the Laude."

For Heaven's Sake

Jesus told His disciples that He was going to prepare a place for them (John 14). Have you wondered what kind of place He meant? What will it be like?

Let's turn to some to some theological experts of the younger set:

"Mom, God's so neat and heaven's supposed to be great. Could me and Gloria go there Saturday for a sleepover?"

Heather heard her mom talk about what it would be like in heaven and that someday people would have glorified bodies. That got her to thinking: "Do you think we'll look like Barbie?"

3-year-old Morgan was visiting at her grandmother's home. She looked around the house for a while and then asked her grandma, "Where's Grandpa?" Her grandmother answered, "Honey, he's in heaven." Surprised, Morgan said, "Still?"

5-year-old Brett liked to go fishing with his dad. One day after a trip to the lake, he was riding in the car and he made an interesting connection. From the backseat: "Hey, Dad, if Grandma's going to heaven with us, God had better have a pretty big fishing rod to haul her in!"

Jenny was four when she asked her mom, "Does heaven have a floor?" Mom wasn't quite sure where this was going. "Well, Jenny, what do you think heaven is like?" Jenny looked up at the blue sky dotted with clouds and replied, "Well, I can't see any floor, so I guess people are just up there on coat hangers."

The Bible gives us glimpses and Jesus spoke about heaven. It's interesting to consider that while He is preparing a place for us, He is preparing us for a place. He is forming and shaping us. He became like we are so that we could become like He is.

"No eye has seen, no ear has heard, and no mind has imagined what God has prepared for those who love Him." (Isaiah 64:4; 1 Corinthians 29)

Wish I Had Thought of That

J. Michael Shannon collected the following pearls of wisdom found inside fortune cookies:

- "No plan will work if you don't."

- "While some dream of a bright future, others are awake making it."

- "Pushing your luck does not count as exercise."

- "He who knows enough is enough will always have enough."

- "Don't be pushed by your problems. Be led by your dreams."

- "You only live once; but if you do it right, once is enough."

Where do you get your wisdom? Do you have a trusted mentor that has your ear? Do you read authors who stretch you? Who speaks truth into your life? Are you willing to listen more than you talk to God?

In Proverbs 9, there are these words: "Reverence for the Lord is the beginning of wisdom. Knowledge of the Holy One results in understanding. Wisdom will multiply your day and add years to your life. If you become wise, you will be the one to benefit."

Who listens to you? Whose life is enriched because of your investment? Who knows that you pray for them, taking them to the throne of grace? Are you being a good steward of your life lessons?

Things to consider:

- It is said that when an elderly person dies, it is like a library burns down.

- Find a wise person and hang around them.

- Age doesn't equal wisdom. Be selective!

- But, you'll never meet someone you can't learn from.

- Record the thoughts and experiences of your grandparents and parents.

- Thank the people who have poured their lives into yours.

- Pass it on. Pour your life into someone else.

- There is a reason God gave you two ears and one mouth. Listen more.

One more ... Just because someone is supposed to wise doesn't mean he is. Solomon, the wisest man in the world, had 700 wives and 300 concubines. Insert joke here ...

Views of God

Sunday morning, we wrestled with our views of God. How do you see Him? Would He say:

- "You're not good enough. Try harder. You could do better."

- "I'm too busy running the universe to worry about your behavior. You know the rules."

- "Nothing you can do will make Me love you more or less."

In UrbanDictionary.com, you can find these definitions of or comments about God:

- "The reason I passed math."

- "The main character in the fiction work, 'The Bible.'"

- "An entity whose opinions on the consumption of pork have been a matter of hot debate among the world's religions."

- "A voice that talks to you from the public address system in stores, 'Clean up in aisle 3.'"

- "Man's most deadly creation."

- "A widely known imaginary friend."

- "The reason for anything currently unexpected or unknown."

- "Some say he doesn't exist, others say he is indifferent. Still others say is the picture of love and he is all-powerful. Some claim to follow him but don't truly do it; some scoff at his followers, and a rare handful of people actually follow him."

According to the editors of the online dictionary, the word 'God' is one of the most popular words to readers and contributors. People have a lot to say about their ideas of God. A little girl named Harriet was concerned that so many people seemed to discount God: "Dear God, Are you real? Some people don't believe it. If you are, you better do something quick."

Does God need defending? Paul wrote to the Romans: "For the truth about God is known to them instinctively. God has put this knowledge in their hearts. From the time the world was created, people have seen the earth and sky and all that God has made. They can clearly see His invisible qualities – His eternal power and divine nature. So they have no excuse whatsoever for not knowing God" (Romans 1:19, 20). Perhaps the problem isn't with God, but with the people who claim to represent Him. Dick Milham once said, "I'm glad I became a Christian before I knew too many of them."

I think I'll go with these two kids. I think they got it right.

Herbie wrote: "Dear God, Count me in. Your friend, Herbie.

Nora wrote: "Dear God, I don't ever feel alone since I found out about you. Nora."

Be Where Your Feet Are

It sounds like common sense: Be where your feet are. Easy, right? Have you ever driven down a stretch of highway and can't remember anything about where you've just been? Have you ever been so focused on what's in the distance that you stumble over what is right in front of you? Somebody wrote: "My brain gets crowded. There is so much going on. I do three things at once and get two of them wrong!"

I can relate. Be where your feet are. I've heard athletes use the phrase. Play your position. Do your job. Get ready for the next play. You can't redo the previous play; you can't anticipate all that will happen in the next quarter.

There is a delightful book written for children by Julia Cook with the same title. *"Be Where Your Feet Are"* ... a hilarious story about learning to be present wherever we are... and what can happen when we're not. [19]

In a day when multi-tasking is promoted as a necessary skill, I notice how easy it is to be distracted or overwhelmed. Doing one thing well trumps doing six things not so well. I like what one observer wrote: "What does it mean to truly be exactly where my feet are? To dwell exactly in this space of time. Not worried for tomorrow or dreaming of yesterday. Not wondering what life will be next month or in five years. Not wondering where you will be or who you will be. Not even worrying about who you will be with. To truly be. Just exactly as you are."

In Psalm 46:10, the psalmist encouraged us to "Be still and know that I am God." I have thought often about the implications of that statement. It could be interpreted in several ways: Be quiet and listen ... Cease striving and trust ... Quit your frettin' and believe ... Take a deep breath and fix your eyes on God ... Let go and let God. With that mind, here's one more:

Be where your feet are ... and remember Who will guide your steps!

[19] Julia Cook, *"Be Where Your Feet Are"* National Center for Youth Issues, 2018

God Is Faithful; Let's Join Him

The John Lewis Department Store chain is well known in Great Britain. A number of years ago, the store in Birmingham, England planned to expand. In developing the plans, it was realized that the tract of land needed for the expansion was occupied by a small Quaker chapel. The lawyers drew up a letter: "Dear sirs. We wish to extend our premises. We see that your building is right in our way. We wish therefore to buy your building and demolish it so that we can expand our store. We will pay any price you care to name for we wish to settle the matter as quickly as possible." The Lewis corporate office received a quick response: "Dear sirs. We in the Friends' meeting house note the desire of Lewis to extend. We observe that our building is right in your way. We would point out, however, that we have been on our site somewhat longer than you have been on yours, and we are determined to stay where we are. We are so determined to stay that we will happily buy your store. If, therefore, you would like to name a suitable price, we will settle the matter as quickly as possible."

At first, the Lewis executives thought the letter was a joke. How could such a small congregation match the financial might of the Lewis enterprise? Then someone noticed the signature at the conclusion of the letter from the Quakers. It was signed, "Cadbury" as in Cadbury, the enormous chocolate and candy manufacturer. That little group of Quakers could have bought the big department store several times over with the resources God had provided. He is still faithful!

Sure, I Can See That

On this day in 1785, Benjamin Franklin announced the invention of bifocals. For all of us who have moved on to the wonderful world of progressive lenses, thanks Ben. If you see someone bobbing his head like a crazed parakeet, you can assume they are wearing progressives. A new disease has been discovered for such unfortunates: Neck-jerk-itis.

On this day in 1876, Boston's Joe Borden threw the first no-hitter in National League history. Watching the Atlanta Braves, I wonder if ole Joe has anything left on his fastball. It would be great if he could also still hit a lick.

On this day in 1618, the 2nd Defenestration of Prague occurred. What is a 'defenestration' you ask? It is the act of throwing someone or something out of a window. The first of these breath-taking events happened in 1419. The second involved two Catholic lord regents and their secretary. Faster than you can say 'defenestration' these three were tossed out the window to land on the street 70 feet below. Here's the good news: None of the men were injured seriously. The bad news: the incident set off the 30 Years War. Here are the rules I just made up for defenestrating somebody:

- Make sure you are higher than the first floor or you lose some of the drama.
- Make sure you have enough help to pick up and throw the miscreant.
- Make sure you open the window.
- Make sure they guy doesn't have a bunch of big, strong friends.
- Make sure you record this for the sake of history - you could have the 3rd Defenestration all to yourself.

So, what will you do to make history today? It's a gift from your Creator. Unwrap the gift and have at it.

A Piece of Rock

It was a piece of rock. A piece of concrete actually. My friend Tom Stallworth brought it to me from Berlin. It was part of the wall that had been torn down – a symbol of an outbreak of freedom in Eastern Europe in late 1991.

It was a vial of sand. Along with my two sons, we scooped it from the Normandy shore at Utah Beach where Warrant Officer Oliver C. Wilbanks waded ashore on D-day+2 with the 90th Division of the US Army in 1944. It was the beginning of the end of the Third Reich.

It was a piece of concrete carried by a man in his mid-sixties aboard a C-130 military transport carrying a USO troupe to Baghdad in June 2003. The man sat beside an actor named Gary Sinise. Perhaps best known for his portrayal of Lt. Dan Taylor in Forrest Gump, Gary was fulfilling a commitment to express his support and appreciation for US forces serving in Operation Iraqi Freedom.

The two men struck up a conversation after Sinise noticed the button pinned to the man's shirt bearing the pictures of two young men. Unlike many on the plane, this man wasn't a celebrity or entertainer. He was a dad. The photos were of his two sons, one NYPD officer and the other NYFD firefighter. They had both died on 9/11. The man passed the piece of rock to Sinise. Gary asked about it. In Sinise's account in his marvelous book, *A Grateful American*, he wrote: "He swallowed once, twice, then his eyes grew wet. He whispered, 'It's a piece of the World Trade Center.'"

Freedom is never free.

[20] Gary Sinise, *A Grateful American,* Nelson Books, 2018

Sacrifice

By nature of the word's definition, sacrifice suggests giving for a greater good, losing something of value for a higher purpose. Certainly, we note the stark implications on a day like Memorial Day. Few of us really have to sacrifice in our comfortable surroundings, our usually predictable world. Then we hear about someone like Oseola McCarty.

Oseola McCarty lived and worked most of her life in a small, wood-framed house in Hattiesburg, Mississippi. She spent most of her days washing, ironing, and folding other people's clothes. She never made much money but somehow, she set some of what she earned aside.

In 1995, word got out. Southern Mississippi University announced that a scholarship was being established for deserving, needy students. The donor of the scholarship was Oseola McCarty. She had willed $150,000 of her life savings to help those who could not afford to go to school. She said, "I want to give others the chance to get the education I never had." Her dream of becoming a nurse died the day she had to drop out of school to support her family (*The Washington Post*, September 27, 1999).

In the original text of Julia Ward Howe's triumphant song, *"Mine Eyes Have Seen the Glory,"* the third line of what was then the fifth verse read: "As He died to make men holy, let us die to make men free." Howe's timeless work was inspired by a battle song during the Civil War. The image of men paying the ultimate sacrifice was a heroic reminder of the cost of freedom.

The text was changed in recent years to read: "As He died to make men holy, let us live to make men free." Sometimes the sacrifice is in the living, not the dying.

- Parents loving and caring for a special-needs child
- Grown children returning the nurturing for an aging parent
- School teachers working in under-resourced People fighting for justice in the face of racism and prejudice
- Missionaries serving in difficult, dangerous places

There are many more you could list. How thankful I am that we are all capable of giving for a greater good, losing something of value for a higher purpose. We honor sacrifice because life is just too precious to hoard or waste.

Respect

Comedian Bob Newhart once said, "I don't like country music, but I don't mean to denigrate those who do. And for the people who like country music, denigrate means 'put down'."

Funny, right? Depends on your perspective. In our over-the-top politically correct world, public discourse is anything but a joke.

Something seems to be missing. Civility? Common courtesy? Dignity? Good manners?

Someone posterized the idea of respect this way:

> "Treat people the way you want to be treated.
> Talk to people the way you want to be talked to.
> Respect is earned, not given."

Okay ... this isn't new. Check out Matthew 7:12. It's been called the Golden Rule. I'm not certain I agree with the last line, though. I wasn't brought up that way. I think you start with respect, not end with it. Paul wrote that wives should respect their husbands; he didn't say that husbands always deserve respect (Ephesians 5:33).

These days you could substitute a number of things for Newhart's dig at country music fans. It's easy to show disrespect in our world. We can always find someone to look down on. Or, we could choose another path.

Too quixotic? I don't have the power or influence to change the world, but I do have the power and influence to affect my world. I don't have to yield to my baser instincts to pre-judge others. I could begin with a page that is blank except for the word "respect" that I could hand to every person I meet. It would require an attitude that starts with this simple truth: I will never meet a person whom God doesn't love.

Regardless of the circumstance, it somehow seems appropriate to honor the highest values we can name, to be truly thankful for those who have paid dearly for our freedom, to leverage that freedom in impacting our world with something other than self-service and absorption. I believe I can respect that.

They're Not Dumb, You Know

Her daughter was staring at her head. Finally, mom asked: "What are you looking at, dear?" The little girl said, "Most of your hair is dark brown but I see some white hair sticking out. How do you get white hair?" Mom thought about it for a moment, then responded: "Well, every time you do something wrong and make me cry or unhappy, one of my hairs turns white."

Silence ... for a moment. Then daughter spoke: "How come all of grandma's hair is white?"

There are perfectly sound reasons why hair turns gray or turns loose. You've got to have a sense of humor as life goes on.

"If grey hair is a sign of wisdom, I must be a genius!"

"There is only one cure for gray hair. It was invented by a Frenchman. It is called the guillotine."

"I don't have grey hair; I have wisdom highlights."

"I don't consider myself bald; I'm just taller than my hair."

"God made a few perfect heads. The rest He covered with hair."

"You can resent that you have little or no hair ... or you could be glad you have a head."

"What hair color do they put on driver's licenses for bald people?"

Now, let's talk about what happens to our bodies as we age ... or not. We can mourn about what we used to look like or what we used to be able to do, but we all know that we can't change the past. We can live fully in the moment and appreciate the gift of life.

Assuming

Two things happened this weekend that I couldn't help but notice. First, our neighbor's mailbox got whacked by somebody cutting a corner too much or not paying attention. There it stood, all catawampus (I've always wanted to use that word in a sentence), pointing crookedly toward the sky. My first thought was that some delivery truck had done a hit-and-run number and didn't bother to report the damage.

Second, somebody stole our Saturday newspaper. How can you live without your Saturday newspaper containing outdated news you could easily find by turning on your computer?

Without knowing the facts, I had made two assumptions. There could be very rational explanations for both, but it is just too easy to assume, usually the worst.

Have you ever been the victim of a false assumption? Not a good feeling. Not easy to explain. Have you ever victimized somebody else with a false assumption? Not a good feeling. Also, not easy to explain.

It's called prejudice. Prejudging others can get us into embarrassing and regrettable situations. We know just enough to make ourselves look foolish. You know, break the word assume down and you understand what assumptions can make you look like.

The subway car was full of tired, cranky commuters on their way home on a late, hot summer evening. At one stop, a man and four children stepped into the car. A seat was open from a departing traveler, so the man slumped into the bench with his hands over his face. The children, ages six to twelve, were loud and boisterous, laughing and pushing and running up the narrow aisle. They quickly became a nuisance. Hard glances were thrown at the children and their father, who didn't seem to even notice that the kids were out of control. Finally, one of the commuters spoke to the man. "Hey, buddy. Can't your control your rowdy kids? They're bothering everybody in here!"

The man looked up, his face tearstained. "I am so sorry. We've been at the hospital since early this morning. The kids don't know it yet, but their mom died an hour ago. I'm lost and don't know what to do next."

There is a reason Jesus cautioned us to leave the judging to the only One capable of knowing all the facts. Lord, forgive me when I assume or jump to an unjustified conclusion. I need to show more grace. I needed to follow the rule, the Golden one: I should treat others as I wish to be treated.

86,400

The story of "The Magic Bank Account" has been around for years. Think about it:

"Imagine that you won a contest that awarded you $86,400, deposited in your bank every morning. You had to follow the rules to keep the money.

- If you don't spend it, you lose it.
- You cannot transfer the money to another account.
- You may only spend it.
- Next day, another $86,400 is deposited.
- The bank can end the game without warning.

What would you do with all that money? Would you spend it on yourself ... give it away ... take care of people you love? Would you spend it all, knowing another deposit happens the next day?"

The story continues: "Actually the game is real. Every person wins the prize. The prize is time."

- Each morning we awaken to receive 86,400 seconds as gift of life.
- When the day is over, we don't get that time back.
- What we haven't used up is gone forever.
- You make decisions about how you spend your gift.
- Each morning the account is refilled, but the game can be over without warning.

Jesus gave us a formula for making the most of the gift: "Your heavenly Father already knows your needs, and He will give you what you need from day to day if you live for Him and make the Kingdom of God your primary concern" (Matthew 6:32,33).

Time is precious. Handle with care!

Another Year, Another Opportunity

People are searching. People are looking for answers. For a growing number, the church has become unnecessary, irrelevant. How do we change that story?

A man named Aaron Earls wrote an interesting article recently entitled: "Searching for a Savior: How comic book movies can point to Christ." We have been deluged in the last few years with movies about larger-than-life action figures and there many more on the way. Why have these films created such a following? Earls writes: "One reason superhero movies have found a wide audience is because people are natural intrigued by battle between good and evil.

In this super-hero obsessed culture, the church has an opportunity to point to the grand story of One who came to rescue us and defeat the enemy – but not without a little bit of drama. As Uncle Ben told Peter Parker, Spider-Man's alter ego, 'With great power comes great responsibility.'"

No, I don't think the answer is for us to each choose a superhero and parade around the neighborhood in a costume. I think we learn from our culture and realize that people do need meaning in their lives, that people want to hope, need to hope. We have a timeless message to share through word and deed. Life affords us another opportunity to deepen our resolve to matter in this world for the cause of Christ.

Signs

Traffic signs are supposed to warn us, inform us, caution us, redirect us, or slow us down. They tell us how fast we are supposed to be going. They help us know where we are and where we are going.

You could preach a series of sermons on traffic signs. I have. If you think about it, life is full of signs. Some of them are relational signs. In a friendship, in a marriage, within a family, with colleagues, with every social interaction, there are signs present to let us know how we are doing. Some relational signs are brightly lit with flashing bulbs warning us that we better pay attention. Some are far more subtle, requiring that we slow down and use all our senses. A man says to his obviously perturbed wife, "What's wrong dear?" She responds, "Nothing." Okay, guys. What's your next step? If you decide on "Well then, everything must be okay," you just missed a sign and there's a big speed bump ahead.

Some signs are health related. Your body is trying to signal you that something's not right. You can see it or feel it but you choose to ignore it. "Stop" signs usually indicate that a behavior doesn't just need to be adjusted; it needs to stop. A "Yield" sign might mean that the stress you're under needs to let up or you'll have a stroke. A "Road Narrows" sign might mean you really need to focus on changing some habits that are hurting you. The doctor holds up a sign in a check-up to warn a patient to start exercising. He says, "I want you to walk five miles a day for two weeks and then call me, so I'll know how you're doing." The man agrees. Two weeks later, the doctor gets a call from the man: "Okay doc, I've been walking just like you said, five miles every day." The doctor congratulates the man and tells him to come into the office the next day. "I don't know if I can make it tomorrow," the man says. When asked why, the man replies, "Well, doc, I've been doing like you told me but now I'm 70 miles from home."

Some signs are a bit confusing, even discouraging, like these actual signs posted side by side:

- "Cemetery Road" and "Dead End" – People are dying to go down that road
- "Welcome to First Baptist" and "Do Not Enter" over driveway – friendly folks
- "Slow Children at Play" and "Hunting with Shotgun Only" – go faster kids
- "School Zone" and "No Passing" – that's a tough school
- "Surgery Parking Only" and "5 Minute Limit" – outpatient surgery on steroids
- "Touching Wires Causes Instant Death" and "$200 Fine"- when do you pay, before or after?

Some signs are spiritual. When our prayer life grows stale or our time in the Word becomes infrequent, there are indications of distance and disconnection in our faith. I appreciate the sign that should be posted on each of us. Paul wrote to the Philippians that there is a construction sign above every believer: "He who began a good work in you will continue His work until it is finished" (11:6). Some construction projects just seem to go on forever. I'm glad the one God is managing will be complete in His time and in His way.

The Positive Side of "You're Not Good Enough"

We want to build people up, not tearing them down. We don't want our children to grow up with an inferiority complex. We hand out participation trophies. We don't keep score because we don't want anyone to feel like a loser.

I can agree with the sentiment behind such statements, but something is missing.

- We want to build people up ... Sometimes the best way to build someone up is to show them the steps to higher achievement, to help them gain greater self-confidence might mean showing them attitudes or behaviors that are holding them down.

- We don't want our children to develop inferiority complexes ... Affirmation is great, but sometimes constructive criticism opens the door to understanding and life change.

- We hand out participation trophies ... I'm sorry, life simply isn't that way. You don't just show up; you contribute to a team, in a class, on the job, in a marriage. Discovering my true value comes when the world benefits from my investment of unique ability.

- We don't keep score ... That might be alright for preschoolers who might not know a glove from a bat. For most of us, keeping score helps us to know how we're doing, if we're making progress toward our goals, if we are progressing in both knowledge and wisdom. If you don't believe me, try that out on your coach, teacher, professor, supervisor: We don't keep score – final score, test results, job achievements?

I have had great teachers in my life, some in formal settings and some in life situations. The ones who I remember most are the ones who, in one way or another, told me "You're not good enough." To me, I wasn't hearing "You're no good." I was hearing "You can do better than that" or "I am expecting more from you." I am grateful for those who believed in me and called for my best. Many of my North Fulton buddies remember Miss Acree who famously told her classes, "If you don't vote, shut up." Anything else wasn't good enough!

You Can Count on It

In a world where there seem to be few absolutes anymore, we would like to be able to count on a few things. With so much uncertainty and confusion shaking our confidence and sense of well-being, we would like to be able to discover and depend on that which is trustworthy.

Perhaps we could identify with the little boy who had to go for a physical examination at his doctor's office. This particular doctor liked to kid around with his young patients to get them to relax. There were a number of items and procedures in a doctor's exam room that could make a boy nervous. Pointing to the boy's ear, the doctor asked, "Is this your nose?"

Turning to his mom with a look of alarm on his face, the little fellow whispered, "Hey, Mom, I think we better find a new doctor."

There are times in our children's lives when they are afraid, when they are lonely, when they feel different, when they make mistakes, and when they don't understand. The love and grace of Christ is a sure thing. Children are not the only people who need to know that God is worthy of our trust. How about you?

Father's Day might take a back seat to Mother's Day, but I am so grateful for dads. I don't know any perfect dads; I'm certainly far from it. But I know a lot of dads who love their families and try so hard to be good stewards of these precious relationships.

- If you're a dad, model your life after the perfect Father who loves without condition, who forgives without reproach, who pays attention to what His children need.
- If you have a dad in your life, pray for him, respect him, and listen to him.
- If your dad is not with you, give thanks for him, learn from him, and honor him.
- If things aren't good between you and your dad, remember time is too short to waste with anger, resentment, and regret.

Our kids need godly parents. Being able to count on strong parenting does more than make healthy homes; it also creates better communities.

Can It Get Darker?

The answer is yes, it can. As broken as our world is, the evil grows stronger. I can only imagine the shock and grief sweeping over Orlando after this horrific weekend. A young entertainer is murdered while signing autographs. A crowded night club is the scene of America's worst mass killing. At least 50 are killed. More than 50 others were wounded, many critically.

When Paul wrote to the Romans, he acknowledged that "all creation is groaning, awaiting freedom from the pain of this life" (Romans 8:18-22). While he was encouraging Christians to hold on during perilous times, he was also predicting an end to this world's suffering.

He wrote to believers in Corinth: "He is the source of every mercy and the God who comforts us. He comforts us in all our troubles so that we can comfort others" (2 Corinthians 1:3,4).

It is tempting to grow cynical. It seems to be trending that God either doesn't exist, is impotent, or indifferent to the human condition. Those views are not new. People have scoffed at the idea of a loving, present God for centuries. Who hasn't wondered: If there is a God, why doesn't He do something?

Is it trite or simplistic to suggest He is doing something? Moreover, He did do something and He will do something.

- He is doing something – He sends us to comfort, to serve, to care, to help, to pray, to give, to witness, to love, to weep, to laugh, to be present, to love justice, to show mercy, and to walk humbly with God. He is working in ways we cannot see presently. He cares more about humanity than any of us ever could.

- He did do something – Galatians 4:4 says that at just the right time, God sent His Son. Jesus did for us what we could not do for ourselves. His rescue announced the death knell of sin, death, and evil. An empty cross and an empty tomb demonstrated that God did something.

- He will do something – There will come a time, perhaps very soon, when God will proclaim, "Enough!" When Jesus returns, He won't arrive as an infant in Bethlehem but as the King of glory.

In that same passage in Romans, Paul declared: "What can we say to these things? If God is for us, who can be against us? Since God did not spare even His own Son but gave Him up for us all, won't God who gave us Christ, also give us everything else?" (8:31,32) People of hope, comfort one another with these words.

Who's Flying This Plane?

Richard Scott was born on April 12, 1908 in Waynesboro, Georgia. At an early age, he fell in love with flying. When he was only five, he witnessed the fatal crash of famed aviator, Eugene Ely. Ely was credited with the first take-off and landing on an aircraft carrier.

Scott was an all-American boy. He didn't just earn his Eagle Scout; he was given the Distinguished Eagle Scout Award. He won appointment to the United States Military Academy at West Point, graduating in 1932. In his distinguished career, he was awarded two Silver Star commendations, 3 Distinguished Flying Crosses, 4 Air Medals, the Army Commendation Medal and numerous other citations. He achieved the coveted status of flying ace. During the 1996 Olympic Games in Atlanta, Scott carried the Olympic Flame along a stretch of Georgia State Route 247, which had been named in his honor. In 1989, Scott was among the first class of inductees to the Georgia Aviation Hall of Fame.

His life story and accomplishments are celebrated in an extensive exhibit at the USAF museum in Warner Robins, Georgia. He wrote his memoir in 1943, entitled *God is My Co-Pilot* – a tribute to the faith he believed carried him through his exemplary career. [21] The book was adapted as a film starring Dennis Morgan as Scott and Raymond Massey as Major General Claire Chennault of the famous Flying Tigers squadron during World War II.

Brigadier General Richard Scott was a patriot who served his country with distinction. This week we celebrate the nation he and so many others have served so well. I am thankful for the life of a man who understood the importance of a personal faith in the midst of incredible challenge and danger.

"God is My Co- Pilot" … Without denigrating in any way what Scott achieved and how he lived, I might change one thing for my own story. I don't think I'm capable of sitting in the pilot's seat. I'd rather have God there instead!

[21] Robert L. Scott, *God is My Co-Pilot,* Buckeye Aviation Book Company, 1943

These Guys Are Good

What is it about golf? I gave up the game years ago. I don't need the stress. I relate to:

- Golf – an endless series of tragedies occasionally interrupted by a miracle.
- Golfing etiquette: hit the ball, swear, look for the ball, repeat
- "It took me 17 years to get 3000 hits in baseball; I did it in 1 afternoon at the golf course." Hank Aaron

- They call it 'golf' because all the other four-letter words were taken.

It's not that I don't admire great golf. I watch two tournaments a year – the Masters and the US Open. I cannot wait until the next idiot screams "Get in the hole!" They used to call golf "the game of kings" – if that's still true the galleries then consist of something less than royalty.

Imagine if other quaint traditions found their way into golf. Like:

- Cheerleaders prancing in pro-shop attire to rev up a crowd
- Squirrels or chipmunks hurled on to the course after a successful putt
- Guys standing near the tee box, yelling, "Swing, golfer, swing!"
- Sideline blondes interviewing players after a triple bogey
- Commentators speaking in their normal voices

I respect the skill required to play the tour – male or female. In some ways, the game reflects the vagaries of life. Even the greatest golfers can hit a bad shot, make a bad judgment, or blow a lead. Even the best cannot win every tournament.

What I like best, however, is that golf, like a few other sports, is a one-player game. You might be playing against the course or other players, but your skill, knowledge, experience and mental toughness matter most. No one else can hit that shot for you. You have to finish what you started. The game is on you.

Life is that way. You have to live your life. You have to use what's in your bag. God made us with unique abilities and personalities. The stakes are high in the game of life. We have to run our race, finish our course. By the grace of God, we can walk up that last fairway with our heads held high. We did the best we could.

Are We There Yet?

Ah, summertime.

Child: When school is out and summer fun begins! Parent: When does school start again?

When humans are trapped in the compartment of some vehicle for a lengthy journey punctuated with such stirring conversation as:

- "I need to go." "I told you to go before you got in the car!" "I didn't need to go then."

- "What's going on back there?" "Don't make me come back there!" "If you don't think I'll turn this car around, you got another think coming!"

- "He's touching me!" "Tell her it's my turn now." "Can't we just get along?"

- "You missed the turn." "Why didn't you tell me?" "You always act like you know where you're going."

- "Are we there yet?"

We need summer if it means a break in the routine, new experiences, favorite destinations, time for relaxation and recreation, family togetherness, and a change of pace. It's a good time to turn off the devices, go outside and play, read a good book, go somewhere you've never been or you always enjoy, do something that you've never done and stretch yourself.

It seems different these days. Summer seems to be shrinking. School around here opens the first week of August. Some say year-round school is inevitable. Economic stress means fewer choices and more careful planning. Families cannot afford to send their kids to this or that camp. Travel is just too expensive, complicated, or risky.

The truth is we have to build some margin in our lives. Releasing the pressure of busy, harried lives is a vital part of healthy living. We cannot keep the valves open all the way all the time. In our day, stress-related illness is on the rise among our children and youth as well as the adult population.

We have to be pro-active if we want our lives to calm and slow down. Take little steps like the dad who told the family that he would prepare a mix of everyone's favorite music to play on their vacation trip. What they didn't know is that he had prepared his own selection – absolute silence. When the kids complained, he simply said, "You got to listen to your music; now I get to listen to mine."

Aim High

The late Henri Nouwen, whose pastoral ministry focused on social justice, compassion, spiritual disciplines, and community, was well-known for his teaching and writing. In one of his books, he related a lesson he had learned at the circus. He evidently knew some of the trapeze artists who soared through the air, thrilling crowds with their daring exploits. They told him about the vital relationship between "flier" and "catcher." The first has to not only know when he has reached the right height, but also to be able to let go at the right time. The second, hanging by his knees, must also master the timing necessary while staying in perfect position. It is a natural instinct for the flier to try to grab the catcher, but he has to wait to let the catcher grab him. He must have complete trust.

In the story of Abraham and Sarah, there were certainly times when complete trust was missing. Both tried to grab on to God instead of waiting for God to catch them. They had to believe that God would keep His word, that He would remain faithful. It is interesting to note that both are listed in the Hall of Faith found in Hebrews 11. Abraham was justified by his faith, not his works. He was called a friend of God, but he had his moments of doubt and times when he acted hastily.

When we get ahead of God, we can experience humiliation and regret … much like Abraham and Sarah did. It is hard to wait for the right moment, to believe God will catch us when we leap.

One thing is true for trapeze artists: If you never let go, you have no show.

Jesus told a story about three servants, each entrusted with differing amounts of money. The first two doubled their funds; the third guy buried his, playing it safe. When it was time for the accounting, the first servants were rewarded while the third one lost what he had been given.

We can try to 'live safe' – take no risks, but isn't there more to life than that? The oft-quoted Wayne Gretzky comes to mind: "You miss 100% of the shots you never take." Keep aiming high!

Slow Down

You gotta slow down! In 1825, a letter of alarm and complaint was sent to the British Parliament. In part it read: "What can be more palpably absurd than the prospect held out of locomotives traveling twice as fast as stagecoaches! We trust that Parliament will, in all railways it may sanction, limit the speed to eight or nine miles an hour, which is as great as can be ventured on with safety."

Yes, 2015 is vastly different than 1825. On some days, we wish we could travel as fast as eight or nine miles an hour in Atlanta traffic. In reality, the speed of life these days is an enemy, not a friend. I see it in my life, the lives of children, youth, and families, in church, in business ... it's hard not to notice the rush.

Dallas Willard spoke truth when he insisted: "You must ruthlessly eliminate hurry from your life." Carl Jung wrote: "Hurry is not of the devil; hurry is the devil." John Ortberg said, "Hurry is the great enemy of spiritual life in our day."

Okay, now that we know the problem, how do we address it?

- Do you remember when we were promised a four-day work week? We cannot hurry and buy more time. We have to work smarter, not harder.

- Do you remember when we were promised that technology would increase our efficiency and effectiveness? But at what price? Our technology tends to isolate us, not connect us. We talk to devices and machines. We have to break free from screens!

What's the rush? I hate being late, so I get 'there' early. So, I sit in my car and try to recalibrate. I listen to music or read a book I carry. Sometimes I just think or take some deep breaths. Often, I can turn my hurry into refreshment.

Perhaps we could have screen-free zones like at the dinner table. How often are we guilty of having a phone or a tablet or a television grab our attention instead of focusing on the people around us?

Instead of driving a familiar route, walk it instead. You will notice things that have escaped your attention, I guarantee.

Schedule a ten-minute nap or rest in your day. Many companies are realizing the value of short breaks for contemplation, rest, and renewal. Instead of staring at your computer or reading one more report, get up and walk around for a few minutes. Pick up your Bible and read a Psalm. Make a short list and bow your head in prayer. Push hurry away, if just for a few moments.

Life is too precious to rush through.

Change

A farmer and his son were making their first visit to the big city. They had never seen skyscrapers, fancy cars, and the like. The farmer had always wanted to see what big city life was all about and he stood slack-jawed at the wonders of modern day. They went into the lobby of a hotel and were overwhelmed by the sights and sounds of a busy, bustling NYC establishment. They watched as an elderly lady approached a big box with lights on the side. She walked in, the doors closed, and lights started blinking. In a few minutes, the doors of the box opened again and out stepped a beautiful young woman. The farmer turned to his son and with a hoarse whisper, said, "Son, go get your mother."

I know. Weak, but I needed a laugh on a Monday morning.

We all know change is a part of life. It happens all around us and it happens to us. Just yesterday, I could hit a golf ball a long way. I didn't know where it was going but I could give it a ride. Just yesterday, my mind was sharp, and my wit was quick. Now, I have to think more about what I need to think about. I have to ask myself, "Did I tell that one already?" way too often.

I need to be content living today. I read some wise words this week: "If I am depressed, I am living in the past. If I am anxious, I am living in the future. If I am at peace, I am living in the present."

I hope your day is full of the present. After all, it is a gift from the Father.

Transitions

Transition: a passing from one condition, form, activity, place, etc. to another; the period of such passing (Webster's New World Dictionary). Life is full of transitions. Life changes. Babies are born, kids grow up, young people mature, adults move through seasons of life. The average person will change jobs 5 to 11 times in adulthood, depending on whose statistics you believe. Technology changes at warp speed. Information overload is smothering us. Life happens, ready or not. Death occurs, ready or not.

Life progresses and we worry about different things. You could follow an interesting trail by focusing on something like hair. A baby is born: "He sure doesn't have much hair." The toddler has a head full of curls: "When will he get his first haircut?" The teenager displays some attitude: "Is there something living in that mess on top of your head?" The young man readies for an important interview: "What does my hair have to do with making a good impression?" A middle age guy checks out the mirror: "Where did all that gray hair come from?" An old dude walks by: "He sure doesn't have much hair."

Having a strong sense of self-worth helps. Hugh O'Brian is a name Baby Boomers will remember. He played Wyatt Earp on television along with starring in movies and on Broadway. Reminiscing over his career, he made this observation: "You go through at least five stages in my business and in life. First stage – "Who is Hugh O'Brian?" Second stage – "Get me Hugh O'Brian!" Third stage – "Get me a Hugh O'Brian type!" Fourth stage – "Get me a younger Hugh O'Brian!" Fifth stage – "Who is Hugh O'Brian?"

Transitions can be tough. We cope in different ways. You've heard the saying: "The older I get, the better I was." Some of us turn to fantasy. Others of us are trapped in the past by memories that can overwhelm us with regret and pain. Some of us seek to relive the glory days, not wanting to realize the glory days won't be coming back.

Paul had a definite approach to transitions in his life. He wrote to the Philippians: "Forgetting the past and looking forward to what lies ahead, I press on to reach the end of the race and receive the heavenly prize for which God, through Christ Jesus, is calling us" (3:13,14).

Today is too important and tomorrow is too promising to live in yesterday. Jesus told us that each day has enough challenge of its own (Matthew 6:34). Carpe Diem! Seize the Day!

What If?

It happened on June 24, 1935. Four young people were double dating. The young man who was driving tried to take a curve going too fast. He lost control. The car flipped several times, ejecting three of the passengers. The fourth was pinned under the car. The others survived their injuries. She didn't. Elizabeth Wilbanks died that night. She was 17 years old. She had just graduated from high school.

The boy she was dating that night was the driver of the car. He was Jewish. Why should that matter? These young people lived in Anniston, northeast Alabama ... in the '30's. A young Baptist girl was dating a Jewish boy in the Deep South. You would have thought there might have been a scandal. No. The community rallied around the young people and the grieving family.

Elizabeth's older brother was a student at the University of Alabama. His parents got word to him; he needed to come home. Something terrible had happened. It wouldn't be the last time. Thirteen years later, he would receive another summons. His younger brother was in the hospital in Anniston. He had suffered a cerebral hemorrhage. He was 24 years old when he died.

He lost both siblings in his young adult years. In between their deaths, he served in the 90th Division of the US army in the European Theater from 1943 to 1945. He came home with a Purple Heart and a Bronze Star. A lot of his buddies were left behind.

Life is full of "what ifs" – you take the left fork instead of the right; circumstances develop that force your hand in unexpected ways; young lives are cut short; dreams are altered or shattered. Misery happens to all of us sooner or later. Our broken world serves up a great deal of pain and heartache. How do you live with the "what ifs" of life?

I wish I had all the answers. Even with the consoling help of Scripture, we can be overwhelmed by the "what ifs" we ponder. The young man who lost so much in those years had two amazing parents. After all, they had lost two children and fretted the loss of their oldest in war. They didn't approach their sorrows and fears with blind faith. Instead, they practiced a willing trust that didn't demand all the answers. They chose to live with hope. They laughed and sang with joy, a joy that sustained them when their hearts were heavy. Their surviving son learned well. He also chose to live with optimistic, joyful faith. He modeled that faith among those he loved and served. If he had lived, he would be 100 on July 17, 2016. We don't mourn his death; we celebrate his life – full of faith, hope, and love. He was my dad.

Now, Where Did I Put That?

You left in a rush this morning. You're not as attentive as you should be. You get to the office and look down. One black sock and one blue one or one black shoe and a brown one.

You walk out of the mall and stop as you gaze out at an ocean of cars. You have no idea where you parked. You start clicking your remote, hoping you're close enough.

You're late and you can't find your keys. Some helpful person in your life asks the inevitable question: "Where were you the last time you had them?" If you knew that, you would go there and pick up your keys.

Someone walks up to you with a sly grin on his face and says, "I'll bet you don't remember me." He's right. You don't.

Possible solutions:

- Keep an extra pair of socks, shoes at the office or in your car or just don't wear socks and shoes.
- It was time to buy a new car anyway.
- Buy a chain and hang your keys around your neck and never take the chain off.
- Smile a lot, pump his hand, slap him on the back, and bluff your way or carry a pictorial directory of every person you ever known.

Life happens. We forget things or misplace things. The older we get, the more often it seems to happen. Give yourself, and others, a break. Try to remember the important things, like:

- How blessed you are and how thankful you should be
- The people in your life who matter so much
- How important it is to pray, to worship, to praise
- How great it is to live in a free country
- How precious time is
- How good God is, all the time

While you're changing socks or looking for your keys, spend a moment thanking God for the gift of your life. You may forget a lot of other things but please remember that!

On Time

He was supposed to be born on July 1. We had been thoroughly schooled as to what to expect. Contractions were speeding up. It was time to go to the hospital. We were certain this was it. They met us in the lobby with a wheelchair ... for her, not me. I told 'em I was feeling a bit faint but they wouldn't listen. They tenderly ministered to my wife with comforting words and gentle actions. They told me to stay out of the way.

Alas, false alarm. They were sending us home. We came up to labor and delivery with a wheelchair. When they sent us out, they just pointed to the elevator. What happened to the comforting words and gentle actions? June 29th came and went. In the early morning hours of the 30th, we were on our way back to the hospital. We weren't taking 'no' for an answer this time – at least that what my wife said. I had heard that tone of voice before. Nurse, doctor, and other medical personnel – be afraid, be very afraid.

We got settled in our room. We were greatly encouraged by the sounds of shrieking coming from the room next to ours. The attending nurse explained that the young lady next door did not have the benefits of the classes we went through. She didn't know what was happening to her. I could have helped. I got a certificate for breathing. I could coach her through it. Someone in our room reminded me I already had a job, and you better be good at it, buster. It wasn't the nurse.

Our first son arrived about six hours before his due date. He was healthy and we were thankful. He was on time, his time, God's time. Seeing him being born is one of life's great highlights.

Tomorrow he turns 37, which makes me ... older. He has grown in every way but most importantly, he is a man of God. He is a good husband, dad, brother, and son. He serves God with passion and creativity and skill. We try to remember how blessed we are every day. We try to rely on God who is always on time, knowing what we need when we need it. He blessed our lives with two sons we love very much, but tomorrow we celebrate our firstborn.

You Shall Know the Truth

Among the many game shows that aired on American television, "To Tell the Truth" has an interesting history. It is one of two game shows in the US that have aired at least one episode in seven decades. Can you guess the other one? Sure, go ahead ... google it, or just check at the end of this column – but only if you read the whole column. Tell the truth, now.

The whole idea was to feature people who either had an unusual job or had been through strange circumstances. The celebrity panel would question the contestants and try to guess which one of the three was telling the truth. The latest version aired its first episode on June 14, 2016. That means the show has been on for 25 seasons.

Are we infatuated with telling the truth or with game shows?

People refer to truth is some strange ways today. Some will tell you that your truth is not necessarily their truth. Others will say that truth is relative depending on the circumstances. We even have different phrases for not telling the truth:

- I might have mis-spoke
- That was taken out of context
- What I meant to say was ...

I grew up when it was a little clearer – not telling the truth meant lying.

Jesus said, "You shall know the truth, and the truth shall set you free" (John 8:32). He also claimed that He was the truth (John 14:6). So, it seems that the path (or way) to freedom means knowing Jesus.

He remains mysterious, controversial, and provocative. Some dismiss Him ... mostly because they make no effort to know Him. Some dismiss Him because of the actions and attitudes of those who claim to follow Him.

When Jesus presented Himself in human form (John 1:14), He came on mission. He did not intend to start another religion. We have enough already. He came to reveal the Father; He came to establish the Kingdom; He came to redeem fallen humanity. He came to present truth.

The truth is that God loved the world so much that Jesus came, full of grace and glory, to rescue us. The truth is we cannot rescue ourselves. The truth is that He came to set us free.

In the game show, the dramatic moment would come when the host would say: "Would the real _____ please stand up!" Compared to the real Jesus, there are no equals. That's the truth!

Trivia answer: The Price is Right

Jesus Loves the Little Children

How did David take down Goliath?

"God gave him the courage to do it. Without God, he would have been just a regular kid." – Robin, age 8

"Goliath was calling the Jews names so somebody had to stand up to him. After it was over, Goliath wasn't calling anybody names no more." – Charles, 9

"It was one of those things you had to do before you could become the king. The other things were, like, hunting animals and having five wives." – Meghan, 9

"David probably carried a spare slingshot with him. You can never tell when you get in an accident and sit on your good one." – Charles, 9

David Keller collected children's ideas and opinions about Bible stories in his book, *Just Build the Ark and the Animals will Come*. Children have something a lot of adults have lost – imagination. They can figure things out. Clare was asked what Bible character reminded her most of herself. She thought of Delilah, Samson's nemesis: "Delilah ... I'm good at cutting hair, too." 8-year-old Robert said, "It sure isn't Satan. I get in trouble sometimes, but I ain't that bad!"

Most of us have some memory of VBS. Many of us learned Bible stories we still remember. Some of those stories have been flavored by our own childhood interpretations. Roger, age 9, captured his convictions about God: "There is only one God, just like it says on the tablets."

I have a picture of a little boy on my desk. Underneath is a caption: "A hundred years from now it will not matter what my bank account was, the sort of house I lived in, or the kind of car I drove ... but the world may be different because I was important in the life of a child."

I don't know who said it, but it makes a lot of sense to me. Think of it this way:

Jesus was surrounded by people who wanted to be near Him, who wanted something from Him. His disciples were conducting crowd control, trying to keep folks from pressing too close. There were children in the crowd. They wanted to be close to Jesus, too. He stopped the efforts of His disciples with these words: "Let the children come to Me. Don't stop them! For the Kingdom of Heaven belongs to those who are like these children" (Matthew 19:14).

I don't think Jesus was describing perfect little creatures. I think He was referring to childlike trust and, yes, innocence and imagination. They felt safe in His company. They knew that He was for real and that He loved them. They were drawn to Him. They wanted to respond to Him.

Jesus was saying to the disciples and to us: Help them find their way to Me.

I hope that happens through you and for you. "Let the little children come to Me.".

Wishes Come True?

The song was written in 1940 for Walt Disney's adaptation of the story a little wooden puppet who became a real boy. The animated character who sang it was a talking cricket named Jiminy. The original version was performed by singer Cliff Edwards. The song continues to be the theme song for the Walt Disney Company. It was the first Disney song to win an Oscar.

"When You Wish upon a Star" suggests a world where dreams come true. Pinocchio's wish was granted. In Disney films, dreams usually do come true. I am a sucker for happy endings.

Life doesn't always work out that way. We live in a broken world where people don't dare to dream because they believe there is no use in dreaming; because hard work doesn't always end in success; because someone else seems to have all the luck; because life can be cruel and heartless.

So, why try?

- Because life is too precious to waste
- Because we don't have to wallow in misery
- Because someone needs us
- Because our dreams open the world to new possibilities
- Because we are children of the King
- Because we were made to be His masterpieces
- Because there is no one else just like us

We can become jaded, cynical, pessimistic, and fatalistic. We can expect the worst because we look for the worst. We can bathe in self-pity and join the ranks of the miserable ...

Or we could choose another path: "Fix your thoughts on what is true, and honorable, and right, and pure, and lovely, and admirable. Think about things that are excellent and worthy of praise." That was Paul's advice in Philippians 4.

Paul might not have had the sweet tenor voice of Jiminy Cricket, but his words sound like a hopeful hymn to me: "Don't worry about anything, but pray about everything. Tell God what you need, and thank Him for all He has done. Then you will experience God's peace, which exceeds anything we can understand. His peace will guard your hearts and minds as you live in Christ Jesus."

What Did You Say?

The G20 summit is over. Leaders of the top twenty economies gathered in Hamburg, Germany to display the brightest minds in government, business, and banking. The wattage in the city had to exceed that of a 60-watt bulb.

As a reminder of how astute and articulate people in positions of power can be, I offer some of these classic lines:

- "Things are more like they are now than they have ever been." President Gerald Ford

- "And what is more, I agree with everything I just said." Piet Koornoff, South African ambassador

- "That's part of American greatness, is discrimination. Yes, sir. Inequality, I think, breeds freedom and gives man opportunity." Lester Maddox, former Georgia governor

- "Wherever I have gone in this country, I have found Americans." Alf Landon, presidential candidate

- "My fellow astronauts …" Dan Quayle, Vice-President at Apollo 11 ceremony

- "That lowdown scoundrel deserves to be kicked to death by a jack-ass, and I'm just the one to do it." Congressional candidate in Texas

- "This is a great day for France!" President Nixon at Charles De Gaulle's funeral

- "If I never get to Mexico again, it wouldn't bother me. I don't like the food or the climate." Dan Eddy, member of the Texas Good Neighbor Commission, charged with promoting Texas-Mexico good relations

- "If English was good enough for Jesus Christ, it's good enough for me." Dr. David Edwards, head of the National Committee on Language

Sometimes it would just be better to keep our mouths closed. James had good advice: "You must be quick to listen, slow to speak, and slow to get angry." After all the blustery rhetoric spewed by our leaders, it would be nice to leave all the spin behind. Jesus said in the Sermon on the Mount that we should treat others as we wish to be treated. How would that change the headlines? Naïve? Simplistic? Of course. I can dream, though ... and pray.

Missed Opportunities

"*E.T. the Extra Terrestrial*" was a huge hit for Steven Spielberg. Filmed in 1981 over a period of three months and costing only $10.5 million, the movie caught the imagination of millions of people around the world. Released on June 11, 1982, by Universal Pictures, E.T. was an immediate blockbuster, surpassing Star Wars to become the highest-grossing film of all time—a record it held for eleven years until Jurassic Park, another Spielberg-directed film, surpassed it in 1993. It is the highest-grossing film of the 1980s.

While the film was in production, Amblin Productions approached Mars, Inc. about utilizing one of its most popular products in the film. The executives of the company decided against the opportunity. Another company, Hershey's Foods, agreed and its bite-sized candy became a sensation. Sales jumped within two weeks in an astounding example of product placement (65 to 85%, depending on who you believe). In fact, Hershey's didn't pay anything except $1 million dollars in a collaborative promotion campaign.

These days, companies pay big bucks to place their products on the big screen. In this case, M&M's took a back seat to Reese's Pieces much to the chagrin of the executives who missed a great opportunity.

You probably can think of a time when you missed an opportunity. It might not have been on the scale of the E.T. story but most of us can point to a moment in our lives when we missed our chance to say the right thing, to do the right thing … to stand up and be counted.

In his old age, Joshua challenged the people of Israel with these words: "If you refuse to serve the Lord, then choose today whom you will serve. As for me and my family, we will serve the Lord" (Joshua 24). He had seen enough waffling from people who were hedging their bets.

I wonder what Joshua would say to us today. I doubt it would be: "Make sure you are politically correct" or "Don't take risks" or "Play it safe." It might be costly, even dangerous, but the people of God need to remember who the only Audience that matters is.

Why Not Now?

Robert G. Lee, a Christian comedian, created a bit based on a conversation he had with a young lady. She asked why Jesus didn't come today instead of 2000 years ago. He came up with reasons why Jesus would have a hard time in today's society. With some liberty taken, here are some to think about:

- Some, if not most, of the disciples would have had a hard time passing the required background checks

- The AMA would have sought to prosecute Jesus for practicing medicine without a license

- The FDA would have fined Jesus for feeding the multitude without individually wrapping and scanning the fish and loaves

- Jesus would have been brought up on charges for hate speech after calling the Pharisees hypocrites and a brood of vipers

- The IRS would have investigated Jesus for undisclosed income, mostly because of His shady accountant, Judas

- The American Psychiatric Association would want Him examined because of His claims of divinity

- In our 24/7 news cycle, He would have been constantly harassed by the media, hyping controversy and looking for dirt

- The Federal Government through a variety of alphabet agencies would surveil Him, perhaps arrest Him for subversive activity

Uh oh … I think I know where this is headed. It would be comical if it weren't so tragic. If Jesus came today instead of 2000 years ago, would He have been treated the same way? Would He be rejected by the intelligentsia and religious establishment of our day? Would folks like you and me recognize Him? Follow Him? Worship Him? Would we choose love and compassion over hate and fear for His sake? Would we build bridges instead of erecting walls for His sake? Would we dare to treat others as we wish to be treated for His sake?

What if He showed up tomorrow? Not for the first time, but the second. He will, you know, and it may come soon. Let's get busy.

Melting Pot or Fiery Cauldron?

On July 1, 1863, the Battle of Gettysburg commenced. Union and Confederate forces met in and around the Pennsylvania town. When the fighting ended on July 3, there were more casualties suffered than in any other conflict of the Civil War and the most costly toll in US history. General Robert E. Lee's Army of Virginia was turned back by General George Meade's forces. The war would continue for almost two years, but the outcome was determined when Lee's second attempt to invade the North was thwarted.

In November, a solemn ceremony was held to dedicate the Soldiers' National Cemetery. The program that day included several prayers, music, and the featured speaker, Edward Edwards. President Abraham Lincoln was asked to make a few remarks. Edwards's speech lasted for two hours and contained over 13,600 words. The president spoke for just over two minutes. His "few appropriate remarks" are remembered as one of the greatest speeches in American history.

In those few minutes, President Lincoln reminded those present of the cost of freedom and the necessity to preserve the union, but his most pressing issue concerned the principle of human equality and dignity.

We could use a Gettysburg address today. We could benefit from a statesman like Abraham Lincoln today. Five different versions of his speech survive, most variations written in the president's own hand. He didn't have professional speech writers or a teleprompter. The Bliss copy, the only one signed by Lincoln and displayed in the Lincoln Room of the White House, was the fifth draft ... "Four score and seven years ago our fathers brought forth on this continent a new nation, conceived in liberty, and dedicated to the proposition that all men are created equal ..."

He spoke of "unfinished work" and "the great task remaining for us" and "a new birth of freedom." That work and task still remains. America was far from perfect when the president spoke over the fresh graves at Gettysburg. She is far from perfect now.

In this season of presidential politics, it is tempting, even easy, to become cynical or to check out. We can be jaded by flawed candidates, toxic rhetoric, empty promises, and broken systems. The freedoms that have been bought with such a terrible price are worth preserving, defending, and cherishing.

May we celebrate our diversity and blessings instead of obsessing over our differences and problems. May we take seriously the unfinished work that remains.

Reaching the Bleachers

For two weeks in October 2015, Daniel Murphy was on top of the world. Playing for the New York Mets, he homered in a record six consecutive playoff games. He batted a superlative .556 in the National League Championship Series. Then his astounding success went into hiatus. Against the Kansas City Royals in the World Series his athletic prowess seemed to disappear. He batted a dismal .150, drove in no runs, and struck out seven times. In the field, he committed two damaging errors.

All professional baseball hitters can relate to hitting everything in sight when things are going well. They can also understand those stretches when the ball looks tiny and you can't find holes in the defense. How did Daniel Murphy respond to his changing fortunes? "Being on top of the mountain and then being at the bottom of the barrel … just felt like a perfect picture of God's grace and love in our lives. Jesus didn't love me any less when I made those errors in the World Series than He did when I was hitting those home runs in NLCS."

His highs and lows don't define him. He now plays for the Washington Nationals (okay, his judgment isn't so great). He is still really good at his craft. But he knows where his true worth is measured and where his trust is placed. "I know where there's hope and where's there's joy and where there's peace."

Growing up in Jacksonville, Florida, Daniel knew the importance of faith in Christ and found community in his church and in Fellowship of Athletes. His rise to the highest levels in his sport was not without challenges, both physical and spiritual.

You don't have to pull for the Nats to understand that guys like Daniel Murphy make a difference on and off the field. He is slotted to play second base on the National League all-stars on July 11th, but his priorities are higher. In FCA's feature article on Murphy, the author writes: "And as skilled as he continues to be at his craft, the fullness of his story is one of personal revival that replaced the idol of baseball with an ever-richer journey with Christ." Along the journey indeed!

Flopping

France wins the World Cup! Most of the world, including a rising number of Americans, was paying attention. We are so America-centric that we often don't realize how popular soccer is around the world. Here in Atlanta the craze around Atlanta United has surprised a lot of people.

When I was in high school back in the late '60's (the 1960's!), I barely remember that we had a soccer team. I couldn't tell you when their season was or who they played. When our boys were small, they played what we called "herd soccer" – where kids ran around in a big cloud of dust kicking each other more than the ball. When our youngest was playing, he was on a team called the Goalbusters. Ironic – they didn't score a goal all season.

Soccer can be a tough game to watch for the uninitiated. Personally, it would help to see more scoring but players have to be in peak condition to last. I heard the accumulated distance they cover is an average of 12 miles.

Still not my favorite game. Probably for one reason mostly: I can't stand the flopping. Here's a definition from the Urban Dictionary:

"A cowardly exaggerated expression of pain or injury heavily utilized by soccer players to get a red card issued on an opponent. In most instances said soccer player shows no sign of injury or pain approximately 3 seconds after desired outcome of flopping. Therefore soccer players are cowards, pansies and cannot play competitive sports like true gentlemen."

Soccer is not the only sport where you see players flopping, but you hate to see someone taking a dive under false pretenses anywhere. It's about character, about playing with integrity and sportsmanship. Do you have to cheat to win? Are you going for an Oscar for your acting?

I think Jesus was disgusted with flopping – people who pretended to be something they weren't. He called them hypocrites. Before we climb into our ivory towers, we need to admit we all have some hypocrite in us. We have probably done some flopping in our day.

Jesus told us to treat others as we would wish to be treated. I think that includes not descending to the level of using dishonesty or deception to get our way. We need the grace that the Lord has offered us but we also need to extend grace to others. Something like: "Lord, forgive our flopping even as we forgive those who flop against us."

Making Your Mark

I believe it is a common desire. Most of us want our lives to count, to stand for something of lasting importance and value. For most of us, it isn't about fame or fortune; we just want to matter – to our family, our friends, our community, our world. But let's be honest, some people go about it in peculiar ways.

Try to answer this: "What is the largest group to recite John 3:16 while standing on one foot inside a skating rink in 24 hours?" Evidently such a record meant so much to the people of Mosaic Church in Ocean Springs, Mississippi that 677 folks of all ages attempted this feat. Now they are the proud owners of a record that will stand until the next group of lemmings does it. Makes you feel all warm and fuzzy inside, doesn't it?

That's not what I had in mind. Luke wrote this about David in Acts (13:36), "After David served his generation according to God's purpose, and then he died." Two things stand out in this verse:

David served his generation – while he was far from perfect and made many mistakes, he is still regarded as the greatest of Israel's kings. Brilliant of mind, gifted of ability, and tender of heart, David made the most of his stewardship of time, talent, and treasure. One of my favorite David quotes: "I will not offer to the Lord that which cost me nothing" (2 Samuel 24:24).

David served according to the purposes of God – From his shepherd days and his confrontation with Goliath, to the height of his power and influence, to the end of his life as he surveyed the bright and dark moments of his days; he was a man after God's own heart. David offered this advice to his son, Solomon: "Observe the requirements of the Lord your God and follow all His ways" (1 Kings 2:3).

We get this treasure, this one and only life. How we spend it, or invest it, is really up to us. For all his faults, David got this right: "I bow before Your holy Temple as I worship. I will give thanks to Your name for Your unfailing love and faithfulness, because Your promises are backed by all the honor of Your name. When I pray, You answer me; You encourage me by giving me the strength I need" (Psalm 138:2,3).

The strength I need ... to live a life that matters.

Well, What's It Going To Be?

C.S. Lewis was a remarkable man. By nature a skeptic, he became a strong apologist for the Christian faith. Here are some of my favorite quotes from him:

- "My argument against God was that the universe seemed so cruel and unjust. But how had I got this idea of just and unjust? A man does not call a line crooked unless he has some idea of a straight line. What was I comparing this universe with when I called it unjust?"

- "Christianity, if false, is of no importance, and if true, of infinite importance. The only thing it cannot be is moderately important."

- "Atheism turns out to be too simple. If the whole universe has no meaning, we should never have found out that it has no meaning…"

- "When you argue against Him you are arguing against the very power that makes you able to argue at all: it is like cutting off the branch you are sitting on."

It seems to be in fashion these days to think of Christians as pitiful dullards … ignorant, backward people who cling to superstition and false hope. Some of the greatest human minds scoffed at the idea of a supreme being and haughtily dismissed the claims of Christianity. Stephen Hawking comes to mind.

I don't think for a moment that I have the intellectual capacity of a man like that. I certainly don't have the answers, but neither do those who summarily dismiss faith as delusion or falsehood. Paul wrote to the Romans in chapter one, "Professing to be wise, they became fools."

I may not be the smartest person around, but I think I will stick with the truth I have found in Jesus. There is not an alternative I can live or die with.

Well, You See...

Dad was talking to his 12-year-old daughter, who really wanted her own computer. She had begun her case with "When you were a kid, how old were you when you got your first computer?" Dad: "When I was a kid, we didn't have computers." Daughter: "Then how did you get on the Internet?"

My youngest son, knowing I grew up in the 50's, used to ask me if everything was black and white back in the old days. One kid was pontificating on what it was like in ancient times (when his parents were his age): "It was harder to study back in those days because they didn't have knowledge yet."

Speaking of knowledge ... do you think your kids and grandkids would know what you're talking about if you ask them to roll up a window or hang up a phone? Most of them have a hard time remembering their phone number. I don't think they even learn cursive anymore. Who needs it?

I know people who remember the Great Depression. There are youngsters who think the Great Depression is missing a concert or losing their phone. Do you remember where you were when JFK was shot? Who? You sound like a broken record. A what?

Ask a millennial where the word "luggage" came from. There was a day when you had to lug your bags around before they made those little wheels or pop-up handles.

What's the point? The world is changing. What my generation remembers, if they can remember anything anymore, may not be what the next and the next will experience. Some of the change will make things better. Some won't. Somehow we have to hold on to what really matters – timeless truths that never change. Where can we possibly find such things? Jesus said, "You will know the truth, and the truth will set you free." Sounds like a good place to start.

Weary and Wary of the Storm

Fidel Lopez and Bennie Newton met on the corner of Florence and Normandie avenues in Los Angeles in the spring of 1992. The backdrop of their meeting was the eruption of the city after the acquittal of the LA police officers in the Rodney King incident. Anger boiled over into the streets. 100 fires were set as businesses and homes were looted and destroyed. Roving mobs attacked vehicles and dragged the occupants out of their cars and trucks.

That's what happened to Fidel Lopez. His boss had given him almost $3000 to buy drywall and insulation for a project. His truck was surrounded and he was pulled into the street. As the Latino man was being pummeled, Newton, an African-American pastor of the Light of Love Church in South Central LA, pushed through the crowd. He covered Lopez with his own body and screamed at the mob, "Kill him and you have to kill me, too!"

The mob moved on. Newton tended to Lopez until he regained consciousness. Trying to summon an ambulance, the pastor realized that no emergency vehicle was going to respond. He put the injured man into his own car and drove him to the hospital.

When Lopez was released from the hospital, he met with Newton. The minister explained that members of his congregation were collecting an offering to replace the money that had been stolen from him during the beating. Lopez was overcome, "I thank you. You saved my life." Newton told him, "Out of tragedy, good will come. The storm is over."

I wish the storm was over. People of God, we have work to do. May we have the courage of Bennie Newton to make a difference in a world still covered with threatening clouds.

Humility

Paul wrote to the Romans this warning: "Don't think you are better than you really are" (12:3).

Pride is dangerous for all of us. We have all fallen victim to our pride. Christ turned a vice into a virtue when He displayed humility (Philippians 2:5) as an example to us. Before Jesus, it was a sign of weakness to be humble. Humility is not something you brag about. It would be hard to take seriously somebody who said, "I'm a modest kind of guy."

Here are some quotes I like about the subject:

- "What kills a skunk is the publicity it gives itself." Abraham Lincoln
- "Humility is like underwear; essential, but indecent if it shows." Helen Nielsen

- "You know what keeps me humble? Mirrors." Phyllis Diller
- "The graveyards are full of indispensable people." Charles de Gaulle

C.S Lewis wrote in his classic work, "Mere Christianity":

> "According to Christian teachers, the essential vice, the utmost evil, is pride. It was through pride that the devil became the devil. Pride leads to every other vice; it is the complete anti-God state of mind."

Paul cautioned his friends in Philippi: "Don't be selfish; don't try to impress others. Be humble, thinking of others as better than yourselves" (2:3). Good advice but not easy to follow, right?

After Captain Sullenberger brought his stricken Flight 1549 to safety on the Hudson River, he was hailed as a hero after saving 150 passengers. Sully deflected the praise with humility, pointing to the training and experience he had received over his career: "One way of looking at this might be that for 42 years I've been making small, regular deposits in this bank of experience, education, and training. On January 15, the balance was sufficient so that I could make a very large withdrawal."

Pride? The quiet confidence of a capable man made a difference to the lives he saved. His example gave the rest of us a lesson of true humility.

Just How Old Are You?

A man received a phone call from his grandson to wish him a happy birthday. In the course of the conversation, the boy asked, "Just how old are you?" The man replied, "I'm 62." There was silence for a moment before the boy spoke: "Did you start at 1?"

Life isn't always measured by length of years but by experiences. A little girl was quizzing her grandmother about how things were when she grew up. Grandma responded: "We used to skate outside on a frozen pond during the winter. I had a swing my dad made out of an old tire; it hung in the front yard from a big oak tree. We rode a pony our grandfather bought for us. We would go out to the woods and pick wild raspberries and blackberries." The girl listened in wild-eyed amazement, trying to take all this in. At last she said, "I sure wish I'd gotten to know you sooner."

Some people do their best stuff later in life. Some start early. Some find their rhythm somewhere along the way. Susan Boyle at 48 was an unknown until she stepped on the stage of "Britain's Got Talent" reality TV show. She sang: "I Dreamed a Dream" from Les Miserables and brought the house down. She launched her singing career that night. Laura Ingalls Wilder, of *Little House in the Big Woods* fame, didn't publish her first book until she was 64. Grandma Moses didn't start to paint until she was 76.

The Bible is full of stories about men and women whose accomplishments exhibit the possibilities of time – not chronos, time measured by seconds, minutes, hours, or years, but kairos, time that refers to opportunity or the right moment. What time is it for you?

Moses was 80 when God called him to lead the Israelites out of slavery in Egypt. Caleb was 85 when he asked to be given the hill country in Canaan. Shadrach, Meshach, and Abednego were young men when they refused to bow before Nebuchadnezzar. Esther was a young woman when she became queen. Joseph was 17 when his world was turned upside down. Jesus was 12 when He amazed the teachers and scribes at the Temple.

So, just how old are you? And what are you going to do with the rest of your life?

A Helping Hand

The creek had risen so high that Herman Ostry's barn was under 29 inches of water. He knew he had to do something so the Bruno, Nebraska farmer invited a few of his closest friends to a different kind of barn raising. He wanted to move his 17,000-pound barn to a new and higher foundation more than 143 feet away. With the help of his son, Mike, Ostry designed and installed a lattice work of steel tubing that he fixed to the interior and exterior of the barn, complete with hundreds of handles.

344 volunteers showed up for the big day. After one practice lift, the group slowly walked the barn up a slight incline to the new foundation. With each lifter supporting less than fifty pounds, the barn was settled on its new site in just three minutes. It's amazing what can be accomplished when folks work together!

Hold out one of your hands and consider how many things you can do with it. You can hurt or help with it. You can make a fist in anger or you can open your hand to heal.

Look closely and you can see your fingerprints. They are unique ... just like you. God created us for community. Sometimes you need the community and sometimes the community needs you. Hands up!

The Joys of Childhood

Have you ever done something you're not proud of? Of course you have. Have you ever done something that you thought was kind of cool even if others didn't? Perhaps. Let me explain.

When I was just a kid, we would spend a week or two at Ridgecrest. If you're a Baptist, you might remember the conference center near Asheville. It was where Baptists would go during the summer when we mostly liked each other. Each week had a different focus – Sunday School, Missions, Music, Casserole-making, etc. My dad used to teach classes there. The adults would go to sessions led by flavor-of-the-month speakers from all over the convention. The youth had camp. But the children went to kids' prison. Volunteers were enlisted to take care of us, watching carefully to make sure we didn't eat the Play-Doh or brain each other with those cardboard bricks. Sometimes we would mess with the flannel graph biblical characters just for fun. Samson vs. Goliath, Moses and the wise men, Bathsheeba and … well, let's not go there. What did we know?

These wardens, I mean workers, would desperately try to find something to occupy us long enough until our parents could spring us. Their ace in the hole was refreshment time when they brought out the unsweetened Kool-Aid and the stale graham crackers that could choke a horse. Their other strategy was to take us on "nature hikes" around the campus. They would chain us together in hopes that we wouldn't wander off. These were thrilling times for us as our wardens, I mean workers, would point out fascinating sights and sounds. "Look kids, that tree has leaves!" or "You have just tromped through a bunch of poison ivy, don't tell your parents."

It's important for me to mention that we often stayed in a cabin that belonged to some friends. On one particular occasion, my grandmother was with us. In the mornings she would sit on the front porch with her handwork and her Bible. Remember this significant point.

One day, our hike took us near the cabin. I recognized where we were so I turned to the boy I was handcuffed to and said, "I'll bet you a million dollars that my grandmother lives in these woods." My chain-mate scoffed at that: "No way. Your grandmother doesn't live in these woods." Scintillating conversation, right? The timing was perfect. We emerged from a stand of trees in front of our cabin and there was my grandmother sitting in her rocking chair. I waved at her and she saw me, "Hello, Mark. I hope you are having a good time."

With that, my fellow convict burst into tears. He wailed so loud that one of the wardens, I mean workers, ran over to see what had happened. I'm certain she thought I had kicked him in the shin, or punched him, or told him his mother was ugly. "What's the matter, Timmy? Why are you crying?" By now there were snot bubbles coming out his nose. Finally he cried out in this sad, distraught way: "I don't have a million dollars!"

I'm pretty sure that my warden, I mean worker, didn't have a clue what had happened. Timmy must have spent years in therapy. I'm just bummed. I never saw one dime of that million dollars.

What's Up With All These Snakes?

What do these stories have in common?

- A 72-year-old Oklahoma woman kills 12 copperhead snakes with a shotgun and a shovel. They were living under her house.

- A woman in Ohio calls 9-1-1 in a panic. A 5.1/2-foot boa constrictor was wrapped around her neck, biting her face. A firefighter had to cut the snake's head off.

- Two guys use a cell phone to video a four-foot snake that emerged from a car hood. They sped up, they slowed down, they swerved – the snake would not budge. It finally slithered off to parts unknown.

- A woman confronts a talking serpent who tempts her to take fruit from a forbidden tree. Later, she entices a male acquaintance to partake as well.

There are people out there who like snakes, who keep them as pets, who consider them some of nature's most interesting creatures. Not me. My encounters with snakes have not been friendly. I am not knowledgeable enough about them to know all the things to look for – shape of head, order of bands, etc. I know Moccasins are mean and Copperheads are poisonous. I've dispatched them without checking with a guidebook.

My grandfather had an interesting experience with a cottonmouth. In his later years, most of his fishing buddies were gone. He still loved to take his boat out on an Alabama lake to try his luck. One day, he had fished for hours without any luck. He pulled his boat out and reached under his seat to pick up his tackle box. Coiled beside it was a Moccasin. It had been there all day. Pop went to his car, opened the trunk, and pulled out his shotgun. He walked back to his boat, lifted his gun, and blew the bottom out of his boat. I get that.

Snakes have been mostly trouble since the Garden of Eden. They seem to represent things that scare us, surprise us, and hurt us. What would have happened if Eve had rebuffed the serpent? What would happen if we resisted temptation? We know the world would be a better place. But the truth is none of has resisted. We need all the help we can get. In the model prayer that Jesus taught His disciples, we find these words: "Deliver us from evil and lead us not into temptation." Jesus understood the lure of the serpent, the power of evil. One day that power will be destroyed. Until then, we count on His peace, His presence, His power.

Leadership

Think of someone who has had a profound influence in your life. A parent, a teacher, a coach, a minister, a supervisor, an older friend, a mentor, a speaker, or a writer. Was their influence expressed or experienced the same way with each one? Of course not. Some led with forceful personalities or authoritative position. Some were far more subtle. Some are connected to significant events while others modeled their influence incrementally over time. Each one made a contribution to your life. Some of them were perhaps negative models, poor teachers, or bad examples. We are shaped by our influencers, both good and bad.

Now, think about those with whom you have had influence. Younger siblings, friends, classmates, teammates, colleagues, employees, young believers, students, and others. What impressions have you left in the lives you have touched? We would have to admit that there are some instances, some relationships we wish we had handled better. We could have had a more positive impact in the lives we have intersected.

Someone said to me this past Sunday, "But I'm not a leader." In the purest sense of the word, our ability and availability to influence others makes us leaders. All of us have people in our lives who think our opinion is important, who value what we think or say, who watch to see how we handle circumstances. A Midwest farmer saw his young son trying to match the footprints his dad had made in a late snow. The little boy had to leap to reach the next impression in the snow. The farmer said to himself, "I'd better watch where I step."

Leaders have to do that. They need to watch where they step because someone might be trying to follow. How do we increase our influence, improve our example? We get better.

When leaders get better, everybody wins. Our commitment is to not only positively affect our church, but to assist people to be better leaders in their homes, their businesses, their communities.

A Great American

I wonder what Will Rogers would say about America today. He never held back. He poked fun at everybody. Politically correct? He would laugh at the very idea.

Born in 1879 to a Cherokee family in the Oklahoma Territory, he became a beloved figure in his country and around the world. He traveled the globe three times, made over 70 movies, and wrote more than 4000 nationally syndicated columns. At one time, he was the highest Hollywood movie star. He came a long way from the prairie. His homespun humor coated his biting wit with keen observations about everything from politicians to gangsters.

He even wrote his own ending: "When I die, my epitaph, or whatever you call those signs on gravestones, is going to read: 'I joked about every prominent man of my time, but I never met a man

I didn't like.' I am so proud of that, I can hardly wait to die so it can be carved."

He did die and the world mourned. While flying with aviator Wiley Post, he died in a plane crash in northern Alaska at 55 years of age.

We could use a Will Rogers today. Here are a few of his best lines:

- "I am not a member of any organized political party. I am a Democrat."

- "Everything is funny, as long as it's happening to somebody else."

- "A fool and his money are soon elected."

- "Good judgment comes from experience, and a lot of that comes from bad judgment."

- "I don't make jokes. I just watch the government and report the facts."

- "If you want to be successful, it's just this simple. Know what you are doing. Love what you are doing. And believe in what you are doing."

- "I bet after seeing us, George Washington would sue us for calling him 'father.'"

We could use some of his common sense, don't you think?

The Perils of Political Correctness

The University of Georgia Redcoat Band made its first appearance in 1906 at a baseball game, not a football game. UGA was playing

Clemson in baseball when the 20 plus-member band put on its first non-military performance. Originally forming through the military department at the university, it now numbers over 400 men and women who are best known for their contribution to Saturdays in the fall between the hedges.

When I was student in the early seventies (1970's for you wise guys out there), there was a parody of the name that today sounds very familiar. Known then as The Dixie Redcoat Marching Band, a tongue-in-cheek suggestion was made:

"It was announced that the band's name had to change because it was offensive.

- It could no longer bear the descriptor "Dixie" because of its obvious association with the Civil War
- "Redcoat" had to be dropped as well due to its connection with colonial oppression
- "Marching" suggested militarism and could not be tolerated in gentler times
- "Band" reeked of exclusivism and defied a more open, welcoming attitude.

Therefore, the University of Georgia proudly proclaimed the new name of its musicians:

"The"

Pretty ridiculous, huh? Haven't we carried this PC thing far enough? Can we no longer have a sense of humor? Is that against the law now, too? Wouldn't it be great if we focused on what we have in common, rather than what tends to divide us?

You Gotta Cheer for the Underdog

I still get chills watching it. *"Miracle"* is the Hollywood version of the 1980 US Hockey Team that stunned the world by winning the gold medal. The gold medal game was almost anticlimactic to another story, the improbable win against the reigning kings of international hockey – the Russian team. The US had won their single gold medal in the Olympics in 1960. The last player to be cut from that team was a young athlete named Herb Brooks. In 1980, Brooks would coach the young US squad.

The US team was a huge underdog, not just against the Soviets. Finishing fourth in 1976 in Innsbruck, the squad now averaged about 20 years of age. Most of the other teams played with veterans of international competition. The Soviets were the most experienced and successful team in the world.

With a raucous, pro-USA crowd in the arena and a disbelieving world-wide audience watching, the US defeated the mighty Russians 4-3. Al Michaels, in the waning seconds of the game, uttered the memorable line: "Do you believe in miracles? Yes?"

Something in us compels us to root for the underdog. We like it when the little guy stands up to the big bully.

David vs. Goliath is often portrayed as the ultimate underdog story. Actually, we might miss who the real underdog was. Goliath was a mountain of a man, a professional soldier, and full of blood lust. Shepherd boy David was on an errand for his father, bringing supplies to his brothers who fought in the Israeli militia. They find themselves facing each other on the valley floor while both armies are watching. Goliath wields his huge spear. David grabs a stone for his slingshot. No contest. Goliath never had a chance. He thought he was fighting a spindly shepherd boy. Oh, how wrong he was.

We are never underdogs when God stands by our side. In Zechariah 4:6, the Lord spoke to Zerubbabel: "It is not by force or by strength, but by My Spirit, says the Lord of Hosts."

Was David's victory the "Miracle on Turf"? Not really. A young man trusted God to come through and He did.

An old joke: An archaeologist discovers a casket with a 3000 year old mummy. He declares that the man died from heart failure. Challenged as to his conclusion, he answers: "I know his age and his cause of death. He held a piece of papyrus in his hand. It read: '10,000 shekels on Goliath.'"

Is That Right?

One of the most interesting passages in the Bible is the story of tragedy and triumph in the book of Ruth. The focal character is Naomi, a woman who suffered great loss but also experienced great gain. Her tale is real life ... all of us are touched by pain and suffering. It is how we respond to those valleys that help define us. Naomi wanted to change her name to Mara, which means 'bitter' because she had lost so much. As the book of Ruth unfolds, we find that her bitterness will fade as she finds new reasons for hope and joy.

Not every story has a happy ending ... at least from our view. Paul wrote to the Romans: "And we know that God causes everything to work together for the good of those who love God and are called according to His purpose for them" 8:28). We know that everything that happens to us isn't good, but can we believe that God can work and move and act in our circumstances for the ultimate good?

The book of Psalms contains the full gamut of human emotion. Glorious praise and flowing gratitude can be coupled with anguished pleading and grieving complaint. Psalm 13 begins with: "O Lord, how long will You forget me? Forever? How long will You look the other way? How long must I struggle with anguish in my soul, with sorrow in my heart every day? How long will my enemy have the upper hand?"

Then the tone changes, much like Naomi's did: "But I trust in Your unfailing love. I will rejoice because You have rescued me. I will sing to the Lord because He is good to me."

So, which is it? We live long enough to realize it's both. There are times when we cry out, when we raise our fist toward heaven and shake it. But there also times when we understand we are not forgotten or forsaken. God is still in control. God still loves us. God does indeed care.

Naomi learned that. Her tears turned to laughter. Perhaps her laughter was sweeter because of the bitterness she endured. God makes a way for us. We matter to Him.

911

Reader's Digest magazine publishes collections of the unusual, the ironic, and sometimes the comedic. This past spring they ran an article entitled "Outrageously Funny 911 Calls." You would think that people who dial 911 are in emergency situations and need immediate help. Something has gone terribly wrong and first responders are required. Evidently, not always.

I needed these on a Monday morning:

- The Regina Fire Department was summoned to battle an inferno that was supposedly raging at a nearby Canadian Football League stadium. Turns out, a video of a burning log was playing on the giant video screen.

- In Lincoln, Nebraska, a man called to report a burglary. What he didn't tell police was that his favorite hookah pipes were missing. What the police did discover were the marijuana plants growing at his house.

- A woman in Dacula, Georgia dialed 911 to report that her Chevy van was missing, presumed stolen. A little while later, she called back to say that her van had been found, parked behind her overgrown backyard.

- In Burnett, Wisconsin, police received a call from a 7 year-old girl. When police arrived, they discovered that the girl was turning in her grandfather for cheating in a game of cards.

Kim and I certainly remember the day when a policeman knocked on our door. Kim answered and asked the officer if there was a problem. He said, "Yes, Ma'am. I am responding to a 911 call from your home." Kim tried to explain that it must be a mistake. "No one from this house had made such a call," she told him. The policeman assured her that the call did indeed come from our house. She was perplexed, until a little head poked around the corner. One of our sons, I won't mention his name, was about three at the time. He had just learned about firemen and policemen at his preschool. Coupled with the fact that he was mad at his mom about something, he decided to dial 911. Of course, he hung up when the call was answered. Thus, the visit from one of Jacksonville's finest.

There is nothing funny or cute about many calls for help. People are in crisis. It seems that more and more folks are desperate for someone to respond, and to do it quickly. Where do you turn? Who do you call? Have you built systems of faith, family, friends, neighbors, fellow Christians, colleagues that are reliable? Are you a part of such systems for others?

Do you find strength, comfort, peace, grace, and assurance from your relationship with God? Does your prayer and devotional life keep you calm when the storms rage? Have you discovered a haven with the One who promised to be our refuge, fortress, rock, shepherd, helper, the Mighty One, and so many others? We all need help from time to time. Just remember to dial the right number.

Okay, God, Please Be You

He had known the man for years. He had offered counsel while the man struggled with a myriad of challenges and crises. Just about the time he thought the man was making progress, the guy would do something or say something that seemed to prove he just didn't get it. Some of his decisions hurt others. Some were self-destructive.

The pastor cringed a bit when his secretary told him the man wanted to see him again. He thought to himself, "What has he gotten into this time?"

When the man came into his office, he didn't wear his usual frown or perplexed look. He actually had a smile on his face. His countenance, his posture suggested something different than the pastor had witnessed before.

Before the pastor could speak, the man burst out, "Preacher, I've got something wonderful to tell you. I've just resigned as general manager of the universe, and it's amazing how quickly my resignation was accepted!"

Have you offered your resignation yet? Aren't you tired of the burden? Don't you grow weary of the responsibility? Haven't you already proven the job's too big to handle? Isn't it time you followed His lead instead of insisting that you're in charge?

Have you considered what God's job description must look like? I certainly don't know all the details but I think I've figured out enough to know I don't have the skill set or the experience or the wisdom.

Life is hard enough. We all struggle with a broken world and broken lives. We have to decide to trust, to live with the questions. A poet named Rainer Marie Rilke wrote: "Be patient toward all that is unresolved in your heart, and try to love the questions themselves, like locked rooms and like books that are now written in a very foreign tongue. Do not seek the answers which cannot be given you, because you would not be able to live them. And the point is, to live everything. Live the questions now. Perhaps you will then gradually, without noticing it, live along some distant day into the answer."

What the poet either missed or didn't say is that we don't have to do this alone. The Creator is also living Word, Comforter, Presence, Healer, and Redeemer. That's His job, not ours.

Okay, God, please be You!

Starting Over

Have you ever made a mistake? Have you ever wished for a mulligan – a do-over? All of us have. We have known failure. We have suffered consequences for words we shouldn't say or ideas we should have forgotten or deeds that have been hurtful.

The author of the first gospel could relate. A young man, full of promise and energy, was invited to join a mission team that included his uncle and the apostle Paul. Heady stuff. There is no record of speech in the book of Acts but his role may have been as scribe. Before Luke joined the team (Acts 16:10), young John Mark may have been responsible for writing down the details of their journey.

Then things went wrong. Perhaps he was just homesick. Perhaps he just wasn't cut out for mission work like this. We are not told the exact reasons but the young man left the team and headed back to Jerusalem (Acts 13:13).

He left a mess behind. His uncle and the apostle would ultimately sever their partnership over the disagreement (Acts 15:37-39). Our mistakes can have a profound impact on others. Too often the consequences can be lingering or even permanent.

The biblical account doesn't fill in the details but it was obvious that John Mark got the chance to start over. Later in Paul's writing, we meet Mark again. In Colossians, Philemon, and 2 Timothy, he is mentioned as being valued, even treasured.

Yes, we make mistakes. But do we have to let our mistakes define us? The best evidence we have that John Mark was restored you can hold in your hands and read with your eyes. Mark was the instrument through whom Peter speaks to us today. Much of Peter's teaching and preaching, providing an eye-witness account of the life and mission of Christ, are found in the pages of Mark's gospel.

We can overcome failure. We can learn from defeat. We can be shaped by the hard times of life to make us more fitting for what God wishes to do in and through us. Just ask John Mark.

A Blast From the Past

Some people remember when you hung your wash on a clothesline. In some places, they still do. Here's an old story with a point that shouldn't be:

A young couple moved into a new neighborhood. On their first morning, they were sitting down for breakfast when she watched her next door neighbor begin to hang her laundry on the line in the back yard. Wife said to husband, "Those clothes don't look very clean. I wonder if she is washing them correctly." The husband didn't say anything. This happened several times with the same comment being made. Each time the husband stayed quiet. Finally, wife noticed a change: "Look, she either learned how to wash better or she got better detergent. I wonder who showed her how." The husband finally spoke: "I got up early this morning and cleaned our windows."

To paraphrase the words of Jesus, perhaps we should clean our windows before we judge someone else's wash. One of the most liberating moments in life should come when we admit our own weaknesses and faults. When we come face to face with our own humanity, we can better see the humanity in others.

C.S. Lewis said that the unique contribution of Christianity to the world was grace. For believers, grace isn't possible, not in its fullest sense, outside of Christ. We see it in His warning about judging others. We recognize it when He told us to treat others as we wish to be treated.

Grace doesn't come from obligation or duty; it flows from gratitude. Being grateful for receiving the gift of grace should encourage us to be more extravagant in sharing it. Who wants to live with dirty windows?

Crutches

If you have ever had to use crutches you know they are both blessing and curse. Having had foot surgery a few weeks ago, I have been reintroduced to the fun of navigating through life with these sticks. I'm keeping score – only one face plant so far. Kim and I spent several days trying to rent, even buy, crutches. A friend came to the rescue. Another friend let me borrow a kneeler. Life is good. I've been challenged by one of our senior adults to a race in the church hallways. I'm in training now.

I've noticed that most often the word "crutches" has a negative connotation. Crutches symbolize weakness, a need you cannot meet without help. Unhealthy relationships, substance abuse, laziness, and stunted growth are just a few of the downside aspects of crutches.

When there is a physical reason for crutches, most people I know can't get rid of them fast enough. Putting them down indicates a return to health and normal activity.

So how do we get rid of crutches? I love the stories about Jesus when He rid people of their crutches. Sometimes He healed them, but He would always urge them to take the first step, to throw away the crutch. Remember the guy who had been a paralytic for 38 years? It's found in John 5. Jesus actually asked the man, "Do you want to get well?" Sounds like a silly question but some people cling to their crutches.

Jesus told the man to pick up the mat he had been lying on for so long and to start walking, He gave the man dignity and accountability. The guy could have just stayed on the mat, physically and mentally. He expected the man to take the first step.

In our world of so many broken people, we yearn to see people be healed in mind, body, and spirit. We have been called to help people get rid of their crutches, to encourage them to get off the mat and get back into life. Perhaps you and I will get the opportunity this week. Let's pray we'll be ready.

God Will See It

A stonemason had been assigned the task of putting the finishing touches on one of the small sculptures for the top of the National Cathedral in Washington, DC. An observer, watching the delicate and meticulous craftsmanship, asked him, "Doesn't it bother you that after all your hard work, no one will be able to see your artistry?" The stonemason replied, "God will see it, and that is enough for me."

Paul wrote to the Colossian Christians: "And whatever you do or say, let it be as a representative of the Lord Jesus, all the while giving thanks through Him to God the Father" (Colossians 3:17).

Peter told believers of his day (and ours) that they were "living stones, being built up as a spiritual house for a holy priesthood, to offer spiritual sacrifices acceptable to God through Jesus Christ" (1 Peter 2:5).

As followers of Christ, we are a part of what God is building in this world. What we are able to accomplish is our tribute to Him. The way we live our lives illustrates our understanding of the "why" we live. When our eyes and hearts are fixed on Him, we can be motivated to honor Him with the best we have to offer.

He gave us gifts, abilities, talents. He will empower, lead and guide us, but we choose how we will utilize our gifts. A woodcutter from the hills was told that he could cut much more wood if he used one of those new-fangled chainsaws instead of the trusty old handsaw that had seen many years of work. Finally convinced, he went to the hardware store and bought one. A week later he was back with the chainsaw and a complaint. He told the salesman that he was cutting far less wood but using far more effort. He wanted his money back. The salesman was puzzled and asked to take a look at the new saw. He pulled the cord and the chainsaw roared to life. The woodcutter was shocked. Over the noise of the whirring chain blades, he said to the salesman, "Will you look at that! What will they think of next?"

It is pathetic when the power available to us is never used!

No, You Don't Have To

You don't have to cheat. Then, why is so much cheating going on? The Rio Olympics is not the first games to be tainted by cheaters. If the IOC wasn't so corrupt, an entire nation's Olympic team would have been banned. State-sponsored cheating!

Alex Rodriguez, Barry Bonds, Sammy Sosa, Roger Clemens ... just a few names from the world of baseball who have been called out for cheating. Football, basketball, cycling, racing, pin-the-tail-on-the-donkey ... the list grows. Wait a minute! Someone cheats at pin-the-tail-on-the- donkey? A little girl was asked how she had gotten so good at the game. She never lost. Her answer was simple: "I peek."

We know cheating touches every area of our lives. Spouses cheat on each other. People cheat on their taxes. Businesses sacrifice ethics. Students grab grades they didn't earn. Builders cut corners in construction. If people think they can away with it, they tend to cheat.

Do we get away with it? It might seem so, but there is always an accounting. Remember this old story? A young preacher found himself in a dilemma. Two brothers were occasional attenders at his church. These men were powerful and rich. In the small town where they lived, they ruled. They were known for shady business practices, monopolizing the market by lies, intimidation, and thievery. One of the brothers died. The other one came to see the preacher. The conversation went like this: "Preacher, I want to biggest and best funeral this town has ever seen. I want you to tell the people what a fine, upstanding man my brother was. You tell 'em my brother was a saint. If you do it right, I'll pay off the debt on this new building you've built."

It didn't take that pastor long to decide how he would handle the service. The church was packed. People wanted to hear what could possibly be said about a man with such an unsavory reputation. The pastor got up to give the eulogy: "Brother Smith was a hard man. He lied and cheated and wrecked the lives of hard-working folks in our town. But next to his brother, he was a saint."

We don't have to cheat. We could recall Paul's words to the Colossians: "And whatever you do or say, let it be as a representative of the Lord Jesus, all the while giving thanks through Him to God the Father" (Colossians 3:17). Let's do the right thing for the right reason.

Beside Myself

Have you heard the expression "I was beside myself"? Have you used it? What does it mean? What are the implications? I need to lie down to contemplate the enormity of this enigma!

I found some definitions: "To be 'beside yourself' is an idiomatic expression indication extreme levels of emotion, usually negative ones such as frustration, anger or grief." Or, this one: "It means experiencing extreme joy. 'Beside' was formerly (15th through 19th centuries) used in phrases to mean out of a mental state or condition as 'beside one's patience, one's gravity, one's wits.'"

So there is a good 'beside yourself' if it means joy, and there's a bad 'beside yourself' if you're really ticked off. When's the last time you were 'beside yourself' and how were you feeling?

It's interesting (at least to me) that there is a biblical reference with this phrase. In Acts 26, Paul appeared before the Roman governor, Festus and King Agrippa. As Festus listened to the impassioned witness of Paul, he exclaimed: "Paul, thou art beside thyself!" (KJV)

Festus evidently thought that Paul was crazy. To the worldly mind of the governor, he wondered how anyone could risk so much to gain so little. Paul didn't see it that way. He had written to the Philippians: "For to me, to live is Christ; to die is gain" (1:21). In some of his final words, he told Timothy: "I have fought good fight, I have finished the course, I have kept the faith. And now the prize awaits me ..." (2 Timothy 4:6-8).

If you're going to be beside yourself, shouldn't the reason have high stakes? Can you think of anything more critical than setting your sights on eternal goals? If I'm going to be beside myself, I want it to be worth it.

William Wilberforce must have been 'beside himself' His holy discontent was the slave trade. His campaign to abolish the horrid blight of slavery took twenty years before the passage of the Slave Trade Act of 1807. He wasn't finished. From 1826 until 1833, he invested so much effort and energy that he had to resign from Parliament due to his failing health. The Slavery Abolition Act of 1833 abolished slavery in most of the British Empire. 3 days after learning of the passage of this landmark legislation, Wilberforce died. He, too, kept the faith.

The next time you feel like being beside yourself, make it a worthy cause.

John Stephen Akhwari from Tanzania was sent to compete in the 1968 Olympic Games in Mexico City. A marathon runner, he had prepared for years to represent his homeland. During the race, he stumbled and fell, severely injuring a knee and ankle. An Ethiopian won the race and the other competitors had long completed the course when Akhwari staggered through the gate into the stadium. Only a handful of spectators remained to see the African with the bloody bandage around his leg complete the final lap around the track. They cheered his every step as they recognized his courage and perseverance.

The media surrounded him, peppering him with questions. The one most asked was: "Why did you continue to race after you were so badly injured?"

John Stephen Akhwari replied, "My country did not send me 7000 miles from home to begin a race; they sent me to finish the race."

Anybody can start; the world is full of those who begin something. What marks our lives is our ability to finish. So we should be careful … careful to run a race worth finishing, careful to finish what we start! Our lives are amazing gifts from God. How we live them is our gift to Him.

Look at Nehemiah, a man who risked his life to do something great for his people. His courage in the face of significant obstacles and opposition was fueled by a consistent prayer and worship life. His most important contribution was not the rebuilding of the walls of Jerusalem. He was able to accomplish that feat in 52 days. I believe it was even more crucial that he and his colleague Ezra led his people to spiritual renewal and revival.

Have you heard the biblical verse: "The joy of the Lord is your strength"? Those words were spoken by Nehemiah. He was calling his people to rediscover the gift of life with God. I pray today that you will experience your own discovery as we worship together.

Things You Shouldn't Say

James wrote a no-nonsense letter to Christians. Among the many significant issues he addressed:

- If you need wisdom, ask believing, trusting, and expecting God will answer.

- Be quick to listen, slow to speak, and slow to get angry.

- Treat people with respect, mercy, and grace. Show favoritism at your peril.

- Show your faith by your actions. Talk is cheap.

- Resist the devil. Draw close to God.

He also warned us about the power of the tongue. How many times have we wished we could recall something we said or how we said it? The tongue can speak blessing or curse, can encourage or deflate, can build up or destroy.

How do you control your tongue? How do you govern your speech? After James described all the damage the tongue can cause, he wrote: "If you are wise and understand God's ways, live a life of steady goodness so that only good deeds will pour forth" (3:13).

Simple, right? I wish. I'm fairly confident that I am not the only one who struggles with living "a life steady of goodness." I know I need to submit myself to His lordship every day, many times during the day. It isn't just the words out of my mouth; it's the condition of my heart. Some days my attitude just stinks. James urged us to come clean about our failings. He encouraged us to pray, to have others pray for us.

His letter is not easy to read or apply, but he spoke the truth. He opened his message in a hopeful tone, claiming that trouble can be turned into triumph. You have heard people say that 10% of life is about our challenges and 90% is about how we respond to them. James might say it another way: "Consider it joy when you face trials. For when your faith is tested, your endurance has a chance to grow. So, let it grow, for when your endurance is fully developed, you will be strong in character and ready for anything" (1:2-4).

So, Lord, we need help controlling our hearts and our mouths. Grow us up in You!

Here's a bonus – things you shouldn't say if pulled over by the police:

- "Aren't you the guy from the Village People?"
- "I thought you had to be in relatively good condition to be a police officer."
- When the officer says, "Your eyes look red. Have you been drinking?" You probably shouldn't say, "Your eyes look glazed. Have you been eating donuts?"

You Can't Get There From Here

The saying supposedly originated in Maine as a way to describe the difficulty of finding your way in a mostly rural state. Maine has actually had several incidents in recent years of motorists driving into remote bodies of water, most recently in the small coastal village of Roque Bluffs, where two women on a foggy evening accidentally drove their car right into the ocean and drowned. It's not known if the women were using a GPS device, but driving along that same road, here's what happened when a GPS was set for Roque Bluffs: "Your destination is straight ahead."

In 1985, R.E.M. had a cut on their album by the name, "You Can't Get There From Here." In the song, a small unincorporated community was mentioned. Philomath, Georgia was settled in 1829 and first called Woodstock. It's a place of "used to" – used to have an all-boys boarding school, Reid Academy, and enjoyed a South-wide reputation; used to have its own post office; used to be a place where politicians and educators made regular visits; used to be known as the place where the government of the Confederacy east of Mississippi broke up. It's just a small place in the southeastern corner of Oglethorpe County.

"You can't get there from here" could also relate to our spiritual lives. You can't get from imperfection to perfection. You can't get from sinful to sinless. You can't get to heaven with good works. The only way to get there from here is not found in religion or philosophy or philanthropy. The way is not a code of rules or a performance chart. The way is not an "it" ... the way is Him. His name is Jesus.

In Every Frame

How's it going? We could give a lot of responses, right? This might be a really good time in your life or you might be experiencing dark days. Today could be miserable while tomorrow might be bright skies and joy. Life is unpredictable, isn't it?

I read a story years ago about a pastor going to see a young man who was battling leukemia. The minister knew that the patient was losing his battle. The man was so weak that the pastor had to bend close. He could see the shadow of death in the face of the weakened man. It wouldn't be long. They both knew it.

The conversation was awkward after the initial greeting. Finally, the dying man said, "Pastor, I have learned something."

"Tell me what you have learned," the minister responded.

"I've learned that life isn't like a DVD."

"What do you mean?"

After a moment, the young man replied: "Life isn't like a DVD … you can't fast-forward past the bad parts."

The room was quiet for a few moments. Then the young man spoke again. "You know what else I've learned? I have learned that Jesus is in every frame, and right now it's just enough."

And right now it's just enough. Is it enough for you? Is He enough for you? I hope so.

How Does He Do That?

"Hush, Rachel's talking to Me." It was a line in a children's musical from years ago. A little girl was kneeling by her bed, saying prayers before she went to sleep. The scene shifts to heaven where the angels are singing and praising God. Holding up His hand, God calls for quiet so he can hear what Rachel is saying.

The point isn't that God has trouble focusing on a little girl's prayer or that heaven's throne room is loud and chaotic. The message was that God cares for each of us so much that our every prayer is important to Him.

The psalmist wrote: "I love the Lord because He hears my voice and my prayer for mercy. Because He bends down to listen, I will pray as long as I have breath" (116:1,2).

I know when we pray we are not passing on news to God. He is never taken by surprise. He knows all there is to know about each of us – our circumstances, our fears, our joys, our minds, our hearts. The ongoing conversation called prayer is an invitation into a deeper relationship with One who cannot love us more or less.

This past week, Kim and I attended a presentation at the Adler Planetarium in Chicago. The universe was displayed before us in all its majesty and immensity. As we traveled deeper into space, we quickly passed through our solar system and began a journey into the vastness of the cosmos that staggers the imagination.

The narrator spoke of billions of stars and systems, characteristics of various constellations, overwhelming distances, and humanity's attempts to penetrate further and further. The one thing he didn't mention was the most important detail. Creation doesn't happen without a Creator. Science that seeks to exclude God is just bad science.

Gazing at the incredible sights in the presentation, we both felt small ... but not insignificant. Like Rachel, when we pray, the God who created the universe pays attention. In Isaiah, we find these words: "But now, O Jacob, listen to the Lord who created you. O Israel, the One who formed you says, 'Do not be afraid, for I have ransomed you. I have called you by name; you are mine" (43:1).

We may live on a small planet in the midst of a huge universe, but each of us matters to God.

"Hush, Rachel's talking to Me." You can fill in your name, if you want.

The Lost Art of Waiting

From *Homiletics Magazine*: "In the late summer of 2012 the Mars rover named 'Curiosity' landed on the surface of the red planet. It took just seven minutes for the rover to enter the atmosphere and touch down successfully – less time that a ride on Splash Mountain at Disney World. While most of the world tuned in and took notice of this amazing feat, many overlooked the fact that it was a long time coming – a very long time in fact. NASA engineers spent roughly 8½ months waiting."

Who likes to wait? You stand in line and notice that another line is moving faster. So what do you do? You move into the apparently faster line only to see the register close or a person with fists full of coupons slow everything down. You pray, "Lord, give me patience." Then He gives you something to be patient about.

We just don't like to wait. We want our food fast. We want faster Internet. We cannot stand to wait. In our instant society, we pay a price for our impatience. We let impatience affect our moods and our actions. Just get behind the guy driving 55 mph in the left lane on the highway and let me know how that feels. Wait a minute, I already know. I'm not proud of the times when I get worked up about somebody's pace of life that doesn't fit mine.

Perhaps we should consider the things worth waiting for:

- A marriage to grow deeper and stronger
- A child to mature into a person who contributes to family and community
- A walk with God that illuminates His love for us
- A God-given ability to blossom
- Brokenness to heal and forgiveness to be experienced

There are plenty of others. Today I was thinking about the father in Luke 15 who had to wait for the prodigal to come to his senses. Not all of our stories come out the way we want them to, but this one does. When the boy comes home, he finds a patient father who waited with a prayerful heart. When he arrives, he is engulfed by loving arms. Yes, he blew it, but now he gets a second chance, a new beginning.

Isn't that the nature of God? We can find Him in the story. We can also find ourselves – either as the prodigal or the older brother. Jesus said we should treat others as we wish to be treated. That may require something that we don't like to do – be patient.

Goldmedalitis

Yeah USA! We love it when Americans step on to that top platform, the flag is raised, and the national anthem is played. We examine the medal count to see how our men and women are doing in sports we couldn't care less about any other time of the year.

The Olympics in its purest form is about more than national pride. The motto for the games is "Citius, altius, fortius" which means "swifter, higher, stronger." Watching the parade of nations on Friday night, you had to be impressed with the diverse display of athletes. Some of the delegations consisted of one or two participants. The American delegation is the largest with over 550.

Many of the athletes will not take home a medal, but they will take home memories of standing shoulder to shoulder with the best in the world. Some will try to turn their prowess into endorsements and celebrity. Others will disappear as quickly as they appeared.

One we should remember competed in the 1968 Mexico Olympics. John Stephen Akhwari was a long-distance runner from Tanzania. He was the last participant in the marathon, finishing long after the winner, Mamo Walde from Ethiopia. Akhwari finally crossed the finish line at 3:25:17, staggering into the stadium before a sprinkling of fans still present.

A reporter asked him why he was so determined to complete a race he had no hope of winning. He replied, "My country did not send me to Mexico City to start the race. They sent me to finish the race."

I think the apostle Paul would have liked Akhwari. He wrote to the Corinthian church: "Remember that in a race everyone runs, but only one person gets the prize. You also must run in such a way that you will win" (1 Corinthians 9:24). 74 men lined up for the marathon in Mexico City. 57 finished. Akhwari was 57th, but he finished what he started.

Finishing well is the goal of every Christian. The prize that awaits is not the praise of men or a medal of gold; it is of far greater value. The starting line is crowded but it is the finish line that counts.

Coke What?

Trying to take my mind off the misery of devastating weather ...

- Coke has a learning problem. Perhaps they have a short memory. Remember what a hit New Coke was? Now they are messing with Coke Zero.

- Then there was the guy who robbed the convenient store wearing his motorcycle helmet. He must have forgotten the nameplate with his name on it just above the visor.

- At church one Sunday, we lost power and the sanctuary was very uncomfortable. A couple of our guys had a bright idea. They brought in electric fans to cool the room. Think about it.

- When an attempted robbery at a Lowes Home Improvement store went awry, Milton J. Hodges fled across the street and jumped a fence ... right into the Cypress Cove Nudist Resort & Spa. As the Orlando Sentinel pointed out, "As one of the only folks wearing clothing," Hodges was easily spotted by police. You think.

- A 12-year-old boy adamantly denied having stolen an iPhone when questioned by police at his home. And then the iPhone rang in his closet. Whoops!

- In July, he turned 104. This November, she will be 93. They have been married for 75 years. It's a first for this Washington state couple: Two hurricanes slamming two different parts of the United States bearing their names, Harvey and Irma Schluter.

This has been a tough stretch for people in the Islands, Mexico, Texas, Florida, and other places. Lives have been lost. Families shattered. The economic impact will be felt for years. We see the worst in people who descend to scams and looting, but we also see the best in people who come to the aid of others. Irma is starting to fade but still brings damage and difficulty. Let's keep praying for those who felt nature's wrath and those still in the path of high winds and rising waters. First Responders, as always, are doing what they do best. God bless each one.

Lost in all the coverage of the storms is the sad reality that we observe another anniversary of the attacks on 9/11. We may have moved on or have become distracted, but for thousands of people this day will always be a nightmare. We must never forget.

Life In the Lions' Den

Have your found yourself thrown to the lions lately? Whether we deserve such company or not, lions do not provide an environment conducive to good health and long life. When things look their bleakest, which way is out? In a delightful book, *Just Build the Ark and the Animals Will Come* by David Heller, kids were asked to answer questions about Daniel in the lions' den (Daniel 6).

Why was Daniel thrown into a lions' den?

- Sondra, age 7: "His hunting was hurting the lion population. A nature group told on him."
- Kerry, 7: "Daniel spelled 'lion' wrong and the government was real tough on spelling."

What advice did the king give Daniel when he had Daniel placed in the lions' den?

- Lori Ann, 8: "Your best chance is if you tell the lions some jokes. Lions have a good sense of humor."
- Ethan, 7: "Just hope they already ate dinner."

Possible prayers uttered by Daniel as the lions approached:

- Howie, 8: "God, there isn't time for a long prayer. So I'll just say HELP and I know You will get the message."
- Dani, 7: "God, please make the lions' teeth fall out real fast."
- Clare, 10: "Heavenly Father, I'm in a little trouble and it's going to take a miracle to get me out of this one."

God heard Daniel. He hears us, too.

Lessons Learned?

William Sloane Coffin, pastor and author, was known for his activism in civil rights issues and war protests. He was also a dad. In 1983, his son Alexander was killed in a car accident when the young man was 24. For all his political arguments and actions, Coffin was humbled by the violent death of one of his children.

In the days soon after the tragedy, he and his family received a healing flood of ministry and messages. One cherished letter ended with a quote from Ernest Hemingway's *A Farewell to Arms*: "The world breaks everyone, then some become strong at the broken places."

In the wake of 9/11, it did not take long for some to become strong at the broken places. First responders, construction workers, medical volunteers, and many others swarmed New York after the towers fell. People donated blood, gave money, organized community events, gathered in houses of worship, volunteered for military service, reached out to neighbors and strangers ...

For a time, our nation and much of the world pushed aside differences and disagreements to become a human family. Many countries lost citizens on that dreadful Tuesday. Most people saw the face of evil that day and chose to respond, not just to vow vengeance but to draw close to those devastated by the attacks.

How has our world changed in 15 years? I wish I could say we learned our lesson, we realized how fragile life is, we work harder to build strong, safe communities, we pay attention to the hurting and displaced, and we refuse to surrender to fear. One of the common declarations following 9/11 was "Never again." It seems we are as vulnerable now as ever.

Our enemy is not just the radical Islamist. Our enemies are complacency, selfishness, willful ignorance, lack of empathy, faith, and grace. For a short while, churches and temples were full of people on their knees in prayer. Today, the scene is far different. Someone wisely said, "Before we stand for anything, we should kneel about everything."

"Lord, listen to Your children praying."

Glad You Noticed

Facebook has its fans and its detractors. There are certainly times when you should ask before you post:

- Am I sharing personal information that needs to stay personal?
- Do I really think someone will be interested in such detail in my life?
- Have I put my identity or safety at risk by sharing too much information?
- Really? Did I just post that?
- Isn't it time to turn off the device and find a real friend?

I love the fact that Facebook allows you to connect with old friends, stay in touch with significant events in the lives of others, learn how to pray more intelligently for people close to you, and catch up with news and notes. At the same time, Facebook can be addictive, draining time and energy that could be invested elsewhere. It can be a poor substitute for authentic relationships.

There's another side to this for one family. A woman in Tennessee posted a recent picture of her daughter. Nothing unusual about that, right? Several people noted something in the photo that seemed odd. There was an odd glow in the little girl's left eye. One would naturally assume that the flash of the camera might have caused the light in the three-year-old's eye, but two friends saw something else. Replies to the mother urged her to have her daughter examined. As the New York Post reported, the mother took the girl to a doctor who diagnosed a rare condition that can cause blindness or significant loss of vision if not properly treated. Early treatment makes all the difference. In this case, a little girl named Rylee was successfully treated. Don't tell that mother that Facebook is a bad thing!

Yes, we should be careful about posting. We should remember that something that belongs in a journal or diary doesn't necessarily belong on a social network. For all of us who read and write on Facebook, it would certainly help to remember Matthew 7:12: "Treat others as you wish to be treated."

Is Jesus There?

Mom wasn't happy. She found the offering envelope in her son's room that Sunday afternoon. Son was called on the carpet. "You were supposed to take your offering to church this morning. What happened?" she asked. He responded, "You told me to give it to Jesus. I didn't see Him at church so I brought it home."

Aren't you supposed to see Jesus at church? The Bible says that where two or more are gathered in His name, He will be in their midst (Matthew 18:20). His presence should be noticeable, don't you think? He should be among us as we greet each other, as we converse, as we pray, as we open the Word, as we worship, as we give, as we serve, and as we go, If He isn't present, why are we?

Today the church takes a lot of heat for her weaknesses and faults. Ask a friend who is not a church-goer what he or she thinks about church. You might not like what you hear.

An old story: A man asked his neighbor why he didn't go to church. His neighbor replied, "The church is full of hypocrites!" The man, far from discouraged, responded, "Oh, don't worry about that. We have room for one more."

The church wasn't man's idea. Jesus established the church. Yes, it is full of faults and hypocrites, but it also the assembly of the forgiven ... an assembly charged with being the presence of Christ in the world. You won't find perfection in the church but you will find it in the One who started it all.

I Quit!

It happened in an NFL game yesterday. A player for the Buffalo Bills decided he had had enough so he just didn't come back to the field after halftime in the game against the Los Angeles Chargers. He quit. Vontae Davis, a 10-year veteran, came to his decision without talking to his coaches or teammates. He just walked away.

He doesn't leave empty-handed. His contract included $2 million in guaranteed money. He does leave with questions. Some of his teammates were less than thrilled with his decision. One said, "Never have seen it ever. Pop Warner, high school, college, pros. Never heard of it. Never seen it. And it's just completely disrespectful to his teammates. ... He didn't say nothing to nobody. ... I found out going into the second half of the game. They said he's not coming out, he retired. That's it."

What makes a person quit? It isn't unusual for NFL players to retire early. The price they pay physically and mentally can mean shortened lives and debilitating injuries. In other professions, grueling schedules, stress, poor health, financial concerns are just a few of the considerations that convince men and women to walk away.

We don't like quitters, perhaps because we know how easy it can be to quit. Bear Bryant used to say: "The first time you quit, it's hard. The second time, it gets easier. The third time, you don't even have to think about it."

I think about what happened in the Garden of Gethsemane. The toughest battle in history was taking place there. Jesus begged His Father, "Let this cup pass from Me." He could have quit. But He didn't. You and I should be really thankful for that.

Anything but Cheap

German pastor and theologian Dietrich Bonhoeffer wrote the classic book, *The Cost of Discipleship*, in 1937. During that time Adolph Hitler had seized power and the Third Reich was beginning to assert itself in Bonhoeffer's beloved country. While one the earliest church leaders to warn of the evil to come, Bonhoeffer was also concerned about the complacency of the church. He spoke out, ultimately at the cost of his life.

Read some of his words: "The essence of grace, we suppose, is that the account has been paid in advance; and because it has been paid, everything can be had for nothing. Since the cost was infinite, the possibilities of using and spending it are infinite. What would grace be if it were not cheap?"

In Paul's writing to the Romans, the apostle was astounded that some believed that the more sin you commit the more grace you receive. "Well, then, should we keep on sinning so that God can show us more and more of His wonderful grace? Of course not! Since we have died to sin, how can we continue to live in it?"

Bonhoeffer was offended by the watering down of the essential nature of grace. "Cheap grace is the preaching of forgiveness without repentance, baptism without church discipline, Communion without confession, absolution without personal confession. Cheap grace is grace without discipleship, grace without the cross, grace without Jesus Christ, living and incarnate."

Richard Niehbur followed this line of thinking when he wrote that American Christianity had grown weak and flabby: "A God without wrath brought men without sin into a kingdom without judgement through the ministrations of a Christ without a cross."

Grace is anything but cheap. It carries a price tag that staggers the imagination, a cost beyond any human's ability to compensate. Can we possible comprehend the value God has placed on every soul?

They had lost their patience. Their teenaged son continued a pattern of disobedience and disrespect. He had been warned of the consequences of his behavior. One of the most striking evidences of his lack of regard for anyone beside himself was that he was constantly late. Dinner time was the only time the family could have together, but he routinely showed up well past the time for the meal. Finally, one night the boy sauntered in to find his parents already seated with their plates served. As he fell into his chair, he was greeted with silence. He looked at his plate and then at theirs.

His plate had a piece of loaf bread with a glass of water next to it. His parents' plate were full of food. No word was spoken as the father stood up, took his plate, and exchanged it for his son's. Something changed that night. The son would later recall, "All my life I've known what God's like by what my father did that night. Grace is never cheap."

Contentment

From the *Orlando Business Journal*: "David and Jackie Siegel, the king and queen of Orlando-based Westgate Resorts, are both well past ready to see the completion of their massive Isleworth home, Versailles — but there's still a ways to go.

The 90,000-square-foot Versailles mansion has been under construction for more than a decade and has its own celebrity status, thanks to the 2012 documentary, 'The Queen of Versailles.' But one thing the house doesn't have yet is tenants, as construction has been off and on for years."

It seems the house isn't big enough with 30 bathrooms, 15 bedrooms, 11 kitchens, 6 pools, 2 movie theaters, 8000-square foot master suite, spa, bowling alley, indoor skating rink, underground parking for 30 cars, and a stadium tennis court seating 200 spectators. "I think I may want a bigger house with a couple more guest houses and a bigger closet," said Jackie Siegel. The Versailles home is slated to be finished before the end of the year after almost 15 years of construction.

Good luck Siegels. We all hope you will be able to manage. I don't know anything about these people, but at first glance I'm a bit nauseated.

Paul wrote to his friends in Philippi: "Not that I was ever in need, for I have learned how to be content with whatever I have" (4:11).

Being content is never about having enough or more than we need. Being content is a state of the soul, living in a deepening trust in our Creator, Sustainer, and Redeemer. I hope the Siegels find contentment. Something tells me it won't be found in a bigger mansion.

What About Me?

From Leadership Network:

"In 1985, Bob Buford decided to create an organization that would address the leadership and organizational needs of large, complex churches and Christian organizations. He wrote a mission statement and business plan for the idea and hired a full-time staff person. To make sure the idea had sufficient resources, he committed 30 percent of his time and funded the budget. The result was Leadership Network.

In 1992, Duncan Campbell, the owner of a timber investment firm, became concerned about high-risk kids in Portland, Oregon. He developed a business plan and put up the money to fund his idea. He committed 50 percent of his time to the organization, Friends, that provides mentors for troubled youth in the Portland area.

In 1994, Tom Luce, a successful attorney, had a dream for an organization that would change the nature of public education in the state of Texas. He wrote a mission statement and business plan, hired a full-time staff person and committed his own money as well as 50 percent of his time. The result is 'Just for the Kids.'"

All three of these social entrepreneurs are still at it today, helping to change things for the better; helping to change lives and organizations for the good. It would be easy to say that we don't have the resources available to these men, but what are we doing with the resources entrusted to us?

Amelia Mohr was 8 years old at the time. Our church was collecting food to help an organization similar to Buckhead Christian Ministry. We distributed grocery bags much like we have done this month and asked our members to bring the bags so we can donate the food to BCM. Amelia wasn't satisfied filling the sack her family picked up at church. She wanted for more bags and went to her neighbors and asked them to fill up a bag to help hungry people. She told her parents that she needed their help to pick up the bags from their neighborhood. She followed up with each neighbor until each had participated.

Stewardship is about life. We have all been given so much. We don't own any of it; we have been entrusted with a sacred charge. Your time, talent, and treasure can make a difference. One day there will be an accounting. "To whom much has been given, much will be required."

I read that somewhere ...

Not One of Your Better Days

The premier of the USSR arrived in the United States on September 15, 1959 for a summit meeting with President Dwight D. Eisenhower Nikita Khrushchev had made it clear to his handlers and to US State Department officials that he had more on his mind. He wanted to go to Hollywood. It might have been seen as the center of western decadence in his worldview, but Khrushchev wanted to meet movie stars and tour Twentieth Century Fox studios. He got to meet Shirley MacLaine and Frank Sinatra. That same day, September 19, he also wanted to go to Disneyland. What had started out to be a good day for the Russian leader had begun to turn sour. He got into an argument with the staunch anti-communist head of the studios, Spyros Skouras.

What pushed him over the edge was when he was told he would not be allowed not visit Disneyland because of concerns over security. They could not guarantee his safety in the open spaces of the amusement park and could not take the chance that something would happen in spite of heavy security. Khrushchev lost it. He threw a tantrum. Already known as a really fun guy, his childish outburst was impossible to hide.

When you and I have a bad day, it is probable that the whole world is not paying attention. We can have a fit in private. But often there is somebody who notices, perhaps is affected by our loss of control and blast of anger. One little boy lifted this fervent prayer: "Dear God, Is it true my father won't get in Heaven if he uses his bowling words in the house? Amen."

James wrote: "Understand this, my dear brothers and sisters. You must be all quick to listen, slow to speak, and slow to get angry. Human anger does not produce the righteousness God desires" (James 1:9). Your mother was right:

- Count to ten first.

- Watch your mouth, young man.

- There's a reason you have two ears and only one mouth.

I am sorry Nikita Khrushchev didn't get to go to Disney land on September 19, 1959. Somehow it would have been appropriate if he had gotten to ride on Dumbo.

"Slow Church Ahead"

I remember seeing this road sign and thinking how punctuation might help. You could read it several ways.

- "Slow down, there is a very active church just ahead and there will be lots of people coming and going." That wouldn't fit on the sign, would it? It's always nice to pass by a church with people streaming in and out, parking lots full.

or

- "There is a slow church ahead. Times have passed them by, and they don't realize it." That wouldn't fit on the sign either, but it might describe too many of our churches.

Church signs tell some interesting stories. One church had a one-way entry that required a sign. The first part of the sign read: "Welcome!" The other part read: "Do not enter." How are you supposed to take that? "You're welcome to not enter?"

Another sign outside a church indicated that the building no longer housed a church. The steeple had been removed and there had been renovations, but you could still tell that at some time it had been a church. The sign on the lawn read: "Antiques for Sale." Is that a parable of too many churches? Someone once said that an antique store was a resting place for rusting relics. We don't like to think that would apply to a church.

When a church is born, no one expects it to one day die. Visions of an ever-expanding ministry serving people, connecting people, inspiring people with the life-changing love and grace of our Lord fill the hearts and minds of a congregation.

Building a church is not about facilities or programs. Peter wrote that we are living stones that God uses to enlarge His Kingdom. He chooses to spread His Word through imperfect people like you and me. We should be both humbled and thrilled with the prospect!

The Dash Between the Dates

In the span of several days, death and life continue their dance. An elderly lady dies in a nursing home. A little boy enters the world, named after his uncle who died as a young man. A college friend, victimized by Alzheimer's, passes away. I think we get it. Death is a part of life. According to statistics, one out of one of us dies. The beginning of life thrills us. The end of life humbles us, hurts us, cautions us.

We didn't determine when we are born. We usually don't have much to say about when we die. What we do have some control over is what happens in the dash between the dates. That's another thing we have in common: we get to fill in the dash.

You hear it said that a person preaches his own funeral. I have been to services where the story of the life just ended inspires, comforts, and challenges. There have been other services that have carried different themes. Regret, wasted opportunities, poor choices, spiritual ambivalence, and doubt weigh heavy on family and friends alike. No life is perfect, but none of us like to think of being remembered as who we could have been or who we weren't.

Having led several hundred such services, I know it isn't always easy to speak the truth in love. One of my favorite stories is about two brothers who terrorized a small town with their corrupt and unethical business practices. Because of their stranglehold on the people, no one challenged their bullying tactics. One of the brothers died. The other brother went to the local pastor to make arrangements. Knowing full well his brother's character, he tried to bribe the pastor to pay tribute to his deceased sibling. He told the young preacher that he would make a sizable donation to a struggling building fund if his brother was portrayed as a saint.

The church was packed for the funeral, not because the man had been so popular but because the townspeople wanted to hear what the preacher would say about him. When the pastor stepped to the pulpit, he took a deep breath. Looking over at the brother, he glanced down at the ornate coffin and began, "This man was a liar, a cheat, an adulterer, and a bully. He stole from hard-working people, he cheated people out of their land, he threatened people weaker than himself ...", then he paused, "but compared to his brother, he was a saint."

I never heard what happened to that young preacher, but you have to admire his courage. Life is too precious to waste dishonoring the gift God has given. We all have our flaws, but the One who created each of us has something better in mind, no matter what the dates may say. He wants us to live abundantly, to love generously, to forgive graciously, and to serve extravagantly. We get to fill in the dash.

Shallow Places

In her book, *A Beautiful Mess*, Danielle Strickland wrote: "God doesn't normally shed light that leads us to shallow places." She then offered an example. The shepherds around Bethlehem were going about their daily routine. Caring for the flocks on the hillsides outside the town was business as usual. Strickland: "They were living small lives, wrapped up in the little drama of their existence. Angels, accompanied by a symphony of light and revelation, invited them into something eternally more grand and wonderful than their puny lives."

It is interesting to examine their reaction to the heavenly interruption. Shock and fear are understandable. They could have been overwhelmed into inaction, shrinking from the moment in terror. They chose something else ... after they gathered their wits. Strickland: "They ran to take the invitation and, in running, plunged into a dimension that was perpetually bigger than anything they could have dreamed of. They ran into the depth of the re-creation of the world."

How can you retreat into shallow places after God speaks? The birth of Christ changed history. The Eternal Word became flesh and lived among us. The shepherds were the first to hear the good news that would bring joy to the world. They refused to remain in shallow places.

I don't think God is through speaking ... I don't think He is through shedding light. Desperately, the world needs light and those of us entrusted with His light cannot retreat to shallow places.

The Nativity stories contrast two very different reactions. First, we have the shepherds who leave their flocks to race to Bethlehem to see what God had done. Second, we have the scribes of Herod who were ordered to search the scrolls for scriptural evidence of a newborn king, find the truth, and report. Then they promptly ignored it, perhaps because of fear or uncertainty or lack of faith.

Perhaps today we are being confronted by the shed light of God as we seek to discern His will for our church. No shallow places for us. We would rather be shepherds than scribes!

Life Stewardship

In his book, *Revolutionary Generosity*, Kirk Nowery wrote about the tragedy that occurred on the morning of May 9, 1980 in the straits between St. Petersburg and Bradenton, Florida. In the midst of horrible weather, the freighter Summit Venture slammed into the #2 pier of the Sunshine Skyway Bridge. The resulting collision caused a quarter mile gap in the southbound span. The fog that covered the bridge prevented oncoming traffic from seeing the missing roadway. A Greyhound bus was the first vehicle to plunge 150 feet into the turbulent waters of Tampa Bay. 19 passengers and the driver fell to their deaths. Other vehicles soon followed. Thirty-five lives were lost that morning. One driver, seeing the danger just in time, stopped his car a mere 14 inches from the edge of the shattered road. Another driver who was never identified left his car and ran toward the approaching traffic, frantically waving his arms in warning. His actions saved untold numbers of people that morning.

Unless you have been in a similar crisis, you may not know how you would react when something terrible has happened. We would all like to think we would be the second guy. It is one thing to make sure you are safe; it's another to have the presence of mind to be concerned about the safety of others.

Isn't that a part of the stewardship of life? Your one and only life surely must be about more than just yourself. Our whole existence is connected with the lives of others. There is nothing more important than the relationships we have. Relationships are not easy, they can often be messy, but we were created for community, for engagement, for loving and being loved.

I heard someone say that the best way to live is with an attitude of grateful generosity. I don't know how you would separate those two words. If we have trouble finding reasons for gratitude, we probably will never experience the exhilaration of generosity. The witness of our lives will tell the story. We either clutch stuff, believing we are the owners of what we survey, or we seek substance, believing that we have been entrusted with that which is truly precious.

There is something holy about caring enough for others that you would risk your life for them. I believe Jesus said something about that (John 15:13). The One who modeled ultimate generosity in sacrificing His life taught us the blessing of blessing. Investing our time, talent, and treasure with grateful generosity reveals the heart of a Christ follower in ways that must bring pleasure to the One who demonstrated how it can be done.

Body Life

Tony, the 8 year-old son of the Deacon chair and his buddy, Mike, the son of the pastor, were having a sleep-over at the pastor's home. The next morning, they sat down to breakfast and were treated to pancakes by the pastor's wife. As the first ones were coming off the griddle, she said to the boys, "Who wants the first batch?" The boys began to argue over who should eat first. The wise mom then interjected, "Now boys, you know Jesus would want you to share. Shouldn't we be like Jesus?" The pastor's son, reaching for the first pancakes, said, "Tony, you be like Jesus. I'm hungry."

We don't always get it right. Being a part of the family of God doesn't make us perfect. In fact, it often reveals how far we have to go. Perhaps now more than ever, we need how to share life together at deeper and more meaningful levels. Opportunities to worship together, serve together, learn together, give together, pray together, play together should help sweeten our fellowship and strengthen our discipleship.

Being like Jesus means in part that we understand how Jesus feels about the church. He never demands perfection, but He does require commitment. If the church is to be like her Founder, we must care about what He cares about. Paul said that Christ loved the church and gave Himself for her. Christ set the example He expects us to follow: to love as we are loved.

The word "Christian" implies two truths: To be like Christ and to do like Christ. Christ followers will not always get it right, but we don't have to go it alone. Grady Nutt used to say that being a Christian is like one beggar telling another beggar where he found bread. We need His Holy Spirit, but we also need each other.

Present

I remember roll call in school. I had to wait a while since my last name started with a "W". Not that I'm complaining or have issues, but why couldn't they start with the "Z's" just once? There was a time when I fervently hoped the teacher wouldn't read out my whole name. I had classmates that would snicker if she read my middle name, Oliver. As I grew up, I realized that name was something to be cherished, not regretted.

You had to answer when your name was called. The correct response was "present". I sometimes wondered why "here" or just a hand-raise wouldn't have worked.

Being present hopefully referred to more than just a physical location. Perhaps our teachers wanted to know if we were ready for a day of learning, or she just wanted to check off the list. Perhaps she was wishing that certain students weren't present.

There are a lot of clichés that refer to being present in life:

- Bloom where you're planted.
- Seize the day (Carpe Diem)
- Be where your feet are
- The only easy day was yesterday

The apostle Paul wrote that he had learned to be content (Philippians 4:11). Jesus encouraged us to live one day at a time (Matthew 6:34). There is a reason why the last commandment in Exodus 20 forbids coveting. It was intended to liberate us from wanting something we didn't or couldn't have. The grass may look greener on the other side, but is it? Art Linkletter once asked one of his young guests what that saying meant. The boy answered, "The grass is greener because that guy uses better fertilizer than you."

Be present today. Live in your moment. Appreciate your life. Count your blessings.

Joy

My friend Don invited me to accompany him and his son on a mission trip to Ghana in 2001. While we were in country, we visited schools, churches, and prisons. We were hosted by a remarkable man, James Baidoo, whose passion for Christ and for His church was incredibly inspiring. While pastoring his church, he was mentoring young leaders and planting new churches. His access to high government officials opened doors for us to share the Gospel in a variety of settings.

We went to several prisons where I preached in conditions that would make American prisons look like plush resorts. On one of those occasions, we were standing in an open courtyard. Above us in a cell block, a group of Muslims were shouting, trying to drown out our worship service. Everywhere we went, there was a hunger for the hope of the Gospel.

We attended several worship services with James and his people. Listening to some of his prize students in Bible study and worship, we realized that God's work was being done with skill and devotion. Speaking to those congregations through an interpreter was both challenging and rewarding. The people were engaged and vocal as they heard God's Word. There were times when I was pretty certain that the interpreter was preaching a better sermon than I was!

There were many lasting impressions from our time in Ghana. James, in humility and joy, let us see his handiwork among students his churches sponsored; in prison ministry where he developed teachers, leaders, and counselors; and in churches where he mentored those who were discipling new believers and leading new congregations.

As encouraging as these scenarios were to each of us, our best shared moments occurred when these Christians in Ghana gave their offerings. I can only describe it as a demonstration of joy. Several offerings were taken in each service. There were different purpose for each. There were no wealthy people present; many had little to give ... but they gave. Plates were not passed. People didn't walk forward to put their gifts in a receptacle. No, they danced to the altar, singing and laughing.

Everybody participated, including the three Americans. I have video of those moments. I will be glad to share that with you for a fee.

It was such an honor to be among such people. We were humbled by their hospitality and their dedication. We learned a great deal from a gifted leader and a joyous people.

All of that experience flooded back to me this week. I want that joy in my life and in yours. We probably won't be instituting an offering dance any time soon, but we need to exhibit more joy in our worship and certainly in our giving.

Transcendent

Arnold Palmer died yesterday. For many too young to know or remember, he burst on the scene when television was finding its legs. He wasn't just good at golf; he turned it into entertainment for a horde of people who couldn't tell the difference between a putter and a driver. His charisma created a persona that transcended the game. Someone said, "He made golf cool." There may have been better technicians of the game, but his "aggressive risk-reward approach" to the game won him fans the world over.

Not too many people transcend their sport or business or discipline. You could say that Tiger Woods was one such person, but he has fallen off his pedestal. He has never looked like he was having any fun. Arnie had so much fun that legions of fans became his army, cheering him on at golf tournaments around the world.

Arnold Palmer wasn't bigger than life just because he could play golf. Almost by force of will, he connected with the powerful and the common. He brought people together. When receiving the Congressional Gold Medal, he joked that finally there was something that the House and Senate were able to agree on. He offered golf tips to presidents and members of the galleries. One of his tips: "I have a tip that will take five strokes off anyone's golf game. It's called an eraser."

In a day when life is so serious and complicated, it is inspiring to be influenced by someone who is in love with life. Joy is contagious. Perhaps that's why it was so easy to pull for Arnie. He knew when to be focused and determined, but he could also be in the moment, sharing a laugh with fellow players or fans.

You and I may never have the same platform that Arnold Palmer occupied, but we can choose to live life with optimism and joy. As Christians, joy comes standard. Let it show. Spread it around.

Motivation

I cannot help it. I love stories about Bear Bryant. I've been an Alabama fan all my life so it's in my blood. One thing you could say about Coach Bryant is that he made his players believe they were probably better than they really were. To say he could motivate them would be an understatement.

Case in point: His team was playing some school in Florida ... lizards or something. One of their tailbacks broke through a hole in the line and was racing down the sideline. A defensive tackle for Bama was in pursuit and actually caught the back, tackling him short of the goal line.

After the game, the Alabama player was asked how in the world he was able to catch up to the much speedier back. The runner had exploded through the gap the tackle was supposed to cover. Knowing what he would face when he returned to his bench where Coach Bryant would be waiting, he did what seemed impossible. Chagrined, the tackle confessed, "He was running for a touchdown but I was running for my life."

Charles Swindoll once wrote, "Life is 10% what happens to you and 90% how you react to it."

There is a lot of truth in what Carol Burnett said, "Only I can change my life. No one can do it for me."

That Alabama player might have been motivated by his coach, but he's the one who tracked that faster player down. It's amazing what we can do when we reach deep into ourselves. I believe God gave us capacities that we haven't fully explored.

Jesus told His disciples, "With God all things are possible." That would be good to remember the next time we are faced with an impossible task.

Put the Device Down

The commercial caught my eye this morning. The exciting news that was being shared was that now, with the latest technology, you can take your favorite movies and TV shows wherever you go. Not a new concept, I know. But I thought it was ironic that people were pictured carrying their tablets, phones, and laptops to the beach or the park or the mountains.

It reminded me of a certain canoe trip we took a number of years ago. Two of us were paddling (I won't mention names in this brief tale) and two of us were reading magazines while making our way down a picturesque view on a glorious Spring morning on the river. The two with the paddles kept saying such insightful things as "Would you look at that?" or "I've never seen anything like that." The other two were engaged in very different activities. With the sounds of birds singing, fish jumping ... the sights of new foliage and sparkling water, we could hear the clear sounds of pages turning and comments about fashion or recipes. There was thought of shocking the two with heads bent over the magazines with alarming shouts of "shark!" or "squirrel" but cooler heads prevailed.

In our modern day, we cannot seem to enjoy the moment without dependence on technological and, I think, artificial stimulation. Do you really need to take "The Walking Dead" to the beach? Can't you enjoy some time away from the normal rush without the latest episode of "Empire?" Is surgery required to separate us from the ever-present device that seems to provide so much of the entertainment we cannot live appear to live without?

We need someone to tell us to go out and play ... or sit down and talk ... or get by yourself and think, meditate, and pray. A friend told me of a long drive she had with her husband. They decided to spend the time in conversation! No radio, no iPod, no tablet, just talk. Wow, Samsung wouldn't be happy about that.

Technology is great, but it can be too invasive. Put down the device and have a real conversation with a real friend. Spend time in solitude without checking your email. Jesus would spend all night in prayer. We have a hard time spending five minutes in prayer. Who would you rather be connected to? The Internet or the Incarnation?

Because It's There

Diane Nyad just completed a dip in the ocean. That's like saying it can be warm in August. She swam 110 miles between Cuba and Florida, the first person to do it without a shark cage and with a specially designed anti-jellyfish mask.

She had tried it before, on several occasions. This time she made it. It took her almost 53 hours to finish on a September Monday. Talk about Labor Day!

 She played mental games including relying on a song list of 85 tunes. "Neil Young is my favorite," she said.

"Experts" have weighed in, opining that she was able to accomplish this amazing feat because she was mentally tough, that she believed in herself, that she had trained her mind to push pass the fatigue, pain, and energy drain.

Diane Nyad is 64. I'm 62. I could swim 110 ... feet.

We could ask how someone could do this. We could also ask why someone would do this.

Why does anyone set a goal, dream a dream, set out to do something grand? Why do people excel when the odds are against them? Why do people attempt what seems impossible or even nutty?

"Because it's there" sounds trite or jingoistic. Okay, what's your reason? What motivates you to do what Charles Swindoll used to say was "living about the level of mediocrity"?

Your goals may not include a grueling 110-mile swim through shark- and jellyfish-infested waters, but you may be trying to build a marriage that lasts or raise a child well or conduct business with integrity or push past your own personal pain and struggle.

It took fantastic effort for Diane Nyad to succeed, but you know what? She didn't do it alone. She gave credit to her team: "Never, ever, could I do this without this team here," she told a news conference.

I don't know if Diane Nyad has a spiritual component to her life. I hope so. I need one and so, I believe, do you. I need relationships with my God and with His people. I need to know I don't have to go it alone. So do you. "Be strong and courageous, for the Lord your God is with you!" (Joshua 1:9)

Here's to You, Mom

Among the tragic stories coming out of the devastation of Harvey is the account of a 41 year-old mother who drowned saving her daughter in a swollen canal in Beaumont, Texas. The woman had left her vehicle when she encountered high water and was swept away in the swirling water. First responders in a boat reached the pair just before they went under a trestle. The police reported: "The mother absolutely saved the child's life. They were in the water for some time. The mother did the best she could to keep her child up over the water.

I think that is a recurring thing with most mothers: they do the best they can. Not all are heroic, not many have to sacrifice like the Beaumont mom, but I see how often the women in our lives protect and provide for their own. My life has been blessed by the example of women who fill this vital role with grace, grit, and love.

So, here's to you mom:

- "She's the only one who knows where the scotch tape is."
- "God used a beautiful morning to make my mother."
- "God makes mothers out of clouds and angel hair and everything nice in the world, and one dab of mean."
- "Mom doesn't want to be boss, but she has to because Dad's such a goofball."
- "Mom knows how to talk to teachers without scaring them."
- "The greatest mom in the world wouldn't make me kiss my fat aunts."

Run the Play

I'm the middle of 3 brothers. My older brother was born in 1947. My younger brother was born in 1957. I was born in 1951. Fascinating facts, right? When my older brother David was around 12, he played for the Buckhead Red Devils. One day he decided that we should practice a play he thought was really cool – a reverse. The play calls for two players running in opposite directions, one handing the ball to the other as they pass by. The intent is to confuse the defense.

That's the intent ... but our practice didn't exactly go as the play was designed.

We collided. My forehead won. He got a gash over his eye. He claimed I ran the play wrong. I claimed he didn't make it clear what side I was to pass him on. To this day, he will tell you I blew it.

I hate blowing it. I've done it many a time. Some of my mistakes were omission – things I should have done, words I should have spoken. Many of them were commission – things I did, words I shouldn't have spoken.

Paul admitted his own frustration in his letter to the Romans: "No matter which way I turn, I can't make myself do right. I want to, but I can't. When I want to do good, I don't. And when I try not to do wrong, I do it anyway."

Can you relate? Probably. I am so thankful we have a God of second chances. He knows our imperfections. He forgives. He renews us. He points in the right way. He loves us no matter what.

Actually, He would have let me run that reverse again so I could get it right!

The Real Thing

The Secret Service was created in 1865, not to protect high government officials, but to combat a rising problem of counterfeit currency. It would not be until 1901 that the agency began its protection mission after the assassination of President William McKinley. Today, the task of securing the financial infrastructure of the nation continues to be a primary responsibility.

When training agents to spot a counterfeit bill, the emphasis is placed on the ability to recognize all the characteristics of a genuine one. It may seem odd to focus on authentic currency instead of fakes, but the skill to tell what is real enables the agent to determine what is phony.

There are plenty of counterfeits in the world. It isn't just the knock-off perfumes, jewelry, or clothing; fakes show up everywhere. Items that look like the real thing, products that imitate but do not replicate the original, people who are phonies – they all have something in common.

Jesus used a harsh term for those who pretended to be one thing while truly being something else. He called such people hypocrites. The word comes from Greek drama when actors would use masks to portray characters and deliver dialogue.

We all have some hypocrite in us. Authenticity is a virtue that is not easily mastered. You probably have heard someone say that the reason he doesn't go to church is that it is full of hypocrites. The best response to such a charge is: "You're right, but we have room for one more. Come on in."

What's the best defense against hypocrisy? Accountability is a good place to start. We are best exposed by being honest with ourselves, by having people in our lives who will tell us the truth, and by seeking deepening spiritual discipline that opens us to the work of the Holy Spirit. After David's great sin, he accepted the accountability of Nathan and then implored God to purify him, to create a clean heart, and renew a right spirit. His path to authenticity wasn't easy, but the road of self-deception and hypocrisy nearly killed him.

Nobody likes a fake. God has a better plan for His children.

A Godly Man

Pop died in 1985. At 93, he just wore out. I wish you could have known him. Life wasn't always fun, but he had fun. In Proverbs 10, we read: "The godly are showered with blessings ... we all have happy memories of the godly ... the hopes of the godly result in happiness."

He was godly. He lived through a great deal of pain. His 18 year-old daughter was killed in an automobile accident. His 24 year-old son died from a cerebral hemorrhage. His eldest served in the European Theater where he was wounded in action. His wife wasted away as dementia robbed him of his companion of so many years.

He made a choice along the way. He didn't allow the circumstances of life determine the condition of his heart. There was a sparkle in his eye and a bounce in his step. His faith was deep and strong. He was a life-long member of one church, sticking with it through thick and thin. He served as a deacon. He sang in the choir. He had an amazing bass voice that could make window panes wiggle. I can't remember too many Sundays when he wasn't in church, at home or on the road.

Proverbs 10 also speaks of people with character: "People with integrity have firm footing ... the words of the godly are like sterling silver, the godly will never be disturbed, the godly give wise advice, the godly speak words that are helpful."

Even after he retired, he kept his office downtown in Anniston, Alabama. We would pile into his giant Mercury sedan and ride with him. He said he had business there and he needed to pick up his mail but we soon learned there was something else to his trips to the office.

In the lobby of the building, there was a newspaper stand. It was manned by an old blind man, an African American gentleman who could recognize regulars by their footsteps. If he didn't know who you were, he would call out to you so he could shake your hand and ask you how your day was going. Pop always stopped to chat, always bought something. These two old guys were friends and had been for years.

Then Pop would head for the elevator. In those days, most elevators were manned by an operator. Inside Pop would find another friend whose skin was also a different color than his. They would tell each other jokes. Pop had huge hands but the elevator guy could match his grip. When Pop told us to shake, our hands would be swallowed by his massive clasp.

I came to realize that Pop was color blind. He was a product of his times but somehow he stepped across lines that in that day were very clear. I remember the signs at water coolers and restrooms. I also learned later that he had served on the school board for many years and had taken risks working for equality in the schools of the area.

Yes, Pop was a lot of fun but he was so much more. At his funeral, the crowd was not made up of just white faces. The godly are indeed showered by blessings.

Dreaming Big

He had always wanted to fly. His dream was to be a pilot in the US Air Force. Poor eyesight kept him grounded. When he was a young teenager, he came up with an idea to use weather balloons, having seen some in a military surplus store. It took him twenty years but he put his idea into action.

On July 2, 1982, he attached 45 helium-filled weather balloons to a lawn chair in his backyard. Aided by his girlfriend and other friends, he prepared for flight. Strapping a parachute on and carrying a pellet gun, Larry Waiters, with a CB radio, sandwiches, and beer on board, was ready for launch. With his creation tied by a stout cord to his Jeep, he gave his friends the signal to cut the cord. Lift off!

It didn't take Larry long to figure out that the balloons were working just fine. In a matter of a few minutes, his home-made flying machine had soared to about 15,000 feet. He was hesitant to use his pellet gun as he went higher and higher, fearing that he might unbalance the load and fall out.

Floating from his point of origin in San Pedro, California, he drifted toward Long Beach and found himself in the flight path of Los Angeles International Airport. Using his CB radio, he contacted a monitoring outfit about his predicament. His message: "Ah, the difficulty is, ah, this was an unauthorized balloon launch, and, uh, I know I'm in federal airspace, and, uh, I'm sure my ground crew has alerted the proper authority. But, uh, just call them and tell them I'm okay."

45 minutes into his wayward flight, Larry decided to shoot some balloons. After deflating several, he accidently dropped his pellet gun. Losing altitude slowly, he got hung in some power lines – causing a 20-minute blackout in a nearby neighborhood. The police were waiting for him, not exactly sure how to charge him for his ill-fated journey. Lawn Chair Larry had his day in the news and in the courts.

Was Larry foolish to make such an attempt? Probably. But you know what? You miss 100% of the shots you never take!

Strength in Numbers

Your spelling word for today: Sequoiadendron gianteum. Named after Sequoyah, the inventor of the syllables in the Cherokee language, the giant redwoods found most notably in groves on the western slopes of the Sierra Nevada Mountains are the largest trees in the world. The tallest have measured over 300 feet. The oldest, based on ring count, is 3500 years old.

You would think that such giants could stand against anything. In fact, they have very shallow root systems. Their ability to survive severe weather, fire, and other stress comes from the interlocking of their roots with each other. These massive trees that are often more than 100 feet in girth are even stronger because of the support and strength of their neighbors.

It is interesting that their greatest predator is man. A guy with a chainsaw, a big one mind you, can fell one of these giants. Think of the implications.

We are stronger in numbers. We were designed for community. We need each other. There are times when I need your shoulder to lean on. There are times when you need the collective strength of others.

Singly, we are easy prey. It is not difficult to cut us down. But when our lives are linked, we present a far more formidable obstacle to those who would do us harm or oppose us. Paul wrote to the Roman Christians: "We are all parts of His one body, and each of us has different work to do. And since we are all one body in Christ, we belong to each other, and each of us needs all the others" (Romans 12:5).

There is even a beautiful picture when we consider the Trinity: Father, Son, and Holy Spirit who exist in perfect communion with each other. We were created for fellowship, to belong to something bigger and greater than ourselves. There is strength in numbers!

The One You Feed

A Cherokee elder was trying to teach the children of his tribe about how to live. He told the youngsters: "I have a war going on inside me. It is a terrible fight between two wolves."

The children's eyes grew wide as the old man went on to explain: 'One wolf represents fear, anger, envy, sorrow, regret, greed, arrogance, self-pity, guilt, resentment, inferiority, lies, false pride, and superiority."

He had his audience's full attention as he went on: "The other stands for joy, peace, love, hope, sharing, serenity, humility, kindness, benevolence, friendship, empathy, generosity, truth, compassion, and faith."

He paused a moment and then said: "The same fight is taking place within you and every person you will ever know."

The oldest child spoke, "But which wolf will win?"

The old man responded: "The one you feed."

If I Could Ask Him Just One Question

They say in heaven it won't matter. All our questions will either be answered or won't need to be asked. But we are inquisitive by nature. God gave us minds; surely He expects us to use them. We contemplate:

- How do you know the difference between partly cloudy and partly sunny?
- How can something be both "new" and "improved"?
- What is another word for thesaurus?
- What do you pack Styrofoam in when shipping it?
- Which baby is the cutest?

(The last one is simple. Just ask first, whose baby is it?)

A great number of questions are not easy. Some of the questions will never be answered. Some of the answers are indecipherable or beyond our capacity to understand. Some we just don't want to know. Most of the big questions always seem to start with 'why?'

 Most of those come out of hearts in agony, confusion, doubt, and grief. We either want an explanation or some way to cope. We want to shake our fist at something or someone. I wish it were not true but suffering happens … to all of us sooner or later.

Yet suffering can accomplish at least two things. It can push us away or draw us close. We reject the platitudes, the bumbling attempts to soothe our pain or we value the "just-being-there" of people who choose to let their presence speak.

I like what Kallistos Ware wrote: "It is not the task of Christianity to provide easy answers to every question, but to make us progressively aware of a mystery. God is not so much the object of our knowledge as the cause of our wonder."

As my life journey continues, I've learned that the more I live the less I know. There are more questions than ever. But there is also a calming of my spirit to trust God with the answers. I hope I keep asking but I also hope I keep trusting.

Whatcha Makin'?

He loved working in his shop. He had turned his garage into a haven. He could lose himself, repairing and fixing, restoring and creating. Since his wife died, he spent more and more time out there.

One day, he was discovered. One of the neighborhood boys found him. The boy had heard the whine of a table saw and followed the sound to investigate. The man was so involved in his project that he didn't notice his young visitor at first. Annoyed at the intrusion into his sanctum, he turned off the saw and spoke gruffly to the boy, "Son, you're trespassing. What are you doing on my property?"

"I just wanted to see what all that noise was," the boy replied. "I didn't mean no harm. I've never seen a place like this. Whatcha makin'?"

It was the beginning of a flood of questions. Before the man could answer one, the boy had ten more. "What's this for?" "How does this work?" "Where did you get all this stuff?" "How much money did you spend on all your tools?" "Whatcha makin'?"

At first, the man was ready to lash out and tell the boy in no uncertain terms that he wasn't invited and certainly not welcome, but something changed. His two boys were grown and gone. Neither had displayed the slightest interest in their father's handiwork and creativity. One had told him once, "Dad, if something is broken, just buy the new, improved replacement."

Not in his lifetime. He could fix most anything. Over the years, he had saved a lot of money tinkering, recrafting, and building. He took pride in his ability to use his hands and mind to work things out. Now, for the first time in forever, someone took an interest in what he could do.

He waited for the boy to take a breath amidst all the questions and then he said, "Hold up there a minute," pointing to his table saw, he explained, "Let me tell you what I can do with this beauty."

The afternoon slipped away as the two became friends - a 10-year-old boy and a 73-year-old retiree. The old man showed the boy a rocking horse he had made for a grandson he hardly ever saw. The boy told him about how he loved to work on his second-hand bike he had gotten for his birthday. The things that made them different faded away; the thing they had in common forged a friendship.

God made us unique. We can focus on our differences or we can celebrate them, learning something new, even life-changing. Just before the young boy headed home, he stuck out his hand toward his new friend, "Nice to meet you. You got neat stuff." The old man took the proffered hand and shook it. "It's been a long time since I made a new friend. Come back anytime, son."

What We Leave Out

On a hospital medical chart, a doctor wrote: "I saw your patient today, who is still under our car for physical therapy." What a strange place to have therapy! Obviously, the 'e' was missing.

We are guilty of leaving things out from time to time. Perhaps that's why our mothers continually reminded us to say "please" and "thank you." We can miss the moment and not notice that something is missing. A word of encouragement that is never spoken ... an act of kindness that never happened ... an expression of gratitude that remained unsaid.

We are busy people, too busy. We can be overcome with the press and pressure of our schedules and not notice the moment that just slipped by.

C.S. Lewis was addressing students at Oxford University in the fall of 1939. Nazi Germany had just invaded Poland. The young men in the audience were beginning to feel tremendous anxiety as the storms of war threatened.

In part, Lewis said: "Happy work is best done by the man who takes his long-term plans somewhat lightly and works from moment to moment as to the Lord. It is only our daily bread that we are encouraged to ask for. The present time is the only time in which any duty can be done or any grace received."

We cannot change yesterday and we have little to say about what the future may bring. We can live this day. We can practice His presence this day. We can open our eyes and hearts to the divine appointments on our daily calendar.

Regret comes when we could have or should have, and we didn't. "Lord, thank You for this day. Help me to live in this moment in time with anticipation of great possibilities!"

"I Used To…"

Time isn't very friendly, is it? I can get stuck in "I used to …"

I used to have trouble gaining weight. Raw eggs in milk shakes, peanut butter sandwiches, bigger meals – I tried everything to change my skinniness. 6' tall and 145 lbs. soaking wet, I looked like a pencil. Now I look more like a sausage.

I used to play basketball. I had a quick first step. I could dunk in the 10th grade. I could run all day. I could drive on just about anybody. Now, my first step is more of a stumble. I'm not sure I can even touch the bottom of the net, much less the rim. The only driving I do now is behind the wheel. After five back surgeries, I would like to just walk without pain.

I used to be quick-witted. Now, I'm more of a half-wit.

I used to have blond hair. Then it turned brown. Then brown-gray. Now gray-brown. At least it turned gray and not loose.

I don't need to live in "I used to." Life changes. I have a beautiful wife who has shared my life for over 40 years. I have two sons who make me proud every day. I have three grandchildren who light up my life. I have a daughter-in-law who is an outstanding mom and schoolteacher. I have another daughter-in-law who is a pediatric nurse. Both young women bring a lot of joy to our lives. I have served in good churches and count my blessings for the privilege.

I can certainly learn from my "I used to" seasons of life. I know I have gained from the experiences, both inspiring and deflating. There is still so much more in whatever time God allows. I am not trapped in the past, but I'm grateful for it.

I like what Walter Purkey wrote: "You've gotta dance like there's nobody watching, Love like you'll never be hurt, sing like there's nobody listening, and live like it's heaven on earth."

And then there was the philosopher Mae West: "You only live once, but if you do it right, once is enough."

The Gracious Hand of God

Nehemiah began the project of rebuilding Jerusalem with his eyes wide open. He knew how desperate the situation was, he understood could no longer accept the current reality that went beyond repairing walls and hanging new gates, he was aware he would need to gather people to join him in the task, and he was cognizant of the opposition he would face.

In chapter two, Nehemiah had a confrontation with the bad guys – Sanballat, Tobiah, and Geshem. Dripping with contempt, they scoffed at the plan to restore the city. Nehemiah's answer displayed his confidence that he was not unequipped for the job: "The God of heaven will help us succeed. We His servants will start rebuilding this wall. But you have no stake or claim in Jerusalem" (Nehemiah 2:20).

I love his fighting spirit. I admire his determination and confidence. He placed his trust in the God who had heard his prayers, guided his planning, and would provide in the challenging days ahead.

We see similar displays of faith and courage in Scripture. David warned Goliath that he was outmatched: "You come to me with sword, spear, and javelin, but I come to you in the name of the Lord Almighty" (1 Samuel 17:45). Shadrach, Meshach, and Abednego defied King Nebuchadnezzar as he condemned them to the fiery furnace: "We do not need to defend ourselves before you. If we are thrown into the blazing furnace, the God whom we serve is able to save us. But even if He doesn't, your majesty can be sure that we will never serve your gods or worship the gold statue you have set up" (Daniel 3:16-18).

Peter and John were arrested by the Sanhedrin and threatened. The two disciples were ordered to never again speak about Jesus. They responded, "Do you think God wants us to obey you rather than Him? We cannot stop telling about the wonderful things we have seen and heard" (Acts 4:19,20).

These and many others depended on the gracious hand of God to guide, to protect, to bless, and to use their lives. God has not changed. His hand is still gracious. Let us claim the same confidence and trust as He leads us!

The Butterfly Effect

In Mark Batterson's book, *All In*, he tells the story of a hypothesis presented to the New York Academy of Science by MIT meteorologist Edward Lorenz in 1963. His hypothesis was entitled "The Butterfly Effect" and theorized that the flapping of a butterfly's wings could conceivably alter wind currents to cause a tornado in Texas. Sounds pretty bizarre, right?

Lorenz had designed a prototype computer program to simulate and forecast weather. We all know how often meteorologists accurately predict the weather. Lorenz hoped to improve such efforts with his program. On a day when he was running late for a meeting, he had hurriedly entered a wrong number in his calculations. Instead of entering .506127, the number he had used in previous trials, he rounded to the nearest thousandth - .506. He figured it wouldn't make any difference, but it did. The numerical difference in his simulation was the equivalent of a puff of wind, but the net difference was the equivalent of a catastrophic weather event. His conclusion: "Miniscule changes in input can make a macroscopic difference in output."

I'm certain that such a revelation will significantly impact your day as you read this, but stay with me for a moment. What's true in science is also true in life. Many of us think we are not important enough, not influential enough, but what happens when we really take our lives seriously? Batterson continued: "This simple discovery has the power to change your life. It can radically alter your spiritual, emotional, relational, or financial forecast. One decision. One change. One risk. One idea. That's all it takes."

What puff of wind can you create? By word or deed, what shift might begin to occur because we seized the moment? If we are to truly put on the character of Christ, there are divine appointments awaiting us every day. With His leadership, we can affect change in our world. Let's pray together that we will heed the words of Paul: "For God has not given us a spirit of fear and timidity, but of power, love, and self-discipline" (2 Timothy 1:7)

You Think We Have Problems

On December 31, 192 AD, Roman emperor Commodus was assassinated. You might wonder what's so unique about an emperor being eliminated violently ... it happened with alarming frequency, In fact, history records his death as the beginning of an era called "Year of the Five Emperors." They tried to poison his food but he spoiled the attempt by vomiting. Then they arranged for his personal trainer-wrestling partner to strangle him in his bath.

You may remember his name at least if you saw the movie Gladiator. The fictionalized Commodus was portrayed by actor Joaquin Phoenix. Hollywood altered the facts a bit, but the man was truly a degenerate. He loved the trappings of power but had no interest in using that power to rule justly. Some have speculated that his reign ushered in the decline of the empire. It is ironic that his murderer was named Narcissus. Commodus loved to parade around dressed like Hercules. He was proud of his physical prowess which he demonstrated regularly in the arena against wounded and crippled soldiers. He didn't need much of an excuse to order Roman citizens, high and lowly, to be executed.

Power does strange things to people. Few of us manage well when entrusted with it. You don't have to be a Roman emperor to abuse the influence and authority that comes with a position or in a relationship.

Perhaps that is why Jesus taught that we should treat others as we would wish to be treated. Perhaps that is why He felt it important to address the vying for special favor among His disciples when He said, "You know that in this world kings are tyrants, and officials lord it over the people beneath them. But among you it should be quite different. Whoever wants to be a leader among you must be you servant. For even I, the Son of Man, came here not be served but to serve others, and to give My life as a ransom for many" (Matthew 20:25-28).

In a political season where people are hiding behind rhetoric and spin, it seems appropriate that we not only remember the words of Jesus, but put them into practice. We could use a few more servant leaders these days.

Advanced in Years

It all started at dinner with the grandkids. We had just finished our meal and were enjoying some time our son's family. The six year old and I had just finished a rousing game of rock-scissors-paper. I got smoked. Then he wanted to play "I spy." In a moment the other two kids joined in. My precious granddaughter took a turn. She said, "I spy something gray." We all looked around – shirts, pants, wall color, pictures ... nothing. Then she said, "Give up? It's your hair."

This is the same young lady who had just learned about Abraham in Sunday School. The lesson was about a man who was very old. So she told me, "Pops, you're advanced in years." I was 0 for 2. Then I remembered the folly of asking how old did she think I was. She responded, "Pops, you're as old as dirt." I was now 0 for 3 and headed for the bench.

Look, I know I'm 67. I have lived almost half my life. I was never very good in math. So to prove things weren't so bad, I decided to take a geological survey of my body. The results were not assuring. My equator is sagging south. It's harder to see my feet now. I detected forestation in my ears and nose. Where did that come from? My polar cap is beginning to look a polar cap. I have lakes and rivers that want to overflow at the most inconvenient times. My pectorals used to resemble mighty mountains of muscle (a slight exaggeration). Now they look like sand dunes being whipped by the wind. I could go on but I need a nap.

Getting old is a part of life. We can whine about it or make the most of it. I love what the apostle Paul wrote to his friends in Philippi: "For to me, living means living for Christ, and dying even better." I hear people say they were glad they woke up on the right side of the grass. I'm not so sure any more. The way this world is going, heaven looks better all the time. No, I'm not ready to quit living. I'm not living to die; I'd rather be dying to live – to cherish each moment with the people I love and the world I'm supposed to serve.

Measuring the Heart

Legendary Coach Vince Lombardi used to say that you could measure everything about a prospective player except the size of his heart. You could determine his strength, his speed, his football acumen, and other factors, but you couldn't measure his desire to become a champion. In describing his All-American quarterback, Pat Trammell, Paul 'Bear' Bryant said, "He can't run, he can't pass, he can't kick – all he can do is beat you."

Life is full of enigmas. One of them certainly has to be that so often the one who seems to have the most promise is not the one who succeeds. The blue chip athlete is a bust. The guy with average ability finds a way to win. On paper, it shouldn't be a contest. The star with all the press clippings should excel. The other fellow with no sterling credentials ought to ride the bench. Funny thing, though – the game isn't played on paper.

Life isn't lived that way, either. Being named the 'most likely to succeed' never guaranteed success. Something has to happen in us if something is going to happen through us. The Bible says that God is always looking for those with the right kind of heart: "The eyes of the Lord search the whole earth in order to strengthen those whose hearts are fully committed to Him" (2 Chronicles 16:9).

The Apostle Paul knew something about promise. He was the finest student of the greatest rabbi. He had the best education one could have in his day. He was a rising star whose pedigree was exceptional. But he found something better than a really strong résumé. He learned a different perspective. He discovered that there was only one prize worth his best effort and highest commitment: "I once thought these things were valuable, but now I consider them worthless because of what Christ has done. Yes, everything else is worthless when compared with the infinite value of knowing Christ Jesus my Lord" (Philippians 3:7-8).

The world might look at the stats; God looks at the heart. "Create in me a clean heart, O God, and renew a right spirit within me" (Psalm 51:10).

Freedom and Faith

Religious liberty is cherished by Baptists (and many others, of course). In its truest sense, such liberty must protect the rights of those who choose to believe in God, to recognize other deities or faith systems, or to hold to no belief at all. As Christians, we read the words of Peter who instructed us to always be ready to present our Christian hope, but to do so with gentleness and respect (1 Peter 3:15,16).

Whether we like it or not, we live in a post-Christian world. The religious landscape has been changing for a while. I can understand that and even agree that a more sensitive tolerance is required by those who claim to live for Christ. But it also seems apparent that the most intolerant people around are those who demand tolerance.

Case in point: There is an organization headquartered in Wisconsin which evidently believes that it has been granted watchdog status over the religious life of our country. Most recently, they have launched a campaign to protest, to harangue, to harass, and to threaten to sue universities who have chaplains associated with their sports programs. Even though the schools do not allow chaplains to be on the staff or receive remuneration from the institution, they are accused of forcing religion on student-athletes.

There have certainly been cases where pastors, chaplains, and others have crossed the line, but the stories are countless where counselors, mentors, and ministers have provided much-needed support, guidance, and spiritual strength to young men and women at critical times in their lives.

A recently released movie entitled *"Woodlawn"* tells such a story. Set in the early 1970's, the narrative deals with a high school in Birmingham, Alabama embroiled in volatile racial tension that threatens to tear the school and community apart. The football team is a microcosm of the larger conflict in the Deep South. White players fight black players on the field and in the locker room. At the games, people in the stands trade insults. Simmering hatred, ignorance, and prejudice seem to be a way of life.

Into this toxic cauldron, steps a volunteer chaplain named Hank Erwin. He asks the football coach if he could speak to the team. Tandy Gerelds is suspicious of the man's motives but grants him five minutes to address his players. What happens in the next hour among those young men could raise the hackles of critics who wish to suppress any spiritual influence in such situations. But the results are beyond debate. Fist fights are traded for Bible study and prayer times. Racial enmity transforms into reconciliation. A deeply divided team becomes a band of brothers. Do you think it's just Hollywood at work? Research it for yourself.

One thing I've noticed about groups who want to snuff out any spiritual influence in public life. There are never any stories of redemption, no lives are turned around, no futures are altered. Hmmmm ...

Intersections

What do you remember about a friend or loved one who is no longer alive or who is no longer near you? Two things stand out:

- The sound of his/her voice – accent, commonly used phrases, laughter. I can close my eyes and listen. I can hold those impressions for a long time. Laughter is one of my favorites – the deep rumble of my dad's dad, the wheeze while my dad's mother would hold one hand to her mouth and slap her leg, the contagious mirth of my sister-in-law – soon to be followed by her three daughters, and many more

- The image of his/her face – the shape of the face, the smile, but mostly the eyes. I can close my eyes and picture many faces I won't get to see again until heaven.

That's one of the reasons I look forward to heaven. I want to look into their eyes and hear the sound of their voices. For some of them, the last thing I saw and heard was caused by the pain of their last days. Those are things I don't dwell on. That's not how I choose to remember them.

As precious as those memories may be, voices and faces are not nearly as significant as the impact their lives had on mine. Mentors, examples, encouragers, teammates, family ... the intersections of our lives with the people God puts in our path gives us a chance to learn, to grow, and to mature. I said "gives us a chance" – it's up to us to heed the advice and follow the counsel.

Who are some of the people who have made such a difference in your life? Are they still around? If they are, let them know of your gratitude. Recently, a friend told me that one of the favorite teachers of his senior class was able to attend a reunion. He watched as, one by one, his classmates greeted their old teacher. There were hugs and handshakes but there were also brief conversations. He overheard a couple:

- "Thanks for expecting the best out of me."
- "You straightened me out even as you kicked my butt."
- "Thanks for loving me when I wasn't very lovable."

Some of those kinds of folks have gone on. You'll have to wait a while. But if they are still around...

The Value of Inheritance

There is an interesting story in 1 Kings 21 about a man named Naboth. He lived in ancient Jezreel and was a subject of King Ahab of Samaria. He owned a vineyard that was adjacent to a palace of the king. Ahab wanted the vineyard for himself and tried to convince Naboth to either exchange the land for another parcel or sell it to the monarch. Naboth refused: "The Lord forbid that I should give you the inheritance that was passed down by my ancestors."

Ahab returned to his palace and sulked: "So Ahab went home angry and sullen because of Naboth's answer. The king went to bed with his face to the wall and refused to eat!"

Really? He didn't get his way so he threw himself a pity party? You may remember his wife, Jezebel. She was vain, ruthless, power hungry, and vengeful. After scorning her husband, she told him she would take care of things. She had Naboth stoned to death and seized the vineyard from his heirs. That wasn't the end of the story.

God sent the prophet Elijah with a chilling warning and prediction. Eventually, Jezebel would suffer a horrible death on the very spot where Naboth's vineyard was located. In 2012, archaeologists discovered the large winery complex that was at the center of Naboth's vineyard.

In a day like ours, it seems that everything and everyone has a price. Naboth paid dearly for refusing to surrender his inheritance but his murder did not go unpunished. There are things in our lives that should not be for sale ... convictions that we will not compromise ... principles that will not be forfeited.

We claim to be people of the Book. Today more than ever, we need to stand on the truth of God's Word. Truth is not for sale.

We Are Family

The 1979 Pittsburgh Pirates adopted the Sister Sledge song, We Are Family, for their title run that won their fifth World Series title.

Willie Stargell led an all-star collection of players who demonstrated a fierce competitive spirit and a close-knit fraternity. The song rocked the stadium and the clubhouse through their historic season.

What does it mean to be family? It doesn't mean everything is perfect. While winning 98 wins that year, the Pirates did lose 64 times. Their best hitter that year, Bill Madlock, hit .328 during the regular season. That means he failed to get a hit almost 7 out of 10 at bats.

I don't know any perfect families. That is certainly true of church families. We all know that.

But families stick together, in good times and not-so-good. We find strength in each other. We celebrate the victories. We mourn the losses. We stand beside the faltering. We encourage the struggling. We depend on each other. We love, extend mercy, and offer grace because we need those things and we need to give those things.

Paul wrote to the Roman Christians: "Don't just pretend that you love others. Really love them. Hate what is wrong. Stand on the side of the good. Love each other with genuine affection. Take delight in honoring each other" (Romans 12:9,10).

That's what families do. I am glad to be a part of this one.

Just Google It

Bob Kaylor is a senior writer for Homiletics online. In a column from April 2014, he wrote about the impact of Google: "Google's reach is ubiquitous, giving us a world in which no problem exists that can't be solved with a few clicks of the mouse or taps on a phone." He noted that Google has brought us data at a speed that has shifted the way we gain information. Trying to remember a song? Google it. Looking for directions to a friend's house? Google it. Need a recipe for a meal? Google it. Instant information available from the Internet, where you know that everything you read is true and accurate, right?

Google debuted in 1998. It has made life simpler because of the incredible access to information. I use it every day. Most of us have trouble remembering when this search engine didn't exist. 'Google' quickly transitioned from noun to verb.

But you can't Google everything. You can find a satellite picture of your house, but you can't make that house a home. You can research the biology of the human heart, but you can't force that heart to love. You can find a church website full of helpful information, but you can't compel a congregation to live out their mission.

Even in this Google world, we still must do the hard work of building, strengthening, and enhancing relationships. Finding out about a person by what you might discover online is not the same as getting to know that person. Google might get you instant, but it won't get you lasting.

In this device-driven world we now inhabit, people can easily hide behind a wall of data. We can pretend to be something or someone we aren't. We need authentic interaction, face-to-face encounters that are just not possible through some date site or chat room. We need real life community.

I believe Jesus established the church for several reasons. First and foremost, the assembly of the redeemed are to share the love of God with the world that so desperately needs it. But there is another purpose. The people of God need each other. We need smiles of encouragement, shoulders of support, loving hands to touch, and open hearts to share. You can't Google that.

It's About Time

Rick Warren, in his book, *The Purpose Driven Life: What on Earth Am I Here For?* wrote:

> "Time is your most precious gift because you only have a set amount of it. You can make more money, but you can't make more time. When you give someone your time, you are giving them a portion of your life that you'll never get back. Your time is your life. That is why the greatest gift you can give someone is your time. It is not enough to just say relationships are important; we must prove it by investing time in them. Words alone are worthless. Relationships take time and effort, and the best way to spell love is T-I-M-E."

We've all said once or many times: "Where does the time go?" The answer might be wherever we spend it. There are so many demands on our time but we still make choices every day about how we will spend our 24 hours. An entire industry of time management consultants, gurus, and experts has blossomed because so many of us need help making the best, the most profitable, the most productive, and the most meaningful use of our time.

In the Sermon on the Mount, Jesus told those who would follow Him that our time was first and best managed by trust. The writer of Proverbs echoed that in chapter 3: "Trust in the Lord with all your heart and lean not on your own understanding. In all your ways acknowledge Him and He will direct your paths" (vv. 5,6).

On my wall, is a reminder to honor the time we have:

> "Take time to work, it is the price of success;
> Play, it is the secret of perpetual youthfulness;
> Think, it is the source of power;
> Read, it is the fountain of wisdom;
> Pray, it is conversation with God;
> Laugh, it is the music of the soul;
> Listen, it is the pathway to understanding;
> Dream, it is hitching your wagon to a star;
> Worship, it is the highway of reverence;
> Love and Be Loved, it is the gift of God."

Let's spend our time wisely. We can't buy anymore.

The Perfect Family

No such thing, right? Whatever a family looks like these days, we can be certain that none is perfect. But a family doesn't have to be perfect to be a place where people are loved, accepted, needed, and safe.

When a family 'works' best, everybody participates, everybody contributes. It's more than a list of chores that are evenly divided. It's the strength that is more than the sum of the parts. At the heart of it all, relationships matter most. Families can be constructed by blood, or friendship, or affinity. Families can experience loss, divorce, distance, and change during the seasons of life, but there is still the potential for bonding and healing. We need each other.

The old man knocked on the door of his granddaughter's bedroom. She was in trouble again. One bad choice followed other bad choices. While she was sulking, locked in her room, she had shut everyone out. She was wrong but she was hurting. Grandpa thought he would try to get through. He knocked again. He heard a muffled, "Go away." He knocked again. From his side of the door, "I'm not going anywhere. We need to talk."

She finally opened the door. They sat together on the edge of her bed and she noticed something in her grandfather's hand. "What's up with the sticks?" The way things had gone she probably thought he would use them on her. He smiled and handed her one stick. "Break this stick for me." She snapped it easily. Handing her the rest, he said, "Now, break this bunch."

She tried then tried again, straining and grunting with effort. She couldn't break the sticks. She looked up at her grandfather, defeated. He put his arm around her. "Honey, I don't think I could break all of them either. Think of it this way: Nobody in this family is perfect. Heck, I've made plenty of mistakes in my day. But this bunch of sticks represents our family. By ourselves, we can be weak, but together, well, that's another story."

The church is a family. If God is our heavenly Father, that makes us brothers and sisters. Paul wrote to the Ephesians, "You are members of God's own family" (Ephesians 2:19). No, we are certainly not perfect, but the One who gives us life and draws us together is. He is the One who adopted us, who chose us for His very own possession.

Maybe, Maybe Not

Do you ever have trouble making up your mind? You don't? How about the guy in front of you at the doughnut shop ... or the fast food store ... or the perpetual lane-changer on the highway? Sometimes it's not easy to come to a decision. Jimmy Buffett once said: "Indecision may or may not be my problem." Another guy admitted: "I used to be indecisive, but now I am not quite sure."

We were visiting friends in the North Georgia mountains recently. They had a neighbor who had a family wedding. The woman's nephew was the groom. The ceremony was on Saturday. As of late Friday night, the groom wasn't sure if he was going to go through with it. Makes you understand what a shotgun wedding might be.

Some things don't matter much. I was standing in my closet trying to decide what shirt to wear. After staring at the rack for way too long, I gave myself a mental kick in the rear – "Pick a shirt for crying out loud!"

There are much more serious issues that confront us that require careful thought and consideration. We know that life is full of challenges when the way forward isn't always clear. The apostle Paul gave this advice: "Fix your thoughts on what is true, and honorable, and right, and pure, and lovely, and admirable. Think about things that are excellent and worthy of praise" (Philippians 4:8).

Another sage recommended that we should reflect on questions like these when we try to make a decision:

- Who will it help?
- Will it hurt anyone?
- Are there acceptable risks involved?
- What do I hope to learn from my decision?
- Will my decision honor God?

Ultimately for people of faith, it always helps to turn to God's Word: "Trust in the Lord with all your heart. Do not depend on your own understanding. In all your ways acknowledge Him and He will direct your paths" (Proverbs 3:5,6).

Years Gone By

North Fulton High School. Bulldogs. I still know the lyrics and can sing the alma mater. "On Atlanta's northern border, reared against the sky, proudly stands North Fulton High as the years go by …" I know you want me to sing it for you. Call me at 1-800-fatchance.

Well, the years have gone by and North Fulton is no longer. It is now the International School (where the movie "Blindside was filmed). In 1969, there were over 200 of us who walked across the stage at Chastain Park in the spring of that year. This coming spring we will celebrate at our 50th reunion.

Last week almost 20 of the guys met for lunch. It was great to catch up. Some of us haven't seen each other since graduation. There were cries of "You look great" and "You haven't changed!" - which means that our eyesight and mental capacity has dimmed over the years.

An objective observer might opine that many of us looked rode hard and put up wet, but I thought that bunch still carried some of the swagger I remember. The conversation shifted from stories of high school shenanigans (the older we get the better we were) to accounts of grandkids and ailments.

We all realized that there were some faces missing. It wasn't the guys who couldn't make it to lunch that day; it was the guys who didn't make it. It is painful to know that we've lost a number of classmates who died too soon.

I think we all know that life is full of twists and turns. Life can take your breath away with moments of exhilaration, wonder, and joy. It can also punch you in the gut with disappointment, heartache, and loss.

My second favorite book in the Bible is Paul's letter to the Philippians. Written while in prison, Paul summed up a philosophy of life that had been shaped through the good and bad times: "Not that I was ever in need, for I have learned how to be content with whatever I have. I know how to live on almost nothing or with everything. I have learned the secret of living in every situation...for I can do everything through Christ who strengthens me."

Through the good times and bad, He is there. He is the same yesterday, today, and forever. Life passes so fast and we better cling to something, or better yet Someone, we can count on.

Stylish Bomb Shelters

CNN reporter Elizabeth Stamp did a feature on billionaire bunkers in April. She discovered a developer who had turned two abandoned U.S. Army Corps of Engineers missile silos into condominiums. For the prosperous survivalist, one can choose a 900 square foot half-floor residence or 2-level penthouse with 3600 square feet. The latter starts at $4.5 million. There are other available comforts in the complex – like a pool, general store, theater, bar, and library.

If you want to get away from it all, why not do it in style?

Talk of apocalypse is on the rise. Volatile and divisive politics, increasing and worsening violence, erratic and deadly weather events ... the list of factors that create a pall over the future grows by the day. Are we on the brink of nuclear war? Are there strains of bacteria we cannot fight off? Will terrorism become the irresistible force? Will an asteroid collide with the earth? Does humanity have a realistic chance for survival?

I don't remember when I heard it first, but I'm glad I did hear it: "I don't know what the future holds, but I do know Who holds the future."

There are indeed many reasons for concern. I am not naïve about the myriad dangers that lurk nearby. But I refuse to live in fear. You won't find this exact quote in Scripture, but there is truth is these three words I can hear the Father saying: "I've got this."

Who Would You Rather Be?

Peter had a reputation. Always mentioned first in any list of the disciples, he was the acknowledged spokesman of the group. His eagerness to speak got him into trouble occasionally. There were times when he suffered from sandal-in-the-mouth disease: speak first then think about it.

He might have been brash and impulsive but you have to give the guy credit. He stuck his neck out. He also stuck his foot out. In a book I hope you have read, John Ortberg wrote about the risks and rewards of stepping into unknown adventure out of our comfort zones: "If You Want to Walk on Water, You've Got to get out of the Boat."

You can read the story in Matthew14:22-33. Peter's impetuous first step was followed by sheer terror. At first, all he could see was Jesus. He asked, Jesus answered: "Come." He came ... until he noticed the wind ripping at his hair, the waves dousing his body, the noise of a dangerous storm. He started sinking when he took his eyes off Jesus. In panic, he screamed for help, "Save me, Lord!"

He could have been like his eleven companions. He could have stayed in the boat. The storm was still raging so they were still in danger. It is interesting to note a couple of things. First, Peter didn't die. Jesus did save him. The safest place to be in the storm is where Christ can grab you. Staying close to Christ seems to be a good idea.

Second, the storm ended after Peter had taken the risk. Jesus had already assured them, "It's all right. I am here! Don't be afraid." I think it's important to be confident that we will never meet a storm so strong Christ can't see us through. Sometimes He stills the storm, but always He is willing to go with us through it.

Was it worth the risk Peter took? Perhaps faltering faith is better than no faith at all. Like the father whose son was desperately ill (Mark 9:24), sometimes all we can say is "Lord, I believe. Help my unbelief."

Thumbs Up!

Picture this: The wedding ceremony is over. My son and his new bride have walked the aisle, the wedding party has departed the platform. I'm standing there, waiting for the moms to be escorted out. I look down at the front row where my 7-year-old grandson is sitting. Earlier, he had performed his ring-bearer role flawlessly. Our eyes meet and he gives me a thumbs-up. My day was complete. I got the approval of a 7-year-old.

Giving a thumbs-up is a part of our culture. It signifies something positive. You see it at movies, at the ball game, after a good performance. When you see it, you know what it means.

There's just one problem. According to historians, we got it wrong. Historians claim that the hand signal originated with gladiatorial contests in ancient Rome. When the victor stood over the conquered, he would look to the crowd. If the crowd turned their thumbs down, it meant "sword down" – the loser was to be spared. "Whenever a combatant was seriously wounded, the presiding judge, or referee, was called upon to determine whether the man should live or die, depending on how well he had put up a fight.

Just like modern day made-for-tv talent shows, "a judge usually based his decision on the passions expressed by the crowds in the stadium; whether they would cheer, applaud, and give the thumbs down if they liked the man. If they didn't then they would give the thumbs up and his opponent would dispatch the fatal blow. Some scholars suggest the thumbs up meant to thrust a sword up into the heart." (Nick Knight)

Okay, then Russell Crowe's *"Gladiator"* got it wrong. All this time, we've been giving each other a 'thumbs up." Who knew?

I don't care. When my grandson gave me a thumbs up, I knew what he meant. Somebody in your life needs one of those today ... not the ancient Rome version. Encourage someone. Let them know of your love and support. Give 'em a thumbs up!

Windows to the World

The church had been constructed on a rise above the village. People came from miles around to gaze at the beauty of the sanctuary. Among its many splendid features were the windows. Memorial gifts had purchased the exquisite stained glass windows that had been made in a mountain studio not too far away. The windows featured biblical scenes and contained Scriptural references. The sanctuary would almost come alive as the morning sun would send its rays through the colored panes. The brilliant hues caused many a gasp as worshipers basked in the warmth and light.

The most impressive window, however, was not made of stained glass. It was a large picture window that overlooked the town. Underneath was the inscription: "Here is our window to the world – the world God loved so much that He gave His Son."

We know that the church is more than impressive buildings, glorious fixtures, and beautiful windows. The church is you and me, every believer who is being transformed from convert to disciple. The church is under orders, a divine mandate to tell the Good News ... to live the Good News. Our target for compassionate and courageous ministry is not the four walls of our buildings. God has called us to be on mission for Him, to be the presence of Christ in the world.

It's just a story but it has implications for the church of today: The angels welcomed Jesus after His ascension. One said to Him, "Now that You have returned, what is Your plan to spread the good news about the Kingdom?" Jesus responded: "I have commissioned believers to take the news throughout the world."

The angels were astounded. "Surely You have a plan B. Do You really believe that entrusting such a vital mission to flawed humans will work?"

Jesus answered, "There is no plan B. I promised them that the Holy Spirit will empower them to accomplish great things. They will never be alone."

I Got Nothin'

It was during a children's sermon. Those things can be dangerous if you toss out an open-ended question to a bunch of kids. I did it anyway. I asked, "Can you tell me a favorite character from the Bible other than Jesus?" Pretty safe, right? A few hands were raised and names began to be mentioned:

Abraham – Moses – Mary – David – Goliath – Peter

I waited just a moment to see if any others would be named. I glanced down at the young lady sitting beside me. She looked up at me and said, "I got nothin.'"

Have you ever had one of those days? Of course, you have. Days or moments or seasons when you 'got nothin'?

He may not have been the first to use the analogy, but Bill Hybels pictured a bucket to represent our lives (*Simplify: Ten Practices to Unclutter Your Soul*). There are relationships and activities than can either fill or drain our lives. The danger of a depleted life can devastate our attitudes and behavior.

We can feel dry and empty because our resources and our energy have not been replenished. We are more susceptible to low self-esteem, lack of confidence, negativity, fatigue, even poor physical health. We are more easily distracted by lesser things. We can isolate ourselves. We can neglect spiritual disciplines. We can easily fall into the "woe is me" doldrums.

Sometimes we have to move past our feelings and cling to assurances, promises, and commitments. Have you ever felt like not going to work? Feel that way long enough and you won't have to worry about work anymore.

Jesus quoted the Shema in Deuteronomy 6 with this important inclusion: "You must love the Lord your God with all your heart, all your soul, and all your strength" (Matthew 22:37). Love is far more than a feeling; it requires intelligent commitment, an act of the will. Love gets us through when the bucket is draining.

When we 'got nothin', we need to remember that the day or the moment or even the season will pass. At the end of his life, Paul trumpeted: "And my God will supply all of your needs according to His riches in Christ Jesus!" We can live with that!

Better Together

The turtle had a dilemma. He wanted to move south for the winter because he couldn't stand another blustery winter and he certainly didn't want to make the long trudge southward. If he was going to pull it off, he would need some help. So he used his mighty turtle brain to come up with idea. He knew a couple of geese that were preparing for the long journey. After all, they were far better equipped for long-distance travel. He discussed his plan with his feathered-friends.

Scrounging around, he found a length of rope. He explained to the geese that each was to hold an end while he grasped the middle with his strong jaws. Away they went.

Things were going well during the flight until someone on the ground happened to glance up and see this strange sight. With admiration in his voice, he shouted, "Who in the world thought of that?" Unable to restrain the impulse to take full credit for the idea, the turtle opened his mouth to say ... "I di – d – d – d ..."

It's amazing what you can accomplish when it doesn't matter who gets the credit. On the flip side, drawing attention to yourself may be a recipe for disaster.

Speaking of recipes, Paul had one for how Christians are to live in community with each other: "Love each other with genuine affection. Take delight in honoring each other... when others are happy, be happy for them. If they are sad, share their sorrow. Live in harmony with each other. Don't try to act important, but enjoy the company of others. Do you part to live in peace with everyone as much as possible" (from Romans 12:9-18).

With the right ingredients, our families and our churches and our communities could look very different. It's worth a try, isn't it?

Who's On First?

It has to be one of the greatest comedic routines of all time. Bud Abbott and Lou Costello first performed it on a radio show, *The Kate Smith Hour*, in March 1938. Over the years, they would delight audiences with the famous descriptions of a baseball team: "Who's on first?"

The rotund Costello would appear to be increasingly frustrated with his cool, calm partner as Abbott tried to explain the names of all the players. It was brilliant, funny theater.

In Mark 10, Jesus had to participate in a very different "Who's on first?" dialogue. The author recorded that two of the disciples (who also were cousins of Jesus) approached Him and ask for special favor. In Matthew's account, the mother of James and John (who was the sister of the mother of Jesus) made the same ask. "When You sit on Your glorious throne, we want to sit in places of honor next to You, one on Your right and the other on Your left" (v. 37).

Costello acted like he was frustrated in his act; Jesus didn't have to act. He told the two, "You don't know what you are asking!" The Lord had just announced for the third time that He would journey to Jerusalem to die. Did they not hear Him? As soon as Jesus made the statement, James and John requested privileged status. Insensitive, clueless?

In His response to their thoughtless question, Jesus explained a new order in His Kingdom: "Whoever wants to be a leader among you must be your servant, and whoever wants to be first among you must be the slaves of everyone else. For even the Son of Man came not to be served but to serve others and to give His life as a ransom for many" (vs. 43-45).

Humility was considered a vice, a sign of weakness until Jesus came. Read again Philippians 2:5-11, the ancient Christian hymn that describes the true power of love through humility and obedience. Revisit the scene in the Upper Room when Jesus washed the feet of His disciples (see John 13).

The Bible tells us that the other disciples were indignant when they heard what James and John did. Were they mad because they didn't think of it first? They all seemed to be tone deaf at this point, but perhaps we should consider the price of pride in our own lives. According to Jesus, trying to be first might be the fastest way to the back of the line!

Make Me a Fire

Some people seem to be born for greatness. Some possess incredible intellect. Some have unusual artistic ability. Some are given physical skills far beyond the norm. And then there is the rest of us. We probably won't find our names in the headlines because of great achievement. The spotlight will shine elsewhere. Our parents' car didn't have the bumper sticker that read: "My child is an honor student."

But you know what? God has given us all talents and passion in this life. In the Bible, Jesus told a parable about three servants who were entrusted by their master with varying levels of funds (Matthew 25). One guy was given five bags of silver; another was given two bags; and the third was handed one bag. The question never centered on the amount; what mattered was what each did with what he was given.

What are we doing with what God has entrusted to us? Time, talent, treasure ...

Amando Nervoz wrote a poem entitled: "Make Me"

> I am only a spark; Make me a fire.
> I am only a string; Make me a lyre.
> I am only a drop; Make me a fountain.
> I am only an anthill; Make me a mountain.
> I am only a feather; Make me a wing.
> I am only a rag; Make me a king.

Paul wrote to his Philippian friends that he could do all things through Christ who strengthened him. Whether he had plenty or nothing, he knew God could do great things through him. He had the confidence that his faith would be rewarded. What he had, he offered to his Lord.

Remember the line from hockey great Wayne Gretzky? "You miss 100% of the shots you don't take." That's what happened to the one bag guy in the parable. Don't let it happen to you.

Healthy Ego

We live in a me-driven society. Egos are out of control. People become "celebrities" on the thinnest of credentials ... or none at all. Do we really care who the Kardashians are sleeping with, what train wreck the latest pop diva has become? What needs to be added to too many menus is simple – how about a serving of humble pie?

Years ago, a famous musician had been hired to perform a very special concert on a beautiful but ancient pump organ. The bellows for the organ had to be pumped by hand. A sturdy young man was enlisted for that purpose. Strong enough for the tiring task, the teen stood dutifully behind the organist and pumped away while the glorious music flowed out of the exquisite old organ.

At the first intermission, the youth whispered to the organist, "We played good, didn't we?"

"What do you mean 'we'," huffed the musician. "I was the one who played, not you."

When it was time to begin again, the organist took his place on the bench and proceeded to press the keys...but no sound came out of the instrument. He realized that there was no air flow coming from the bellows. Over his shoulder, he hissed urgently, "Pump!"

The boy responded, "Say 'we'."

The Apostle Paul warned Christians in Rome to keep their egos in check. "Love each other with genuine affection. Take delight in honoring each other. Live in harmony with each other. Don't try to act important and don't think you know it all" (Romans 12). It's a timeless message, one that needs to be trumpeted often. You may think this is your world and we get to live in it, but a little humility would do us all well.

Crackpots

You have heard the term 'crackpot' before, right? Did you know there was a village in the UK named Crackpot? Did you know there was an Australian band with that name? Useless information you say. Let's dig a little deeper.

Anything that is cracked suggests imperfection or flaw. When you hear the word associated with a person, it usually refers to something strange or eccentric. Often when something is cracked, we either fix it, throw it away, or live with it. Tree roots crack pavement. A building settles and cracks appear.

Perhaps the most famous crack is found on one of America's most iconic symbols. Just after its arrival in Philadelphia in 1752, the Liberty Bell was rung for the first time and the crack appeared. The Whitechapel Foundry in London had forged a flawed bell. Repairs were undertaken by two local craftsmen, John Pass and John Stow. You can see their names inscribed on the side.

The repair lasted through the public reading of the Declaration of Independence in July of 1776.

But in 1835, the bell cracked again when tolling for Chief Justice John Marshall upon his death. The crack remains to this day, a significant part of its character.

Truth be told we all have cracks or flaws. People are much like cracked vessels: we either try to fix them, cast them out, or live with their imperfections. David, confronted with his own flaws, finally came clean: "Have mercy on me, O God because of Your unfailing love. Because of your great compassion, blot out the stain of my sins. Wash me clean ... purify me ... create in me a clean heart" (Psalm 51).

Cracked pots don't have to be ugly. In Japan, cracked pots have been turned into something beautiful. Kintsugi is the Japanese art of putting broken pottery pieces back together with gold — built on the idea that in embracing flaws and imperfections, you can create an even stronger, more beautiful piece of art.

Some flaws we must live with. Isn't it amazing that God can fill in those cracks with His grace? He isn't finished with us. As Paul wrote, "He who began a good work in you will continue until it is finished." Yeah, I'm a cracked pot but I'll leave my life in the hands of the Master Potter.

Time Change

It happens twice a year. The best one happens this weekend when we fall back. I like getting that extra hour. I'm tempted to go ahead and change my clocks early so I can begin enjoying the extra time right now.

Time is the commodity of our day. I found some interesting observations about the subject:

- William Penn: "Time is what we want most but use worst."
- Harvey Mackay: "Time is free but it's priceless. You can't own it, but you can use it. You can't keep it, but you can spend it. Once you've lost it you can never get it back."

- Robert Orben: "Time flies. It's up to you to be the navigator."

- Margaret Peters: "Time has a wonderful way of showing us what really matters."

The way we squander our time can lead to deep regret. The words we wished we had said. The moments we let slip away. The friends we've lost touch with. The broken relationships we should have tried to heal. The risk we never took.

One of my favorite humorists was Erma Bombeck. She was asked once what she would have done differently if given the chance. You can find her column easily but here are just a few of her musings:

"I would have talked less and listened more. I would have taken time to listen to my grandfather ramble about his youth. I would have cried and laughed less while watching television and more while watching life. There would be more 'I love you's'. More 'I'm sorry.' But mostly given another shot at life, I would seize every minute ... look at it and really see it ... live it and never give it back. Stop sweating the small stuff. Don't worry about who doesn't like you, who has more, or who's doing what. Let's think about what God has blessed us with."

In this one and only life, time is to be cherished not wasted. I hope to be a better steward of God's precious gift. How about you?

Acting Like the Rest of Us

A congregation was excited about its new, young pastor. He was energetic, preached inspiring sermons and worked with the youth. Then one night he was late for the church council meeting.

Another time, he failed to show up for a committee meeting. He even started coming late to worship. Then one Sunday, he failed to show up at all for worship.

The council voted to dismiss the pastor.

Then the council had the following message posted at the church entrance: "We have fired our pastor for acting like the rest of us."

A preacher wrote that story, right? Sounds like one, doesn't it?

Was Brother Lawrence right? "Our only business is to love and delight ourselves in God." How can we practice the presence of Christ in a hurried, distracted life?

Who Are You Supposed to Be?

Halloween used to be fun. It used to be simple. You dressed up in your store-bought or hand-made costume and made the rounds. It was usually a neighborhood event. You knew who was who because kids talked about their costumes for weeks. You knew who gave out the best candy. You knew where the old grouch lived and stayed away. You watched the sun makes its agonizingly slow descent so you could hit the streets as close to dark as possible. Everybody watched out for everybody.

If you were cool, you had a great mask ... not the ones with the thin rubber bands that kept breaking. The best ones were scary or funny or weird. I remember the 3-foot tall Frankenstein who showed up at our door one time. I always thought the monster was about 7 feet tall, must have been his kid. Sometimes you had to guess what character stood before you. And then there are the middle school kids who don't even bother to dress up – they just want free candy or else. If you turn them away, they might come back with something you don't want.

Things change. One guy started giving out tooth brushes. I didn't think Scrooge showed up until Christmas. Then there are the people who handed out granola bars. Really? Then people started into tricks instead of treats, vandalizing homes, cars, and lawns. Not cool.

Today, you don't see as many kids in many places on Halloween. Churches and schools offer festivals to provide a safe place – "trunk or treats" have become popular. Parents are afraid their children won't be safe in their own neighborhoods. You have to be more careful these days with the items in their bags. One young man approached us with the traditional "Trick or Treat" and then added "no peanuts please."

It's sad when the simple becomes complicated. Sometimes I need to remember that not everything was good about the "good old days" but I'll still be at my post tomorrow night ready to ask "Who are you supposed to be?"

The Cup of Wonder

In his marvelous collection of meditations on the Lord's Supper, Lloyd John Ogilvie wrote of the wine of astonishment, citing Psalm 60. The setting was one of staggering events, both personally and corporately. Hard times had sent the people reeling. Yet there was a message beyond the judgment the nation had experienced. God promised rescue and salvation. In verse 4, we find these magnificent words: "But You have raised a banner for those who honor You – a rallying point in the face of attack."

Think about that. Almighty God has raised a banner of protection and victory over His beloved. Whatever you and I face, we belong to God and "With His help we will do mighty things" (v. 12).

Thanksgiving affords us the significant opportunity to express our gratitude for the blessings we enjoy. For those to whom much has been given, much should be expected. Let's pray together how we can give of our time, talent, and treasure in this wonderful season.

Any time we are invited to the table of the Lord, we are reminded of the mystery of our faith. We can rest and revel in the wonder of God's love for sinners like you and me.

Tables occupy a significant role in Scripture. The Hebrews established a tradition around their tables to observe Passover. Jesus gathered His disciples in the Upper Room and instituted what we call the Lord's Supper. The early church met together constantly around tables of fellowship and worship. The Feast of the Lamb in the book of Revelation features a great table for the redeemed.

Over each of those tables hung the banner of God's care for His children. In awe and wonder we rejoice because of His bounty and blessing.

It Sounded Like a Good Idea at the Time

Do you remember "New Coke?" Coca-Cola launched their reformulation of their famous beverage in April of 1985. Their market share had been taking some hits from Pepsi and other competitors, dropping from 60% to 24%. So the company executives decided to tinker with their flagship product. It sounded like a good idea at the time.

Mike Kami is a strategic planning consultant. He met with the Coke folks prior to the introduction of their new formula. They told him they had conducted numerous taste tests and were convinced they had found a winner. They were wrong. Mike was brought back in when it became obvious that "New Coke" was received so poorly.

Mike was also hired by Bob Buford, founder of Leadership Network and author of the classic work *Halftime – Changing Your Game Plan from Success to Significance*. At the time Kami entered Buford's life, Bob was asking himself some tough questions: What should I do? How could I be most useful? Where should I invest my talents, time, and treasure? What are the values that give purpose to my life?

Mike asked him one more question: What's in the box? As an avowed atheist, Mike Kami wasn't coming from the same place as Bob Buford. But Buford was convinced that God used Mike Kami to awaken something in him. What's in the box? What is the most important thing in your life? What receives your primary loyalty? Bob Buford decided that his answer had to be Jesus Christ. His answer changed his life.

When asked back by the Coke company, he posed the same question. They had originally thought "great taste" was in their box. They found out the hard way, the expensive way, that it was something they had missed. He told them, "Let's try again." They came up with a different response: "American Tradition."

Sometimes we can outsmart ourselves. Going back to the basics is not a bad approach for most of us. Maybe you don't need to reinvent yourself. Maybe you just need to be who God created you to be.

Tapestry

Corrie ten Boom was a remarkable woman. Her Dutch family took great and costly risks to hide Jews from the Nazis during the occupation of the Netherlands in World War II. Helping a number of Jewish neighbors to escape, the Ten Booms were determine to provide a hiding place while the German Gestapo and Dutch collaborators hunted them.

Betrayed by a Dutch informer, the entire family was arrested on February 28, 1944. Corrie and her sister, Betsie, were transported to several camps until arriving at the infamous Ravensbrück women's labor camp. They endured the horrors of their captivity while leading worship services with a Bible they had snuck into the camp. Betsie grew weaker and it became obvious that she would not survive. On December 16, 1944, Betsie ten Boom died. Just before slipping away, she told her sister: "There is no pit so deep that God is not deeper still."

After the war, Corrie returned home to set up a rehabilitation center for camp survivors and collaborators. Traveling the world to tell her story, she even came face to face with one of her guards. She overcame her feelings of anger and resentment to offer the man forgiveness.

She had a victorious perspective of a life of suffering and hardship. She chose to trust God with a larger picture than she could see. One of her poems demonstrates her amazing faith:

> "My life is but a weaving between God and me.
> I cannot choose the colors He weaveth steadily.
> Oft times He weaveth sorrow; and I in foolish pride
> Forget He sees the upper and I the underside."

Few of us will ever be exposed to such deprivation and devastation. Even so, we can choose to trust the Weaver of our tapestry. O God, help us to lean on You!

In My Seat

Most of us can remember exactly where we were on that horrific Tuesday morning. Our world changed that day. A great deal was lost – almost 3,000 lives, the dreams of families and friends, billions of dollars in destruction and damage, the sense of security and protection, and so much more.

Stories emerged from that day. Some of the stories were overwhelmingly tragic. Some captured heroic and courageous sacrifice. Some revealed people who had planned to be in one of those buildings or planes but escaped the carnage. People overslept and were late to work that day. Some had appointments away from the office. Some missed their flight.

For an American Airlines pilot, a reassignment changed his future: "Steve Scheibner went to bed September 10, 2001, with his bags packed and ready to go. He was scheduled to be the pilot on American Airlines Flight 11 the next day. When he awoke in the morning, however, a rare last-minute substitution meant someone else would pilot that plane ... the first plane that hit the World Trade Center on 9/11. Steve knows firsthand what it means to have someone else die in his place, not once ... but twice" (from In My Seat).

Who was the man who took Steve Scheibner's seat that fateful day? On that September morning, Tom McGuinness kissed his wife, Cheryl, goodbye at their Portsmouth, New Hampshire home. He was headed to Boston's Logan airport to serve as co-pilot and first officer on American Airlines Flight 11. One of the last things Tom, a 42 year-old former Navy fighter pilot, had told his wife was: "If anything ever happens to me, you have to trust God. God will get you through it. Just surround yourself with loving people, people who know Christ, people who will surround you in Christ-like love."

Like so many others, Cheryl and the children, Jennifer and Tommy, had no idea that they would never see their loved one again. Mohammed Atta and his henchmen gained control of the jet on their mission of hate and murder. Tom McGuinness along with 81 passengers and flight crew perished in the crash.

For both families, Steve's and Tom's, tragedy has given way to hope and purpose. Yes, they do believe Romans 8:28: "And we know that God causes everything to work together for the good of those who love God and are called according to His purpose for them." Regardless of how those fanatics viewed their devastating deeds, God did not cause that horror and heartbreak. The testimony of the Scheibner and McGuinness families might be best captured in the title of Cheryl's book: *Beauty Beyond the Ashes: Choosing Hope After Crisis*.

For the Bible Tells Me So

No, Joan of Arc wasn't Noah's wife. No, John, Paul, George, and Ringo were not the gospel writers. There is no book of Hesitations. You won't find some of these common sayings in the pages of Scripture:

- "God helps those who help themselves."

- "No pain, no gain."

It is frightening what people think is in the Bible. It is perhaps even more disturbing that the tidbits above actually came from a survey of Christians.

We sometimes take for granted the importance of Bible reading, Bible study, and Bible teaching. Most of us have multiple Bibles in our home. The Bible continues to be the best-selling book in history. Our problem is not having a Bible; our challenge is to pick one up, read it, and apply it!

What does the Bible mean to you? Is it a part of your daily life? Do you turn to it in times of crisis? Do you find it hard to read and harder to understand?

In the longest chapter in the book of Psalms, we find great encouragement to make the Bible an integral part of our lives: "Your Word is a lamp for my feet and a light for my path" (119:105).

There is a personal commitment to read, study, and apply the truth of Scripture and there is a corporate commitment to raise a high standard in the church for the Bible teaching program. When the church does not honor that commitment, we stray from the heart of discipleship. The early church devoted themselves to the apostles' teaching (Acts 2:42). Paul made it clear how he felt about the importance of personal spiritual growth (2 Timothy 2:15) and devotion to God's Word (2 Timothy 3:16,17).

In a world like ours, we can be overwhelmed by the cacophony of opinions and declarations. We are told that truth is relative and situational. The loudest voice often carries the room.

With all that noise, it would be helpful to remember the words of the psalmist: "Be still and know that I am God." He is still speaking. Are we listening?

"You're Not Wearing That?"

It's time for true confession. Come on, Mark, you can do it. Take a deep breath and just spill it.

"I'm color blind. A little."

Like a lot of guys, I have trouble with certain shades. I have been known to wear articles of clothing items that didn't quite match. I have a color blind advisor. I have learned through painful trial and error that it is wiser to just ask: "Does this go with that?" Sometimes gently and sometimes with eye-rolls ... okay, sometimes with guffaws, corrections have to be made. Some unfortunate fashion selections have been made with both color blindness and early morning darkness fighting against me. Only in the light of day and with keen observer commentary have I learned I should have just stayed home that morning.

I have learned a few things about what we wear:

- If you want to bring laughter into the lives of your children, pull out your high school yearbooks or your wedding pictures.
- If you don't, burn those suckers.
- I cling to the hope that one day their children will laugh at them, too.

- I have learned the futility of believing that one day I will be able to wear that again.

- Whoever invented neck ties and panty hose came from the same torture chamber.

- Teenaged boys still don't know how to pull their pants up.

- My philosophy about clothing has changed from what looks good to what feels good.

- I am now the old guy I used to make fun of.

It's interesting to me that the Bible contains helpful hints about what we wear. Paul wrote to the Colossians: "So, chosen by God for this new life, dress in the wardrobe God picked out for you: compassion, kindness, humility, quiet strength, discipline. Be even-tempered, content with second place, quick to forgive an offense. Forgive as quickly and completely as the Master forgave you. And regardless of what else you put on, wear love. It's your basic, all-purpose garment. Never be without it" (Colossians 3:12-14, The Message).

How about that? Clothing that never goes out of style!

And Jesus Had Compassion

Over and over, the New Testament bears witness to how Jesus viewed those He came to save. In Matthew 9, we are told: "When He saw the crowds, He had compassion on them because they were confused and helpless, like sheep without a shepherd." In Mark 8, Jesus spoke to His disciples: "I feel sorry for these people. They have been here with Me for three days, and they have nothing left to eat."

In Matthew 25, we are given a picture of judgment when Jesus acknowledged those who had compassion on the "least of these."

When the Lord gazes over our world today, He sees this poor, the despairing, the grieving, the confused, and the misguided. These past weeks have been horrific. The ravages of fierce storms have wrecked so many lives. The senseless violence in Las Vegas has taken a devastating toll among so many. We are staggered by the disruption and discouragement.

And Jesus had compassion.

A man was complaining to his pastor, listing all the events and circumstances that caused pain and loss. "Why doesn't God do something?" The minister thought for a moment and then said, "I don't believe God needs me to defend Him, but I think He is doing something. He is sending you and me into those moments when we can show the compassion of Christ."

We don't have all the answers, perhaps very few of them. But we can impact our world with our attention and care. An elderly man, affectionately known as Mr. Ben, who lived on their street had recently been widowed. A mother was explaining to her six-year-old what had happened. He sat silently for a while and then left the room. The woman got busy with some chores and realized that she hadn't heard anything from him for a few minutes. She went looking for him. When she couldn't find him in the house, she stepped out her front door. He was walking up the sidewalk toward her. "Where have you been, honey?" The boy's face was streaked with tears. "What's wrong? Are you okay?" she asked. "I'm okay. I just went over to Mr. Ben's so I could cry with him for a while."

And the followers of Jesus had compassion.

When Is It Over?

A man invited a friend to attend a service at his church. The friend had not been to any church since he was a child. After being asked multiple times, he finally agreed to come. If nothing else, at least he wouldn't have to be bugged anymore. What he didn't know was that the service was a prayer meeting. It was a service of silence. He sat there growing more and more impatient. There was no music, no speaking, just quiet. Finally, he leaned over to the man who had invited him and whispered, "When does the service begin?" His friend replied, "When we leave."

Does it bother you how bent out of shape we get over worship? The preacher is boring. I don't like the music. Nobody better sit in my seat! I've preached over 2000 sermons in my ministry. Every one of them was fantastic. Okay, maybe not all of them. Alright, a few of them were real stinkers. One thing I tried to remember: the only audience that truly matters is not the one sitting in the sanctuary.

If I applied that to every aspect of a worship service, then I think we can know what worship really means. The word comes from old English and means "worth ship" – it tells us that the Audience we seek to honor is worthy. We cannot allow our preferences to rob us of seeking to encounter and experience God. Worship is our highest calling and our greatest privilege. Tim Keller wrote: "The Christian breathes in God's goodness and exhales worship."

One study, published in the journal *Demography*, found that in general people who attend worship services one or more times a week live about eight years longer than those who never attend religious services. There you have it, the secret to a longer life is to go to church!

Attending worship services is important, but as the story of the two men reminds us, true worship leads to service. We leave our holy huddle to be the hands and feet of Christ in the world He died to save. If we don't, can we truly say we have worshipped?

I know church can be boring. Leaders do have the responsibility to plan and lead well. We also have the responsibility to give the Holy Spirit room to work! Sometimes it goes well, and sometimes ... children writing to the preacher:

- Dear Pastor, I liked your sermon today, especially when it was over.

- Dear Pastor, I like to go to church on Sunday because I don't have any choice.

- Dear Pastor, Thank you for your sermon. I will write more when my mother explains to me what you said.

- Dear Pastor, I think more people would come to church if you would move it to Disneyworld.

Amazing Grace

John Newton was 11 years old when he went to sea with his father, a shipmaster on merchant ships. After six voyages, his father retired and made plans for his young son to work at a sugar plantation in Jamaica. Those plans were interrupted when he was captured and pressed into service in the Royal Navy. After a miserable experience in the navy, he transferred to a slave ship bound for West Africa. While there the young man was treated much like a slave by an African duchess. He was alone, abused, and angry. Finally rescued by a sea captain enlisted by his father to search for his lost son,

Newton returned to England. For almost ten years, he continued to be involved in the slave trade. He captained his own ships on three voyages with human cargo. Over this regrettable period of his life, the stench of the ships finally seeped into his soul. His own spiritual struggle would one day serve as a source of warning and encouragement to those who wrestled with faith and needed direction.

One of those who sought him out was a young member of Parliament named William Wilberforce. The young politician was suffering a crisis of conscience and spiritual doubt, and was contemplating a departure from the political scene. Newton pleaded with him to stay in Parliament and told him to "serve God where he was."

Criticized for not separating completely from the heinous trade upon his conversion, Newton finally came to terms with himself and his faith. He became a fervent ally to Wilberforce and others who sought to abolish the African slave trade. He lived to see the passage of the landmark legislation, the Slave Trade Act of 1807.

With the collaboration of poet William Cowper, Newton wrote a number of hymns late in his life. His life testimony is not one of perfection; he admitted his flaws: "I was greatly deficient in many respects." His story is best told in his most well-known hymn, Amazing Grace. "I once was lost, but now am found; was blind but now I see."

John Newton was a work in progress ... much like your life and mine. The grace he acknowledged was a gift he didn't deserve. Neither do we. Amazing.

Of Course I Pray

Following a Sunday morning service, a man said to his friend, "I'll bet you can't recite the Lord's Prayer." The other man responded, "Yes, I can! Listen: 'Now I lay me down to sleep, I pray the Lord my soul to keep...'"

"Wow!" said the first man. "I was sure you wouldn't know it!"

Do you remember how you learned to pray? Did it start at your bedside or at the table? Was church the place you first began to pray? Was it a crisis that brought you to your knees? Was there a moment of awe and wonder that made you shout for joy and pray with praise?

Sometimes I think we make it more difficult than it needs to be. Prayer should be so natural. The psalmist wrote, "I love the Lord because He has heard my appeal for mercy. Because He has turned His ear to me, I will call out to Him as long as I live" (Psalm 116:1,2).

It is just that simple. God loves each of us like He loves all of us. He cares about His children. He invites us into an intimate relationship with Him. He wants us to share our lives, our hopes, our fears, our needs, our hurts for our sake. He knows. He really does.

Jim Cymbala noted: "I have discovered an astonishing truth. God is attracted to weakness. He can't resist those who humbly and honestly admit how desperately they need Him."

The week ahead offers us opportunities to pray in private and together in community. Prayer should happen naturally in a fellowship of believers. It should be characterized by expectancy and confidence. We approach the throne of grace boldly, said the writer of Hebrews (4:16). Robert Smith wrote: "You want prayer to be something that's a powerful expression of faith and belief that God can touch those around you." Prayer changes us as we pray for things to change. Here are some key factors for praying churches:

- Praying churches experience breakthroughs – barriers are torn down, pathways are cleared, new directions are forged

- Praying churches have praying leaders – leaders must first be followers who seek the true Leader

- Praying churches anticipate answers – stories are told, answers are celebrated, a climate of expectation is fostered

- Praying churches attempt great things for God – when God's people pray, God works. When God works, transformation occurs

It's time to pray!

Whoops!

The guys were pretty young. Big brother decided to give little brother a haircut. For some reason little brother agreed. Do you have an idea how this turned out? We had a pair of clippers that big brother thought he could use. Little brother was sitting still, listening to the buzz until he heard from behind one word: "Whoops!"

There was no blood, just less hair ... in one spot. It was like you could peer into his brain. Not really. You would have thought so for a moment. Another crisis at the Wilbanks house.

Things worked out. They usually do. Little brother's hair grew back ... by the time he graduated from high school. If you look closely, you can still tell. Not really.

Families go through "whoops" times. Friendships go through "whoops' times. None of us is perfect. We make mistakes with words and actions. We hurt each other and sometimes the hurt lasts and lasts.

There is a reason that Jesus wanted us to understand the essential nature of forgiveness. We know that God is a loving, forgiving God but Jesus made it clear. To fully experience God's forgiveness we have to be willing to forgive.

I think a good way to look at God's forgiveness is to realize that God chooses not to remember all our stumbles. The Bible says He casts our sin as far as the east is from the west. Could He call up all our wrongs if He wanted to? Certainly. But He chooses to not remember, to cleanse us, to give us a fresh start.

Forgiving is not always easy, but the cross reminds us that while we were yet sinners Christ died for us. The next time we hear "whoops" we should remember that.

The Empty Chair

Sunday dinner used to be a big deal. I don't mean going out to a nice place to eat. Dinner followed church and usually involved the family and perhaps a friend or two. Traditions might have included a roast or fried chicken, plenty of vegetables, and a favorite dessert. It was a lot of work but it might be one of the few times when the entire family sat down together.

In some parts of the country, another tradition was observed. There was always an empty chair. There was always room for one more. The tradition has a long history. In Jewish heritage, there was always an empty chair during the observance of Passover. Symbolically, it was a sign of expectation and hope that this year Elijah would come, announcing the arrival of the Messiah.

We are fast approaching another tradition-rich occasion – Thanksgiving. Will there be an empty chair at your table? Perhaps a loved one or dear friend is no longer alive. Perhaps someone couldn't make it home this year. Perhaps there is someone who has nowhere to go. Perhaps we could fill that empty chair with someone who needs to be included.

Where Is the Body?

Researchers in Jerusalem, continuing their investigation into the traditional site of the burial place of Jesus, claim to have confirmed that they have determined that portions of the original tomb are still present. According to National Geographic, the tomb has survived centuries of wear and tear of the Church of the Holy Sepulchre in Jerusalem's Old City.

On the night of October 26, researchers removed marble cladding that had been placed to protect the original limestone burial bed. Sixty hours later, they had cleared a layer of fill material to find the slab intact. Was it really the tomb where the body of Jesus lay after His crucifixion? "While it is archaeologically impossible to say that the tomb recently uncovered is the burial site of a Jew named Jesus of Nazareth, there is indirect evidence to suggest that identification of the site by representatives of the Roman emperor Constantine some 300 year later may be a reasonable one" (Kristin Romey, National Geographic).

If they found the tomb, where is the body? There are two answers to the question.

- Christians believe that Jesus was resurrected on the third day. The tomb was a temporary resting place that was no longer necessary.

- Christians also believe that Jesus established the church as His body on earth. Paul wrote to the Corinthians: "Now all of you together are Christ's body, and each one of you is a separate and necessary part of it" (1 Corinthians 12:27).

Where is His body? You certainly do not need to be searching tombs in Jerusalem for it. The body of Christ appears ...

... every time Christians model the example Jesus set of love, grace, and mercy

... every time Christians express compassion

... every time Christians stand on biblical truth

... every time Christians live out the promises and principles in God's Word

... every time Christians choose to be in the world, but not of the world

... every time Christians give witness by word and deed of their changed lives

We are the body of Christ!

Won't You Be My Neighbor?

Fred Rogers, a non-assuming and beloved character in American culture, hosted a television show for children. His message could be summarized in simple terms: "He gave us the most precious gift of all: the courage to be kind" (Morgan Deville). For over thirty years, "Mr. Rogers' Neighborhood" was a fixture on PBS. Millions of children watched a show that was critically acclaimed for focusing on children's emotional and physical concerns.

The courage to be kind … how often do we see that kind of courage in a world torn by a lack of courtesy and respect? His message is still needed. Tom Hanks portrays Fred Rogers in the new film. I cannot think of anyone better suited to portray him in the movie that premieres this week.

I have been reflecting on what it means to be a friend. Webster's Dictionary defined friend this way: "One who is attached to another by affection; one who entertains for another sentiments of esteem, respect and affection, which lead him to desire his company, and to seek to promote his happiness and prosperity."

The Bible helps us understand what a friend is;

- "A friend is always loyal." (Proverbs 17:17)
- "There is a friend that sticks closer than a brother." (Proverbs 13:20)

In the letter of James, Abraham was called a friend of God. In John 15, Jesus told His disciples that He considered them His friends. He told them: "Greater love has no one than to lay down his life for his friends" (John 15:13).

In our circles of relationship, we have many acquaintances but not many friends. My mother, who demonstrated friendship better than anyone I know, used to tell us "to have friends you have to be a friend." We need friends who love us no matter what, who tell us the truth and hold us accountable, who stand behind us and stand with us, who enrich our lives by their very presence.

I hope you work hard to be the friend that people you know need. I hope you have the courage to be kind.

Live This Day

The fall of 1939 indicated that the world was about to enter the horrific years of another war. Hitler's forces had invaded neighboring Poland. In the Far East, Japan had already launched a violent, aggressive expansion of its empire. America, still reeling from the Depression, seemed determine to stay out of the fray.

At Oxford University in England, a middle-aged professor was asked to speak to the students. His topic: "Learning in War Time." Many in his audience that day would soon trade their academic gowns for military uniforms. In trying to calm and comfort these young men, C.S. Lewis spoke about the importance of trusting the future to God.

In part, he said, "Happy work is best done by the man who takes his long-term plans somewhat lightly and works from moment to moment 'as to the Lord.' It is only our daily bread that we are encouraged to ask for. The present is the only time in which any duty can be done or any grace received."

It's an old cliché but still appropriate: "I may not know what the future holds but I do know Who holds the future."

We live in uncertain times. All we are promised is the present. I recently attended a funeral at a national cemetery. Gazing out the window at the precise rows of white markers, I was reminded of how fragile life can be. I was deeply moved to think of the sacrifice that so many have made. Soon our family will make the journey to another national cemetery where the earthly remains of a good man will be interred.

Tom Perrin stood for all the right things. He loved his family. He was a patriot who served his country. He was faithful to his Lord and to the churches he belonged to. He was a good businessman who had high integrity. He was a good friend to many. He was generous with his time and his resources. He was a pragmatist who saw life in clear terms. He didn't claim to know the future but he did all he could to prepare for what might come. A man, who said more than a few times that he wasn't going to buy any green bananas, was thankful for the life he had been given. His legacy is enduring. It has been my honor to be his son-in-law.

Heavens to Betsy!

We say some strange things. One that always confused me: "I'm just beside myself." Does that mean there are two of me standing here? One is plenty. Or how about: "Heavens to Betsy!" No one knows who Betsy was or why heaven was involved.

Some of these sayings have an easily understood back story. A "scapegoat" comes from Jewish history. A scapegoat is a person who is a convenient fall-guy or unfairly blamed for problems. The concept originally comes from Leviticus, in which a goat is designated to driven into the desert symbolically bearing the sins of the community.

What if you were trying to learn English and heard some of these?

- As Cool as a Cucumber ...
- Hold Your Horses ...
- Kick the Bucket ...
- Blue in the Face ...
- Storm in a Teacup ...
- Head in The Clouds ...
- Dead as a Doornail

I'm certain people have their favorites and every culture has their strange idioms. The truth of the matter is that communication is hard enough without navigating through colloquialisms. But that doesn't mean we shouldn't exercise more diligence in expressing our thoughts and feelings.

It might be as easy as falling off a log or you could gum up the works. I'm not pulling your leg that you probably have bats in your belfry. See how easy this is? You try it.

It Used to Be a Church

Many Atlantans are familiar with Fred Craddock through his association with the Candler School of Theology. Early in his ministry he served a church in the hills of eastern Tennessee. Like a number of small churches, the congregation mostly consisted of individuals and families who had lived and worked in the area for a long time. As a young pastor, Craddock tried to open the hearts and minds of his members to reach out to new people moving into the community. The nearby Oak Ridge National Laboratory was expanding, and new jobs were attracting new neighbors.

Craddock's efforts to launch an outreach program were rebuffed. One man told him, "They wouldn't fit in here." Another made a motion in a church conference that in order for someone to become a member he or she had to own property in the county. The pastor spoke in opposition to the motion, but it passed.

Years later, the Craddocks were on vacation in the area and decided to drive by the church to see how things were going. When they pulled into the parking lot of the old building, they were amazed at the number of cars, trucks, and motorcycles. A sign over the door announced that the church was now a BBQ restaurant. Obviously, people from all over the area had discovered it. When the Craddocks went inside and looked around, he couldn't help it. He said to his wife: "It's a good thing it's not a church anymore or these people couldn't be in here."

Rise Up, O Church of God!

Somebody said to me this morning: "So, this is the end, right?" I knew what he meant. Are we seeing the close of history unfolding? Is the fulfillment of prophecy so apparent that it is most certainly the end of days?

Perhaps there are two things we all need to do right now. The first and most important must be to bathe our world in prayer. Let's pour out our hearts to the Father. Let's make ourselves available to the moving and prompting of the Holy Spirit. Let's claim the peace that He promises and follow Paul's advice: "Don't worry about anything but pray about everything. Tell God what you need and thank Him for all He has done" (Philippians 4:6).

The second I believe is to care for what matters most. Paul also wrote: "Fix your thoughts on what is true, and honorable, and right, and pure, and lovely, and admirable. Think about things that are excellent and worthy of praise" (Philippians 4:8). What fits that description in your life? I imagine that the 'what' quickly becomes the 'who.'

Evil spreads like a devastating cancer. We have seen its face and felt its destructive power. But evil didn't first appear on the streets of Paris last Friday night. It isn't found just in a twisted, perverse ideology that destroys life and relishes death.

When ISIS and its ilk fade from the scene, evil will find another way to diminish humanity and oppose divine truth. There is a battle underway according to Paul: "Be strong in the Lord and in His mighty power. Put on all God's armor so that you will be able to stand firm against all strategies of the devil. For we are not fighting against flesh and blood enemies, but against evil rulers and authorities of the unseen world, against might power in this dark world, and evil spirits in the heavenly places" (Ephesians 6:10-12).

Evil will have its day but its reign is temporary. An empty cross and an empty tomb speak to a different conclusion. Even so, come quickly Lord Jesus.

A Walk in the Dark

Let's go for a walk. I need to stretch my legs. It's a beautiful day. It's time for some exercise.

There are a number of reasons why we take a walk. Most often, it is not out of necessity. We have cars, bikes, and public transportation so we don't have to walk ... far.

If we get thirsty, we can walk to the refrigerator or the water fountain. We can just turn on the tap or reach for a bottle.

What if we had to walk, not a few feet, but a number of miles to find water? In too many places around the world, water is not so easy to obtain. Clean water is even more difficult to find.

Sometimes people will begin their walk to the water before the sun comes up. The two-way trip can take most of a day.

We need water to survive. When we say "I'm thirsty" we don't normally mean we have reached a crisis point. We just want something to drink.

We partner with World Vision on several fronts. This week has been the Matthew 25 Challenge. I hope it has been eye and heart-opening for those who have participated. Much of the work of World Vision is to provide clean water for people in many parts of the world. Last year 4.6 million new people were able to have clean water. Many of them were children.

From their website: "We believe in children. Water changes the lives of children. They have better health, improved nutrition, and can go to school instead of spending the day fetching water."

The next time you go for a walk, remember those who walk to survive. The next time you sit down to enjoy a meal, remember those near and far who may go hungry today. The next time you put on a warm coat, remember those who shiver in the cold. We can make a difference.

Press On

I love the story of Esther in the Bible. The name of God is never mentioned but you sense His presence, protection, and provision throughout. Esther was a courageous woman who seized her moment, a moment that could have easily cost her life. When her kinsman, Mordecai, came to her to tell her the grave danger the Jews were facing, Esther realized her dilemma. She could only approach the king if he summoned her. If she broke protocol, he could have her executed. The knowledge she then possessed that her people would be exterminated weighed heavily on her heart. What would she do?

Mordecai's message to her: "Don't think for a moment that because you're in the palace you will escape when all other Jews are killed. If you keep quiet at a time like this, deliverance and relief for the Jews will arise from some other place, but you and your relatives will die. Who knows if perhaps you were made queen for just such a time as this?"

To her credit, her reply was decisive and bold. She sent word to call the people to a solemn assembly of prayer and fasting. She also made it clear that she would take the risk. She would go before the king.

We know how the story ends. The king welcomed Esther, granted her requests. Esther's strategy to expose the villain in the story worked beautifully. Mordecai was rewarded. The people were saved. A strong woman rose to the occasion.

People who press on despite the obstacles and difficulties are inspiring, aren't they? You and I may never face a challenge like the one that confronted Esther, but we are called to persevere, to endure in our circumstances. Like Esther, there is Someone who is always near, always able, even when it is hard to see Him at work. I believe in the old saying: "When you cannot trace His hand, trust His heart."

How do we respond to a loving God who is generous, gracious, and giving? We do it best when we seize our moments to influence and impact the lives around us. I can imagine God cheering on Esther when she displayed her selfless bravery. I can imagine God cheering us on when we do the right thing, regardless. We were born for such moments!

Unstoppable

I guess they are trying to hype the rugged safety and security of their new SUV. Threatening skies, rumbles of thunder form the backdrop of a family outing in their new vehicle. The narrator scoffs at the idea that their brand new car has anything to fear from Mother Nature. The tag line: Unstoppable.

Really? How many times do we need a reminder that man vs. nature is often an unfair contest. Hurricanes, tornadoes, typhoons, floods, ice storms, blizzards, drought, thunderstorms, and heavy winds come to mind.

In 1974, our seminary was in the path of a tornado that was carving its way through Louisville, Kentucky. Hearing the sound, watching the funnel cloud coming straight at me, I don't remember thinking I was unstoppable; I thought that tornado was unstoppable.

Surveying the damage after Hurricane Andrew crushed South Florida in 1992, I felt small and defenseless in the face of such destructive power. I never felt the need to thrust out my chest, shake my fist at the heavens, and shout, "Bring it on!"

Nature did bring it and we were helpless to resist such power.

I know the commercial was not suggesting that Mother Nature is no threat. I know they are just trying to sell the next generation of a popular SUV. Still, a little more humility is called for.

I think that is part of the human dilemma. We seem to be able to convince ourselves that we are invincible, indestructible ... until an accident occurs or a doctor gives us bad test results. James wrote: "How do you know what will happen tomorrow? For your life is like the morning fog – it's" here a little while, then it's gone."

Perhaps it is time to drag out an old cliché: "I may not know what the future holds, but I do know Who holds the future."

We can live in fear or we can live in trust. The only thing that is truly unstoppable is the love of God.

Expanding My World

For as long as I can remember, I knew about missionaries. From the time they let me go to Sunbeams, I heard stories about these people who told people about Jesus in various places around the world. Missionaries came to our church, they stayed in our home, we met them at Foreign Missions week at Ridgecrest every summer, and mom would read devotionals about them at mealtime.

We used to joke that you could tell a missionary by the Bible in one hand and a slide projector in the other one. It's not joking matter to consider what many have sacrificed to answer God's call. Many of us have attended commissioning services where we got a deeper sense of the cost these men, women, children, and extended families were willing to pay.

Many have traveled far more extensively than I have, but I will always carry treasured memories of missionaries in the field in Colombia, Thailand, Burma, Ghana, Mexico, and here in the states. You marvel at their skill, determination, passion, conviction, and compassion. You hear about their victories, disappointments, and frustrations. Again and again, they thank you for support, interest, and prayers. Every one of them stressed that prayer was what they needed most.

While it is discouraging to see Christmas becoming more and more secularized, I do see signs of hope. I see individuals and families who are moving away from getting and giving for themselves toward serving and supporting great causes. God plants us in a sphere of influence that is unique. We are all called to make a positive difference in our world. The most generous people I have known are also the most grateful people I have known. There's a reason that Scripture tells us that God loves a cheerful giver!

Stick the Landing

Okay, I have to admit I don't watch a great deal of gymnastic or figure skating competition. My interest in sports tracks along what most guys enjoy, obsess over, blow out of proportion, and develop inexplicable amount of trivial knowledge about. I have inspired more than a few eye rolls, head shakes, and expressions of exasperation. I am not alone in this sad fraternity. It helps to remember that 'fan' is short for 'fanatic.'

There seems to be a fine line between obsession and dedication. In any pursuit in life, passion, determined effort, keen focus, and skill development are necessary attributes ... perhaps not for the guy in the stands or in front of the TV ... but certainly for the competitor.

Usually, the only time I watch gymnasts is during the Olympics. I see these remarkable athletes who demonstrate such control over their minds and bodies as they seek scores that approach perfection. Regardless of the nations or teams they represent, they are appropriately applauded when they perform at a high level. One of the most obvious goals is to stick the landing.

Definition: When a gymnast lands a tumbling pass, vault, or dismount without moving his/her feet, it is referred to as sticking the landing. The aim of every gymnast is to stick -- if the gymnast moves his/her feet at all it is a deduction.

Perhaps another way to say this is with the phrase 'finishing well.' You don't have to be a world-class athlete to want to finish well. This past weekend, a woman's life was celebrated. She was my favorite teacher. I would guess that many Garden Hills Elementary alums in Atlanta would say the same. Virginia Powell was not just an amazing educator; she was deeply invested in the lives of her students. She taught with grace and compassion while demanding and expecting the best from her pupils. She was woman of deep faith, a person who made a lasting difference.

She stuck the landing. I was honored to be one of her students.

Blessed

This is a bit dated but can you guess who said these words? "Happiness is not on my list of priorities. I just deal with day-to-day things. If I'm happy, I'm happy – and if I'm not, I don't know the difference. You know these are yuppie words, happiness and unhappiness. It's not happiness or unhappiness; it's either blessed or unblessed. As the Bible says, 'Blessed is the man who walketh not in the counsel of the ungodly.' Now, that must be a happy man. Knowing that you are the person you were put on earth to be – that's much more important than just being happy."

I've met a lot of unhappy people. If happiness depends on circumstances, it doesn't take much to be unhappy. Happiness seems to come and go, turn on a dime. It seems we have to have something far deeper and more lasting than happiness.

I've never met an unblessed person. I've met plenty of people who either ignore their blessings or feel they are somehow owed more. I've met people who have chosen to focus on the pain and disappointment of life and never quite see that, even when the storms are fierce, that good can result. People who have experienced tragedy and suffering often speak of lessons learned and character strengthened.

Paul wrote to the Romans: "We can rejoice, too, when we run into problems and trials, for we know they are good for us – they help us learn to endure. And endurance develops strength of character in us, and character strengthens our confident hope of salvation. And this expectation will not disappoint us. For we know how dearly God loves us, because He has given us the Holy Spirit to fill our hearts with love" (Romans 5:3-5).

Nobody said it was going to be easy or pain-free. Life can be cruel, crushing our spirits under the weight of hurt and difficulty. Yet, we don't have to face the hardships without hope. Our blessings include ourselves – mind, spirit, body; our friends and family; our community; and most importantly, the God who will sustain us.

You are blessed. Count your blessings. Start now. I dare you to stop.

By the way, the man quoted above gave an interview to Rolling Stones magazine in 1991. When the interviewer asked him if he was happy, that's how Bob Dylan responded.

"And Another Thing…"

Don't you hate that? You think someone is just about finished and then he winds up again and keeps going. It's as bad as a pastor saying the fateful words: "In conclusion" – you know the preacher ain't done yet! We all know what it means when the preacher takes off the watch and sets it on the pulpit – absolutely nothing.

It would be okay if "another thing" really added value. There are times when I finish a sermon but keep preaching anyway. Sometimes we just don't know when we're done. When the eyes of our listeners look like doughnuts, we ought to recognize "glazed" for what it actually means.

There are times, though, when "another thing" is worth hearing or knowing or experiencing. In the book of Lamentations, there is this wonderful message: "The unfailing love of the Lord never ends! By His mercies we have been kept from utter destruction. Great is His faithfulness; His mercies begin afresh each day. I say to myself, 'The Lord is my inheritance; therefore, I will hope in Him'" (Lamentations 3:22-24).

It's like Jeremiah is saying, "And another thing." His people were suffering greatly, in large part because of their disobedience and stubbornness. Even so, God chose to extend mercy. He gave them a reason to hope.

We, too, can be the architects of our own messes. Some of the difficulty we experience is because of poor choices, hard-headedness, and foolishness. In those times, I'm glad for "another thing." I need second chances. I need grace. I need to be forgiven. I need hope that will not disappoint.

Perhaps you need "another thing" right about now. Great is His faithfulness. His mercies are new every day!

Gotcha!

We live in a day when vulnerability is a fact of life. With cell phone cameras catching awkward, embarrassing moments, "journalists" looking for dirt, politicians who play loose with the truth, exposés of sexual abuse and oppression lighting up the news, our society is painfully open to "gotcha" sound bites and video clips.

We might think this is a product of our 24-7, nothing is off limits age, but Jesus was often confronted with the "gotcha" crowd. In a study of Mark's gospel, you can encounter numerous confrontations when His critics and opponents tried to trap and discredit Him. Finding their efforts futile, they finally conspired to kill Him.

One of those attempts is found in all of the synoptic gospels. Frustrated because they had such difficulty cornering Jesus on theological and cultural issues, they decided to go political. Sounds familiar, doesn't it?

"Teacher, we know how honest You are. You are impartial and don't play favorites. You teach the way of God truthfully. Now tell us – is it right to pay taxes to Caesar or not?"

You would think Jesus was subjected to a modern-day press conference with loaded questions and not-so-subtle insinuations. Surely they had Him this time. He would be walking another fine line of insulting His Jewish brethren or promoting civil disobedience.

As usual, they had underestimated their man. Jesus deftly called for a Roman coin. "Whose picture is on this?" In response to the obvious answer, Jesus said, "Give Caesar what belongs to him and give God what belongs to God."

This really wasn't about taxation; it was about truth. Instead of trying to trap Jesus, I wished they would have tried trusting Jesus. They would keep on trying to trap Jesus until they thought they had won. How sad. The Truth stood before them and they couldn't see. They were the victims of their own "gotcha" moment.

Who's in Charge Here?

Jim Carrey played the lead role in *"Bruce Almighty"* released in 2003. Carrey's character was Bruce Nolan, a TV reporter who suffers a series of setbacks. Angry about his life, he complains to God (played by noted agnostic Morgan Freeman) that He is not doing His job correctly. God decides to offer Nolan the chance to try being God for one week. The results are predictable, but the movie at least stirs one's imagination.

What would I do if I were God for even a short period of time? What would I fix? What would I stop? How could I do better than the real Almighty?

People who have a God complex are not unusual. One such individual became a patient of a psychiatrist. In their first session, the doctor wasn't quite certain about the man's situation, but he began with: "I'm not fully aware of your problem, so perhaps you should start at the very beginning." His new patient responded, "Of course." Clearing his throat, the man said, "In the beginning, I created the heavens and the earth ..."

Who is more foolish? Is it the person who does not believe in God or is it the person who thinks he could do a better job than God?

Let's be honest. We don't have to look very far to see the struggle and suffering that surrounds us. The brilliant physicist Stephen Hawking, who suffered with ALS, was often asked if he believed in God. In one interview, he said, "Before we understand science, it is natural to believe that God created the universe. But now science offers a more convincing explanation. What I meant by 'we would know the mind of God' is, we would know everything that God would know, if there were a God, which there isn't. I'm an atheist."

Another brilliant man who lived 2000 years ago, was convinced otherwise. He wrote to Christians in Rome: "For ever since the world was created, people have seen the earth and sky. Through everything God made, they can clearly see His invisible qualities – His eternal power and divine nature. So, they have no excuse for not knowing God" (Romans 1:20).

Who's right? Both of those very accomplished men have tasted death. They now know the truth. At my advanced age, I have realized that the longer I live, the more I don't know. Can I conclude with my limited knowledge that there can't possibly be a God? The darkness of evil, the inexplicable suffering, the depravity of humanity all seems to point to a nonexistent deity or one who is powerless or uncaring to change this world.

Then I look at the cross. I see a ravaged figure bearing the sin of every person – Stephen Hawking, the Apostle Paul, me and everyone who has lived or will live. The God dismissed by the brilliant physicist displayed His true character by defeating the power of sin, evil, and death. I'll let God be God. I may not understand His ways or thoughts, but I'd rather trust Him than depend on finite minds even as brilliant as Hawking.

If It's Up to Me...

Have you ever wondered how you would do if it was up to you? I remember standing on a foul line at the end of a basketball game with a one-and-one situation. I was ten years old. Make the first free throw, you get a second. Make 'em both, we win. No pressure, right?

You want to know what happened? I made both shots, of course. Then I went on to a successful career in the NBA. Then I woke up. Actually, I was only 10 at the time but I can still remember that moment. Our team went 29-1 that year, the best team I ever played on, I was really glad that number of losses stayed at one. It was up to me and I got it right ... that time.

In settings far more important, people have wondered what would happen if it was up to them. An airline pilot in horrific weather ... a surgeon in the midst of a life-or-death procedure ... an executive with the fate of the company at stake ... a combat soldier with comrades in danger.

For most of us, life might not be so dramatic but there are those moments. Parents wonder if they can get it right when raising their kids ... teachers who yearn to challenge students to excel ... friends who know they need to tell someone they really care about the truth about destructive behavior ... pastors who need to be bold enough to lead with conviction ... voters who know a ballot represents a stewardship of freedom.

Leaders find themselves in critical moments all the time. There are moments when there is no one else to ask, no one else to turn to, no one else with the responsibility. The best leaders I have known fell forward, not backward. I never met a good leader who didn't make mistakes. But the really effective ones owned their decisions. They didn't blame others. They didn't make excuses. Most often, their errors led to better leadership. They were willing and able to try again. They learned and grew.

Leaders are everywhere. If you have influence over just one person, you are a leader. There will be moments when it's your turn. It will be up to you. Take a deep breath. Calm yourself. Step up to the line. Drain that shot.

"I'm So Glad You Came"

I overheard a conversation recently on a Sunday morning. I was waiting to speak to a first-time guest. One of our members was there ahead of me. After a few welcoming comments and questions, our member held out her hand and said with feeling, "I'm so glad you came."

I can't read minds but I can tell a look. The smile on that young woman's face told me that she recognized authentic friendliness. We have many challenges as a church, but I am always grateful to see people genuinely care.

Caring reaches far beyond the Sunday morning service. We know that. In a hospital room with a sick friend, in a neighboring home with a lonely senior, in a harried office with a struggling colleague, in a classroom with a feeling-left-out youth, at the register with an overwhelmed sales person, in a restaurant with a worn-out server ... the moments are plentiful, if we choose to seize them.

Authentic faith involves investment. The good guy in Jesus' story about the man on the Jericho road was an unexpected hero. Samaritans were despised and dismissed. The one who stopped to help a severely injured traveler has inspired the building of hospitals, schools, and helping organizations around the world.

The ministry of Jesus wasn't a display of power; it was a demonstration of compassion. The Lord of lords and the King of kings stooped to wash the dirty feet of His disciples. Then He told them to apply the lesson.

Whose feet have we washed lately? Whose battered life has received empathetic concern and action from us recently? Where has our faith showed up? When is the last time we extended our hands and hearts to those who might really need authentic compassion?

I learned the hard lesson years ago. Church isn't for me or any other already-convinced person. Church is for the people who are disconnected, disenfranchised, discarded, distracted, and defeated. The "least of these" might be right next to us – people who need hope and help.

The Bible tells us that Mary wrapped Jesus in swaddling clothes. One writer noted that swaddling clothes were a symbol, not of poverty as some have tried to characterize her action but of maternal care, affection, and tenderness. He wrote: "What are you wrapping people you meet in? Are you swaddling them in compassion, tenderness, generosity, and devotion?"

Perhaps you might hear someone tell you: "I'm so glad you came."

Any Color You Want

Henry Ford, according to Wikipedia, was a famous "American captain of industry and a business magnate, the founder of the Ford Motor Company, and the sponsor of the development of the assembly line technique of mass production." He was also known for some pithy quotes.

The one most folks might know concerns the ground-breaking Model T automobile: "You can have it in any color you want, as long as it is black."

Some of my favorites:

- "Don't find fault; find a remedy."
- "Whether you think you can, or you think you can't – you're right."
- "To do more for the world than the world does for you – that is success."

Ford was more than a brilliant capitalist; he was progressive in his practices and innovative in his business. He was also generous. That quality was expressed in his association with Martha Berry. The long-lasting friendship between Martha Berry and the Fords began when, in 1921, Miss Berry accepted a dinner invitation from Thomas Edison, who at the time was a friend of the Fords. At this dinner, Martha Berry met the Fords and began her life-long friendship with them.

What a combination! Martha Berry's commitment to making educational opportunities available for any person and Henry Ford's willingness to do more for the world that the world did for him changed many lives.

We can follow Ford's advice. Success is indeed making a difference for all the right reasons.

Please Get It Right

Did you happen to see Russell Crowe's "biblically inspired epic" entitled *Noah*? The movie had so many rewrites that the final version left most people scratching their heads. Scott Franklin, who produced the film, said, "Noah is a very short section of the Bible with a lot of gaps, so we definitely had to take some creative expression in it. But I think we stayed very true to the story and didn't really deviate from the Bible, despite the six-armed angels."

Really? Leave it to Hollywood to produce movies with the generic disclaimer: based on a true story. Evidently that gives you license to push your own agenda at the expense of the truth. Everybody loves a good story, but it seems in vogue to take the Bible as a source and then disregard it.

Louis Zamperini died at 97 July of 2014. This amazing man survived. He survived the reckless years as a youth on the streets of Los Angeles. He survived the crash of his B-24 bomber while on a rescue mission. He survived 47 days at sea in a life raft before being captured by the Japanese. He survived the torture and degradation inflicted by his Japanese captors. He survived the anger, the bitterness, and the determination to return to Japan and hunt down his tormentors. He survived posttraumatic stress disorder and heavy drinking. He survived the impending doom of a wrecked marriage due to his fits of rage fueled by his alcohol binges and horrible memories.

His wife Cynthia was desperate to help her husband. A young evangelist was in Los Angeles for a series of services. She had gone, hoping for encouragement and fortitude while she listened to Billy Graham preach. She asked Louie to go with her, but he refused. She didn't give up, either. She finally convinced him to go with her.

His life changed that night. He found Christ. The drinking stopped; the rage dissipated. He still wanted to return to Japan, but not for revenge. He wanted to find the Japanese soldiers and officers who had cause so much pain for him and too many others so that he could offer his forgiveness.

Books, movies, documentaries ... all were written or planned, but the story could not gain enough traction. Then Laura Hillenbrand, the author of the best-seller Seabiscuit, found an old clipping about the famous racehorse. On the back of that newspaper there was a story about young phenom who had run in the 1936 Olympics in Hitler's Germany, Louie Zamperini. A phone call started a relationship that became another best-seller, Unbroken. With the resulting success, the movie rights were snapped up by Angeline Jolie. The film was finished in time for Zamperini to see it, albeit twenty minutes at a time.

The story of Louis Zamperini is a tale of unbelievable courage. It is a story of triumphant faith. Please, Hollywood, get it right.

Changing Lives

These words are written on a tomb of an Anglican bishop in Westminster Abbey:

> When I was young and free and my imagination had no limits, I dreamed of changing the world. As I grew older and wiser, I discovered the world would not change.
>
> So I shortened my sights somewhat and decided to change my country. But it, too, seemed immovable.
>
> As I grew into my twilight years, in one desperate attempt, I settled for changing only my family, those closest to me, But, alas, they would have none of it.
>
> And now as I lie on my deathbed, I suddenly realize: If I had only changed myself first, then by example I would have changed my family. From their inspiration and encouragement, I would have been able to better my country and, who knows, I may have even changed the world.

We cannot leave our own spiritual growth and development for someone else. I need to take responsibility for my life. You need to do the same for yours. No one can pray your prayers. No one can settle issues of faith in your heart but you. If I am to be a fully devoted follower of Christ, I must begin with self-surrender.

Take a step today. Your journey will take you places you never dreamed. Change is inevitable so let's make the most of every moment.

Freedom

Austrian Viktor Frankl died in 1997. He was a famous neurologist and psychiatrist. He was also a survivor of the Holocaust. During that horrible time in history and in his life, Frankl lost his father, mother, brother, and wife. His family was wiped out; all except his sister perished in the death camps of Nazi Germany. How could he pick up the pieces of his shattered life? How could he, with every possession lost, every value destroyed, most of his family murdered … suffering from brutality, hunger, disease, miserable conditions … how could he dare to believe his life was worth fighting for? He saw many who died, not from the ovens or the beatings or the horrific health issues, but from lack of hope. They just gave up and died. Why didn't he die? Why didn't he give up? He found a way to go on. He never surrendered his hope.

This is what he wrote: "One day, a few days after the liberation, I walked through the country, past flowering meadows for miles and miles, toward the town near the camp. Larks rose to the sky and I could hear their joyous song. There was no one to be seen for miles around; there was nothing but the wide earth and sky and the larks' jubilation and the freedom of space. I stopped, looked around and up to the sky – and then I went down on my knees. At that moment there was very little I knew of myself or of the world … I had but one sentence in mind … always the same: I called to the Lord from my narrow prison and He answered me in the freedom of space. How long I knelt there and repeated this sentence, memory can no longer recall. But I know on that day, in that hour, my new life started. Step by step I progressed until I again became a human being."

We can live without a lot of things, but we cannot live without hope. Whatever is happening in your life today, there is always room for hope, the freedom of space ... and in that space One waits for you to reach out to Him. Does that sound corny to you? Why don't you try it? Who knows what freedom awaits?

What Do You Need?

Our group of CBF pastors had traveled into the hills of northern Thailand. We were introduced to a wonderful couple who served among the Bisu people. Kirk and Susie had brought their family to this primitive setting – it was a long way from Texas.

We listened as they told stories about trying to overcome the lack of trust, to allay the suspicion, to understand the culture in the village. They told us about the mixed bag of superstition and Buddhism that formed the basis of the religious life in the community. They showed us the spirit houses where the village spirits lived. They explained how the men would have to pass through the spirit gates at the edge of the forest to appease the forest gods. On the way home from their work in the woods, streams, and fields, they would have to rub against the gates to make sure they didn't take any of the spirits back to their huts.

How do you begin to bear witness to the freedom, grace, and love of the Gospel in such a place? These Americans did not try to import customs and traditions from back home. They learned the language. They ate the food. They abided by the ways of the people.

While supported by Cooperative Baptist Fellowship resources, Kirk was also working in association with the Wycliffe Bible Translators to develop a written language for the Bisu. The tribe had migrated from Myanmar (Burma) years ago. They had never had a written language. Using Scripture as a guide, Kirk was making it possible for the villagers to not only receive a language they could see and read as well as speak; he was also introducing them to the truth of God's Word.

Here's an example. In the culture of the village, you would never come to the door and knock at a neighbor's door. Instead you would stand in the yard and call out their name. So Revelation 3:20 ("Behold, I stand at the door and knock ...") became "I stand outside and call your name."

As our time was ending, we asked this wonderful family, "What do you need?" They explained that CBF gifts provided many things, but the one thing they really needed was prayer. The work was hard and slow. Only one young woman had professed faith in Christ in all the time they had been there. I turned to Kirk and asked one more time, "What do you need?" He looked down at his feet. "These boots get a lot of wear and tear. I probably need to get some new ones." I asked him what size he wore. Then I started unlacing mine. I had bought boots for the trip and they were still in good shape. I was just glad they fit him.

When we left the village that day, I left behind more than a pair of boots. Part of me will always be there, knowing that we are helping to support a family willing to sacrifice so much to be faithful to their call to serve.

Living the Dream

Something special happened on Saturday, November 19th. 55 year-old Joe Thomas, Sr. got his wish. While such statistics are not definite with the NCAA, it is believed that Joe was the oldest D-1 football player to take the field for South Carolina State. His game stat: a run for 3 yards.

Joe's story includes overcoming economic and physical challenges growing up in Blackville, South Carolina. In high school, he was a gifted, strong player who played on both sides of the ball. His athletic career seemed to come to an end with no prospects of attending or playing in college.

Fast forward. His son, Joe Jr., was a budding star at State. Dad decided to join him in the classroom and on the field. His son, who now plays for the Green Bay Packers, helped him put a highlight video so he could walk on to the team. They never got to play together but Joe Senior would not give up. Since his first interview with the head coach in 2012 until that Saturday, he patiently went to work to earn his shot. Four years later, his tenacity paid off. His son said of his dad, "When my teammates first found out, they'd say things like, 'Your dad is coming for your spot.' But he's a grown man, and I wasn't going to get in the way of his dreams. I'm happy for him."

What gets in the way of your dreams? Reading a more complete version of the story of Joe Thomas, you get a sense that he had plenty of moments when he could have quit. He built a business that hit the skids. He fell behind on his financial obligations. He couldn't find a job that did not require a college education. So he asked his wife, Sarah, to help him fill out a college application, then drove the 40 miles to the SC State campus. He asked his son if he would be okay with him if his father joined him in college.

I like stories of overcomers. I like being challenged to push through even when obstacles are plenty. Joe is living the dream. I hope we can live ours.

The Right Thing, the Godly Thing

I have always admired him yet I know next to nothing about him. Only a handful of verses mention him. Someone described him as the forgotten man in an unforgettable story. He was engaged to a young woman in his hometown. Imagine how he felt when he learned that his bride-to-be was pregnant. He is portrayed as a just man, a man who did the right things. At that moment when his life was being shattered, he had a choice. He could do the right thing. He could divorce her, shame her, and move on. He was well within his rights to do so. Instead of the right thing, he did the godly thing. I've never had an angel appear with a message from on high, but this guy did. While he was asleep, he had a vision that changed the course of his life. Instead of doing the right thing, Joseph did the godly thing. He kept his vow to Mary. He provided a home for the infant Jesus. We last see him in Luke 2, fulfilling his role as husband and father. A man who was used to doing the right thing had done the godly thing.

It almost seems contradictory to think that you could choose to do the godly thing over the right thing. As early as 1933, Pastor Dietrich Bonhoeffer recognized the lurking evil in Adolph Hitler. He took a public stance at a time when it was increasingly dangerous to speak out against the rising Nazi regime. In 1939, he was invited to the United States and urged by friends in America to stay because of the dangers he faced in Germany. They tried to convince him of all the good things he could do. It seemed to be the right thing. Bonhoeffer chose otherwise. He wrote to a friend: "I must live through this difficult period in our national history with the people of Germany."

Bonhoeffer returned to his native land. It cost him dearly. Arrested and charged with participating in the resistance against the Third

Reich and conspiracy against the Fuhrer, he spent several years in prison. In April of 1945, he was taken to the Flossenbűrg concentration camp. He was hanged at dawn on April 9. Two weeks later, American troops from my dad's outfit, the 90th Division, would liberate that camp.

I would like to think that the two are complementary – the right thing and the godly thing – but sometimes the choice has to be made. Paul wrote that Jesus did the godly thing: "Though He was God, He did not demand and cling to His rights as God. He made Himself nothing, He took the humble position of a slave and appeared in human form" (Philippians 2:6,7). Jesus had the right to the crown of gold but He chose the crown of thorns. At Christmas, it matters to recognize the godly thing – and then do it.

A Gatekeeper in the House of the Lord

Jim Hudson died this past Tuesday. On the way home from church this past Sunday, Jim suffered a heart attack and was rushed to the hospital. He never regained consciousness and slipped away around noon, surrounded by his family. His death was a shock to them and to so many who knew and loved him.

Sunday morning, he was in his usual place, taking care of us. A word of welcome, a handshake, a worship guide, and a smile were his tools. This kind and gracious gentleman, gentle man, served his church for many years. Often, he was the first to greet a guest. Many passed by his station on their way into worship. Choir members shook his hand as they entered the loft.

The men and women, who participate in this vital ministry of a church, faithfully serve before, during, and after services. They help create positive first impressions as they minister to those who walk through the doors for their initial visit. They are vigilant to guard people's safety and security. They view the people who come not as a crowd but as brothers and sisters in the family. They assist in ways that many will never know.

In Psalm 84, the songwriter wrote of the joy experienced in the courts of the Lord: "How lovely is Your dwelling place, O Lord Almighty. I long, yes, I faint with longing to enter the courts of the Lord. With my whole being, body, and soul, I will shout joyfully to the living God … A single day in your courts is better than a thousand anywhere else! I would rather be a gatekeeper in the house of my God than live the good life in the homes of the wicked."

Jim was a gatekeeper in the house of the Lord. His absence will be painfully noted. Our consolation is the certainty that he will celebrate his first Christmas in heaven. Jim, you will be missed.

Dumb Things You Say…or Do…or Think

My mom told us we shouldn't call people dumb. Calling people stupid was a capital offense. But you know we all say, do, and think dumb from time to time. Here are just a few examples:

- Guy robs a convenient store wearing his motorcycle helmet, but he forgot that his name was plastered on his helmet. Bright.

- In a courtroom, the attorney asks the witness if the man who robbed her was in the courtroom. The guy at the defense table stood up. Very helpful.

- A girl I know (who will remain nameless) once asked her father how to change the blinker fluid in her car. She was serious.

- Just before he was hit by a Confederate sharpshooter, General John Sedgwick reportedly said, "They couldn't hit an elephant at this distance." Wrong.

- Mohammed Ali to the flight attendant who had told him to fasten his seatbelt: "Superman don't need no seatbelt." The attendant replied, "Superman don't need no airplane."

- Vice President Dan Quayle speaking at Nasa: "Greetings fellow astronauts!" Spacy.

- In the 8th grade, Mark Wilbanks makes a basket for the other team. Well, it was a good shot.

We could all make a list, right? Sometimes we speak before we think, act before we consider the consequences. We are fallible, prone to mistakes. We don't get it right all the time.

But there's dumb and then there is DUMB.

- I'll have a double cheeseburger, large fries, and a Diet Coke. We need balance.

- I don't need to buckle up; I'm only going to the store.

- Oh, that engine light? It's been on so long I just ignore it.

- I know my family has a history of _____ disease but it won't affect me.

There's dumb and DUMB and then there is DUMB. Like the guy in Luke 12 known as the rich fool. He decided by his words, actions, and thoughts that he was the master of his domain. He took full credit for his good fortune, "I'll sit back and say to myself, 'My friend, you have enough stored away for years to come. Now take it easy! Eat, drink, and be merry." God had a message for him: "You fool! You will die this very night. Then who will get everything you worked for?"

No one can live his life as if there is no God and get away with it. Now that's dumb.

There's an App for That

Of course there is. A blogger named Corey Eridon has compiled some weird apps you might have to have ... or not. Here's a sample:

- Cuddlr - Cuddly, a location-based networking app. It lets you find people in your area you can cuddle with.

- Carrr Matey – This app will help you find where you parked your car, in a pirate voice.

- Demotivational Pics – An app that reminds you that, yes, things are bad and could get worse.

- Run Pee – A helpful app that can alert you in a movie that you have time to get to the restroom before you miss anything important.

- Yo – An app to aid your communication skills by saying "yo" to someone you meet.

- Spirit Story Box: Ghost Hunting Tool – An app that speaks 'ghost' will help you decipher what the ghosts around you are really saying.

There are some on the list not suitable to repeat or just too stupid to mention (even more than the ones above). Some apps are really helpful. Are you constantly running late? You may need the 'Bounce' app or the 'Running Late' app to notify your friends that you're going to be late. Or you could have enough respect for your friends to change your behavior and arrive on time for once.

There are certainly a number of apps that have proved to be a great way to access information, accomplish tasks, schedule appointments, etc. I just wonder how tied we are to all our technological wizardry.

One man's tombstone reflects our current reality: "I was so busy programming my life that I forgot to live."

Whether you are photo shopping your cat or planning your next trip to the john, remember that more information is not always better. Life still comes down to what and who matters most. Someone has said that the best app is a face-to-face conversation. You can get all the updates you could ever want.

"You're Not the One I Wanted."

From Max Lucado's *You'll Get Through This*:

"Once, just minutes before I officiated at a wedding, the groom leaned over to me and said, 'You weren't my first choice.' Lucado responded, 'I wasn't?' Here's the rest of the conversation:

'No, the preacher I wanted couldn't make it. But thanks for filling in.'

'Sure. Anytime.'"

Lucado said he considered signing the wedding license: "Substitute."

Have you ever felt that way? Ever been someone's second, third, or worse choice? Really builds your self-image, right? Who wants to be 'settled for' or not wanted at all? It reminds of the political candidate who asked a potential voter if he had made up his mind. The man said he was down to two choices – the politician's main rival and another guy. The politician was a little miffed, "Well, who's the other guy?" The voter replied, "Anybody else."

If you have ever stood waiting and waiting to be chosen in a pick-up game or wondered why the gang went to lunch without asking you, you know the feeling. If you have ever had your heart broken by someone you cherished, you know the pain. "You're not the one I wanted."

There are times when we may feel that way about God. We may feel picked on or ignored. We may feel we don't deserve His love or attention. We may feel unworthy.

You know what? I am unworthy. I don't deserve His attention or favor. I have done nothing to earn anything from God. I might even think God could say to me, "You're not the one I wanted."

I would be wrong.

Lucado wrote: "You'll never hear such words from God. He chose you. The choice wasn't obligatory, required, compulsory, forced, or compelled. He selected you because He wanted to. You are His open, willful, voluntary choice. He walked onto the auction block where you stood, and He proclaimed, 'This child is mine.'"

And He bought you with the precious blood of His Son. I cannot make Him love me more or less than He already does. I am, you are, the one He wanted.

He wants you on His team. He wants you to sit at the table with Him. He wants you to be His forever.

Perhaps this week, we need to be reminded how precious we are to Him. When you're going through a tough time or having a bad day, remember Who loves you. You are the one He wanted.

Give Him the Glory

Russell Wilson plays quarterback for the Seattle Seahawks NFL team. He led his team to the 2015 Super Bowl. He was one play away from consecutive championships. On the one-yard line with 20 seconds to go, Wilson threw a pass on a slant route that was intended for teammate Doug Baldwin. Down 28-24, the pass reception would have won the game. New England Patriot Malcolm Butler jumped the route, intercepted the pass, and sealed the game.

In typical fashion, Wilson accepted responsibility for the play: "I put the blame on me – I'm the one who threw it. It's something you learn from, it's something you grow from."

In many ways, Russell Wilson isn't typical. In a game where huge egos are on full display, he goes about his business with higher priorities than jaw-dropping stats or staggering contracts. When he was drafted by the Seahawks with the 12th pick in the third round in 2012, few people believed that he would be the success he has proved to be. He was too small; he didn't possess an NFL arm. He just won.

If you followed him into the locker room before a game, you would notice his earphones. Most players listen to music before games. But he is listening to contemporary Christian music. Then you will see him bow by his locker to pray. "I'm not a hyped person. I try to stay relaxed," he says. During the game, you can hear him sing softly one of his favorite Gospel songs in the heat of the contest.

Wilson makes it clear when interviewed that his life isn't centered on the fame and glory of success in the NFL; his life is focused on his relationship with Jesus Christ. "It's like I put on the whole armor of God so I can take God everywhere I go – mentally, physically, and spiritually."

His life verse comes from John 3:30: "He must increase, but I must decrease."

With all his success, Russell Wilson has a firm handle on what matters most. "Win or lose, it's about Him for me. It doesn't matter the ups and downs, the good and the bad, just keep Him first."

You and I don't have to perform on a stage with millions watching. But the only Audience that matters is watching. He deserves our best even as He deserves our trust and obedience. He deserves the glory.

April 15

We normally associate April 15 with income tax deadlines. In 2013, that date took on a different meaning. At 2:49 pm, near the finish line for the Boston Marathon, two bombs exploded within 550 feet of each other on Boylston Street. Three people were killed; more than 260 people were injured by the blasts. In the devastation and confusion, many flee understandably frightened. Many others run, not away but toward the scene. Stories of compassion, bravery, and service begin to be shaped as the minutes become hours on that horrific day.

In 2014, approximately 36,000 people took part in the Boston Marathon, scheduled for Monday, April 21. Boston Strong indeed became Boston Stronger. At least one Wieucan, a young lady married here in our church who has run in numerous races and marathons, was one of the participants. I wished her good luck the Sunday before the race and promised that I would pray for her.

While much of the world's attention will be turned toward Boston, the marathon is not the big event of the weekend. "For God so loved the world that He gave His only Son, that whoever believes in Him will not perish but will have eternal life."

Those familiar words from John help to frame what happened two thousand years ago this weekend. Evil reared its ugly head then, too. Violent death suffered by the innocent took place. An excited crowd had gathered earlier in the week to watch a parade. On the darkest day in history, the cheering crowd had become a jeering mob. A young man hung broken and bleeding. His body would be enclosed in a borrowed tomb. Tears flowed, hearts were broken.

As I have heard and read the stories of those who are putting their lives back together after the Boston bombing, I am inspired by the courage and determination of those who refuse to allow this tragedy define their lives. I am encouraged by the many acts of ministry that took place that day and since.

As I reread and listen to the words of what took place 2000 years, I find strength, comfort, and assurance that sin and death falter in the face of love. The cloak of despair and darkness was ripped away to reveal the glory of the One who burst from the grave. Christ claimed victory from the jaws of defeat.

I will stand and applaud those who compete and those who finish their race on Monday, but on Sunday I will bow and worship the One who finished a race I could never win. He is risen!

Point Guard

A class reunion is bringing them back to town. In my brother's senior year, two high schools merged – North Fulton and Dykes. That transition wasn't easy, particularly when it came to blending athletic teams. John played point guard on a basketball team that was instantly much better than the year before.

Better at the game we all loved, little brother had been a gym rat. He shot for hours, increased his ball handling skills, and most of all learned the game. Point guards are like quarterbacks on a football field. The good ones not only know their position, they also know everyone else's. As the point guard brings the ball up the court, he has to recognize defenses, he has to guide the pace of the game, and he has to follow instruction from the sidelines.

John did all that well. Oh yeah, he could score, too. He could shoot over you or drive around you. But that wasn't his primary job. He had to see the floor, run the team, and distribute the ball. Dishing the ball to four other guys who each felt it was his turn wasn't easy.

For a long time, John held assist records at Anderson College and Texas – Pan Am where he played. He was a playmaker, a floor general, a key to the success of his teams. I'm not biased at all, right?

I've noticed that he continues to see the floor well, run the team, and distribute the ball. He does these things in life ... in his family life, his church ministry, his professional career. John is a great servant leader wherever God has placed him. He is a faithful steward of his time, talent, and treasure. He can still run the point but he really knows how to follow the Coach.

Among my many blessings, I have two brothers who are good and godly men. When we get together, we tell stories from back in the day – the older we get the better we were - but I have witnessed how both have played the game of life. I am a proud brother.

Halftime

In the world of sports, there are certain points in a competitive environment when scheduled or called breaks occur. In a basketball game, there are periods dictated by the clock. There are also timeouts called to correct a team's play or stop the other team's momentum. The same is true of other sports. Some coaches are known for their ability to react to what is happening on the field of play and make necessary adjustments.

I have given away a number of books in my ministry. One book stands apart as the one I have given away most often. It was written by Bob Buford, a man whose success in business ventures was unquestioned. But he came to a point in life when he realized all of his success wasn't fulfilling. He became convinced that there had to be more.

His book, *Halftime*, is a classic. If you have not read it, you should. I'll even give you a copy. The premise of the book, in my estimation, is quite simple. Living a life that is large in the ways God intended is about significance, not success.

While it does not always involve crisis, the search for meaning and fulfillment for Buford was impacted by the tragic death of his son. He could have surrendered to the overwhelming grief that broke his heart. He had reached one of those pivotal moments when he had to make adjustments. He had to recalibrate. He chose to do so from an eternal perspective. He chose to make a Kingdom difference. Today, his influence and the networks he has built with the help of other significance champions are impacting the world.

Churches have such moments. It is time to make adjustments, to recalibrate, to choose integration not segregation. One quote is appropriate here regarding churches that reinvent themselves to have maximum Gospel impact. He called them 50/50 churches – churches who allocate 50% of their resources to themselves and the other half to serving their community and the world: "The 50/50 church reaches out to serve its surrounding community, living out its proclamation of the Gospel rather than imposing an unwelcome ideology on others. Its witness is first by example, then by proclamation. It places carriers of faith back into all of the contradictions, tensions, and paradoxes of the community, rather than isolate people in an unrealistic, cloistered atmosphere for a couple of hours on Sunday morning."

Hmmm. I think he is on to something ...

Win At All Cost?

"I will not be a loser!"

This was the title of an article about Jimmy Johnson years ago when he was the new coach of the Miami Dolphins. Johnson was a successful coach at both college and professional levels of football. Today he is one of the talking heads that tells us more than we ever wanted to know about pro football. When the article was published in 1993, Johnson was a rising star. He won championships with the Miami Hurricanes and the Dallas Cowboys. He was a real success ... or was he?

In the article he was quoted as saying, "I've prepared my entire life – 48 years, 24 hours a day, 365 days a year – for 16 Sundays. Everybody out there in the world judges whether I'm a successful human being based on how I do on those Sundays. If we lose, I'm a complete bum, a worthless human being. If we win, I'm a success. That's the way the business is. I will not be a loser!"

This from a man who once said he couldn't remember his son's birthday and he "doesn't do Christmas" because it conflicts with game preparation.

I wonder how he feels about it now. He is still tied to the game, sitting at an expanded desk in a TV studio with other retired coaches and players.

The sad truth is that he is partially correct – our infatuation with sports is at an all-time high. The "What have you done for me lately?" mentality has doomed many a coach, athletic director, general manager, and player.

The Apostle Paul used a great deal of athletic imagery in his writing. He could teach Jimmy Johnson and others a few things about winning, because he had a higher purpose than winning a game or a championship. Paul kept his eyes on the ultimate victory: "I press on toward the goal for the prize of the upward call of God in Christ Jesus" (Philippians 3:14). Jimmy Johnson did his thing before an audience of thousands in the stands when he was coaching, but the only Audience that ever mattered sees our worth differently. He isn't going to count to see how many rings adorn our fingers; He is more interested in the condition of our hearts.

Every Life is Precious

Gene Stallings was old school as a player and coach. In his years of coaching, he was an assistant to some of the great coaches of his or any day – Tom Landry and Paul Bryant. Born in Paris, Texas, he was recruited to play at Texas A&M. He was one of the 'Junction Boys' who survived Bear Bryant.

Football has always played a big part in his life, but there was much more. He married Ruth Ann Jack after college graduation. Five children were born to the Stallings – four girls and a son. Their son, John Mark, was born with Down syndrome. That wasn't exactly how it was supposed to play out. Stallings wrote: "Often, I dreamed of the day when my son would carry on the family tradition of playing football. Maybe he'd play for me and for Coach Bryant. There'd be times when I'd look at one of my players, and for an instant I'd see my imaginary son."

In a cold, matter-of-fact manner, the doctor who delivered the little boy answered the worried father's question: "Is there some kind of problem?" The response: "Yes, we think maybe your baby is a mongoloid." Angry enough to hit the insensitive physician, Stallings sank to the floor in a faint. When he recovered, he made the slow walk to his wife's room to tell her the bad news. They were understandably devastated.

It was 1962; 'mongoloids' were monsters. People with Down syndrome were retarded. They were laughed at, ridiculed, avoided, ignored. Stallings had known a boy with that syndrome growing up in Paris, Texas. He and his buddies had made fun of him unmercifully. Now his son would be subjected to the same treatment.

They were going to name their son after Gene's father to carry on the family name. They decided instead to give the boy a biblical name – John Mark Stallings. Still reeling from the news, they were told that their child also had a serious heart defect. With the challenges he faced, he probably wouldn't live very long.

John Mark did die – not in a few days or a few years. He lived 46 years. He accompanied his dad to practice fields and stadiums, cheering on the teams his dad coached. He helped his dad as Gene Stallings became an advocate for the developmentally disabled. With the ever-present smile on his face, he lived life. One said of him, "He had a way of lighting up a room." Another wrote: "There weren't any lives John Mark touched that weren't made better by his influence."

There is no such thing as an unimportant life. Ask Gene Stallings. Celebrate life, every life. That's what John Mark did. You can read more of the story in *"Another Season – A Coach's Story of Raising An Exceptional Son"* (St. Martin's Press, 1997).

MRE's

Ask a veteran or an active duty soldier or Marine. Ask them what MRE's are. Some would tell you "Meals Ready to Eat" – a lot would say "Meals Rejected by Everybody." If you know a veteran old enough, he could tell you about K or C-rations. Improvements have been made since the Civil War when soldiers might carry hardtack and salt pork. Some soldiers joked that the hard crackers could stop a bullet. But providing nutritious food that would not turn the stomach has always been a challenge. These days, vacuum-sealed pouches contain a wide variety of foods, but bland is bland. If you checked the equipment and supplies a typical soldier would carry, you probably will find a bottle of Tabasco to either add some flavor or kill the taste.

Complaining has been around a long time – probably since Adam complained that Eve got the fruit first. The people of Israel complained as they were escaping the bondage of Egypt. Don't get them started on having to eat manna and quail. They moaned and whined – "It's too hot."

"There's no water." "How long until we get there?" Their gripes sank to the outrageous "We would be better off back in Egypt" whimper.

While MRE's would never be compared to culinary delights, those rations weren't designed to please the palate. They were created to be nutritious and energy-producing in eat-on-the-march conditions. The meal was never as important as the mission.

The manna God provided for the Israelites would only last a day. That required the people to trust God to provide for them every day. He had promised to deliver them. With the memory of their miraculous rescue from the clutches of Pharaoh, you would think trust would come easy. Does trust come easy to us?

God promised to deliver us. An empty cross and an empty tomb prove His power. He has promised to guide, bless, provide, correct, sustain, and redeem us. He asked us to seek Him every day. He asks us to trust Him. Does trust come easy to us?

We, too, need to remember that the mission is more important than the meal. We are a part of a great adventure He has invited us to join. Perhaps our MRE should stand for "Mission Ready to Engage."

Remembering

Memorial Day approaches. For any country who has suffered the loss of life among its citizenry, remembering their sacrifice is a sacred duty. For Americans, the last Monday in May is far more than just a holiday or break in our routine. It is a day for remembering.

On Memorial Day, we recognize and honor those who have served our country and paid the ultimate sacrifice. The day will be more poignant with the tragic news of the helicopter crash that claimed the lives of six Marines and two Nepalese soldiers. They died, not in a combat operation, but in a relief mission for those in need after another earthquake hit the region.

Every life is precious. Those who risk their lives for their comrades and their countries deserve our respect and gratitude. The families and friends they leave behind deserve our prayerful support and tribute.

In a perfect world, we would need no military or police force. We have not solved humanity's problems and ills through force of arms.

Are there times when evil must be confronted? History answers with a resounding "yes." But we yearn for the day when peace is not just the temporary cessation of hostilities. We pray for the day when the Prince of Peace will return. Perhaps it will be soon.

God does wrap Himself in the red, white, and blue, but perhaps not the way we might think. Take a look at the Christian flag. The red stands for the sacrifice of Christ for our ultimate freedom. The white stands for purity and peace. The blue represents the faithfulness of Jesus and the hope we have of heaven.

As I write this, I am looking at a picture of a 28 year-old US Army Warrant Officer, standing at parade rest. He served his country and risked his life. If, like so many, he had fallen while fighting Nazi Germany, many lives including my own would have been affected. I consider that when I think about those who have lost a loved one. As grateful as I am that my father returned safely, I cannot help but grieve over broken dreams and hearts ... people who have not been as fortunate.

Whatever you do this Memorial Day, make sure you remember.

Remember Memorial Day

Wars and rumors of wars ... Jesus warned us that they would plague humanity for all of time. There have been few periods in history when people weren't killing each other in some conflict around our globe. The horrific toll of war robs us of many things but the most costly loss is in human life. In America alone, over 683,000 died in our first 100 years. Since then, another 626,000 plus have been killed. Sons and daughters, fathers and mothers, brothers and sisters ... futures terminated, families devastated, generations gone.

One day war will cease to exist. One day no parent will have to receive the dreaded "notification of next of kin" visit. One day we will not have to escort one more flag-draped coffin to its final resting place. In this dark and dangerous world, the valley of the shadow of death will one day give way to the light of the high pasture. As we yearn for that day, we stand alongside those whose grief and loss will be too fresh and too present on this Memorial Day.

D-Day Remembered

He was 19 years old. PFC John Robertson was a soldier with Company F, 116th Infantry in the 29th Division. In the early hours of June 6, 1944, he was one of thousands storming the Normandy beaches. In his landing craft, most of the men were seasick. He recalled heaving over the side, seasick and terrified. His sergeant yelled at him to get his head down. Robertson replied, "I'm dying of seasickness, it won't make much difference." Then the ramp went down and hell arrived. Everywhere he looked, men were dying. His lieutenant was killed by a shell. One man carrying a flamethrower disappeared in a blinding flash. Men were crying, screaming, frozen in fear. Omaha Beach was taking a terrible toll. The invading forces would suffer almost 2400 casualties on that stretch of sand.

Carrying 60 pounds of gear, Robertson staggered into the surf in a foot of water and stopped. Machine gun fire raked the water as he tried to make himself small. Then he heard the rumbling of a tank from behind. He looked around and saw a Sherman tank bearing down on him. "It wasn't long before I made a quick decision. I had two choices. How I made it, I'll never know. But I got to the shingle and tried to survive."

June 6, 2018, we mark the 74th anniversary of the beginning of the assault on Fortress Europe, the beginning of the end for Hitler's Third Reich. Of the 16 million Americans who served in World War II, only about 550,000 are still alive. They may be fading but the memory of their service and sacrifice must never fade.

America

Bob Kaylor worked as a historical, perhaps hysterical, interpreter at the Gettysburg battlefield for two years. His hysterics may have come from some of the actual questions he was asked by visitors to the Civil War site:

- Did the soldiers hide behind the monuments when they fought?
- What was Abraham Lincoln's Gettysburg address? Do you mean he had a house here?
- Why were so many Civil War battles fought on National Park Service land?

Makes you proud, right? How about these answers to American History tests:

- Q. What ended in 1896? A. 1895
- Q. If you could go back in time and meet Abraham Lincoln, what would you say to him? A. Don't go to the theater.
- Part of an essay: "Soon the Constitution of the United States was adopted to secure domestic hostility. Under the constitution people enjoyed the right to bare arms.

America will celebrate her 239th birthday next weekend. For all our stumbles and challenges, our country deserves the support of her citizens. Our moral drift is frighteningly similar to the fall of other countries/kingdoms in history, which demands more, not less, of those who care about faith and values. It isn't politically correct these days, but engagement still trumps entitlement.

We may have lost some of our standing in the world these last few years, but who does the world turn to in times of disaster and conflict? Who normally is the first to respond when catastrophe strikes? Who continues to demonstrate generosity and compassion when other nations hesitate?

Yes, we have external threats that seem to grow closer each day. We live in scary times but I refuse to live in fear. Frankly, I'm more concerned about internal decay. Our pulpits need to grow bolder. Our witness needs to combine our words with our ways. We may live in a post-Christian age, but we know the truth and the truth will set us free.

Happy Birthday America ... now, go study your history.

A Day That Changed History

On this day seventy five years ago, the supreme commander of Allied forces in Europe issued the order to launch the largest amphibious military operation in history. 6000 landing craft, ships, and other vessels were carrying 176,000 troops and heading for the beaches of Normandy. 822 aircraft, some carrying paratroopers and some towing gliders, were scheduled to arrive before the landings. 13,000 bombers, fighters, and observation aircraft were mobilized to cover the invasion.

It didn't happen. Not that day, June 5, 1944. General Eisenhower had to postpone the original D-Day because of bad weather. Consulting with his staff, he realized there was a small window that would signal a break in the weather and allow the invasion to occur ... on June 6th. If he had waited until July, any element of surprise as well as the readiness of his forces would be affected. He wrote two letters to his troops on that occasion.

The first was a letter to stir his forces to accept nothing but total victory. The second was quite different. This note was written hurriedly, with words crossed out, to respond to another outcome. "Our landings in the Cherbourg-Havre area have failed ..."

He closed the message with these words: "If any blame or fault attaches to the attempt it is mine alone."

Failure is a part of life. Few of our failures would be measured with the magnitude the Allied forces would have endured in their mighty attempt to break through Fortress Europe. But we fail, in mostly small but sometimes large ways.

It's what we do after we fail that matters. When we fall, do we get back up or wallow in our shame and grief? Do we learn the lessons painfully gained or do we look for someone to blame? Sometimes we bask in the glory of success to our detriment. Sometimes the agony of failure reveals character traits that will do us well in the challenges ahead.

Eisenhower didn't have to send that second letter. At great cost, the invasion succeeded. It was indeed the beginning of the end of Hitler's third Reich. To his credit, the commander was willing to take responsibility, regardless. How refreshing in our day of fault-finding and excuse-making!

I like these words from Denis Waitley: "Failure should be our teacher, not our undertaker. Failure is delay, not defeat. It is a temporary detour, not a dead end. Failure is something we can avoid only by saying nothing, doing nothing, and being nothing."

A Soldier's Story

He wrote his journal when he was in late 20's. He tried to chronicle his experiences, describing scenes no person should ever have to witness. He served as a Warrant Officer in the 358th Infantry Regiment of the US Army's 90th Division, an outfit consisting mostly of men from Texas and Oklahoma. He enlisted after finishing seminary in Ft. Worth.

In 2012, my two sons and I visited some of the places he wrote about, his journal in hand. We stood near where his unit landed on D-Day plus two on Utah Beach. We traveled to some of the villages in Normandy where his outfit fought Hitler's troops through hedgerow country. We walked through the ordered rows of graves overlooking Omaha Beach as well as the cemeteries in Luxemburg and Belgium where so many who made the ultimate sacrifice now rest.

Andy was just a little older, Jordan just a little younger than the age of their grandfather when he went to war. They gained a lasting perspective, realizing that people their age accomplished so much at such a price. It's a trip I wanted to take for many years to understand better what it took and what it cost.

We went to honor him, a young man who hailed from northeast Alabama and had seen little of the world before he went aboard a liberty ship in New York Harbor. We also went to give thanks he came home. So many didn't.

He arrived back in the states on January 6, 1946. He wed Betty Howell on January 12 in Florence, Alabama. Oliver Wilbanks was a man who served all his life ... his God, his family, the church, and his country. Well done, Big O.

Labor Day

There is something very right about doing something productive with your day. It is interesting to note that soon after God created Adam He gave the first man a job (Genesis 2:15). There is dignity in the partnership between Creator and creature to take care of the world in which we live. As we observe Labor Day, note the description from the US Department of Labor:

"Labor Day, the first Monday in September, is a creation of the labor movement and is dedicated to the social and economic achievements of American workers. It constitutes a yearly national tribute to the contributions workers have made to the strength, prosperity, and well-being of our country."

Here are some appropriate quotes about the value and significance of work:

- "Genius begins with great works; labor alone finishes them." Joseph Joubert
- "Nobody can think straight who does not work. Idleness warps the mind." Henry Ford
- "Choose a job you love, and you will never work a day in your life." Confucius

- "Thunder is good; thunder is impressive, but it is lightning that does the work." Mark Twain
- "I am a great believer in luck, and I find the harder I work the more I have of it." Thomas Jefferson
- "All labor that uplifts humanity has dignity and importance and should be undertaken with painstaking excellence." Martin Luther King, Jr.
- "There is no substitute for hard work." Thomas Edison
- "Those who are unwilling to work will not get to eat." Paul
- "Every day is a gift from God for us to use. How we use is it is our gift to God."
- "And in everything you do or say, do it as a representative of the Lord Jesus, giving thanks through Him to God the Father." (Colossians 3:17)

"Almost" Isn't There

Since I was old enough to understand the meaning of December 7, 1941, I have wanted to go to Pearl Harbor and visit the USS Arizona memorial site. It's been on my bucket list before I even knew I had a bucket list.

My wish came true as Kim and I took our 35th anniversary trip to Hawaii. We did the things you're supposed to do there. Standing on the deck of the USS Missouri and knowing the historic significance of what took place there as the war came to a close was inspiring. The displays, the films, the tours all added to our experience. But when it came time to board the launch to cross the harbor for the memorial, there was a rope and a sign barring our way. The commander of the base had determined that wind conditions were such that further tours were not possible. I could see the familiar white shape of the memorial across the water but I could not get any closer. I was almost there …

"Disappointment" doesn't quite catch the sentiment I felt when I realized that "almost" wasn't being there. Life is that way so often. Things don't always work out like we would want. Stuff happens that we can never anticipate. Sometimes we don't measure up. Sometimes people let us down. Sometimes circumstances and situations change unexpectedly.

I have realized that the ministry of Jesus was so often affected by interruptions: teaching moments that presented themselves; healing opportunities when hurting, needy people approached; and confrontations when His enemies and critics tried to trap Him. You can find these interruptions through the four Gospels. Jesus turned the unexpected and inconvenient into life-changing events.

I hope I can go back one day, but if I don't I will have to be satisfied with "almost" there. I learned so much about that awful day that launched a nation into war. I was humbled and saddened by the sacrifice and suffering of so many. I was once again reminded that the price of even one life is higher than any of us can fully appreciate.

You can count on interruptions and disappointments in life. You and I can turn those moments into something bright and hopeful if we choose … even when it is really hard. Compared to what so many go through, my disappointment seems almost trivial. Let me just remind us all that we can trust the One who walked among us. He knew what it was like. He offers us grace and wisdom and strength to handle whatever comes.

Veteran's Day

Sunday is Veterans Day. I am writing this on Election Day. Somehow I think that is fitting. America today goes to the polls to exercise one of our most cherished freedoms. On November 11, 1918 – on the eleventh hour of the eleventh day of the eleventh month – an armistice was signed between the Allies and Germany. It was the truce that marked the end of "the war to end all wars." When the Treaty of Versailles was signed on June 28, 1919, the war was officially ended. President Wilson, on the first commemoration of Armistice Day in November 1919, spoke these words: "To us in America, the reflections of Armistice Day will be filled with solemn pride in the heroism of those who died in the country's service and with gratitude for the victory, both because of the thing from which it has freed us and because of the opportunity it has given America to show her sympathy with peace and justice in the councils of nations ..."

Solemn pride ... gratitude – those are fitting words as we mark this important day in our nation's history. Men and women who have worn and who now wear the uniform of our country deserve our expressions of solemn pride and gratitude. Someone has written that Veterans Day is "a celebration to honor America's veterans for their patriotism, love of country, and willingness to serve and sacrifice for the common good."

Today we salute and thank those who have served. Today we hope for a day when humanity might find other ways to survive and thrive. Jesus told us there would be wars and rumors of wars, but one day the Prince of Peace will change all that. We pray that day will come soon.

Sacrifice

Gary Gordon died in a hellhole called Mogadishu in 1993. He was a Master Sergeant in the United States Army Rangers, part of an elite fighting force called Delta. You may know his story. After one of the Black Hawk helicopters was shot down over the Somalian capital, Gordon volunteered along with his buddies, Randall Shughart and Brad Hallings to be inserted to provide cover for a second helicopter that also was disabled. At first, their request was denied. The area was crawling with hostile Somalis. Twice more Gordon and his colleagues asked to be given permission to protect the downed airmen. Gordon and Shughart were finally allowed to go in. Fighting their way to the downed aircraft, they fought off overwhelming odds until they ran out of ammunition. The after action report determined that Gordon was the first to die. Shughart was killed not too long after. The pilot they gave their lives for was ultimately rescued. For their heroic efforts, both Gordon and Shughart were awarded posthumously the Medal of Honor. In the award ceremony for Gary Gordon, the president of the United States remarked, "Gary Gordon died in the most courageous and selfless way any human being can act."

Gary Gordon left behind a family – wife, Carmen and son, Ian and daughter, Brittany. He also left behind a letter he had written to Carmen: "My love, you are strong and you will do well in life. I love you and my children deeply. Today and tomorrow, let each day grow and grow. Keep smiling and never give up, even when things get you down. So, in closing, my love, tuck my children in bed warmly. Tell them I love them. Love, Gary."

Gary Gordon also left behind a legacy of character and conviction. He knew the situation that day. He knew he had little chance of survival. He was willing to do what he could, even if it meant losing his life.

I don't glorify war. It is horrible and carries an awful cost. One general is credited with the quote: "War is hell." You might have heard of him, William Tecumseh Sherman. If you know Georgia history, you know what Sherman did to bring hell this way.

No, we don't have to glorify war, but we can honor the sacrifices made. Don't forget that as another Veterans Day comes and goes.

Freedom

She stands over 151 feet tall on her pedestal on Liberty Island in New York Harbor. Designed by Frederic Auguste Barholdi, the statue of a robed female figure representing Libertas, the Roman goddess of freedom, holds aloft a torch and clutches a tablet inscribed with the date of the American Declaration of Independence. A gift from the people of France, the statue is an iconic figure recognized around the world.

Dedicated on October 1886, the original concept was born in the mind of a French abolitionist, Édouard René Lefebvre de Laboulaye, who wished to acknowledge the defeat of slavery in the United States. It was intended to convey the congratulations of the French nation. Initially, Lady Liberty was supposed to hold a broken chain. The design was changed so that a set of broken shackles would lie at her feet. The tablet she held with July 4, 1776 took the place of the chains. Twenty years after the end of the Civil War the nation was still healing, so the sculpture was altered because there was concern that the held chains would be too provocative.

Too provocative? With the vantage point of history, we can wonder about such things. It would be great if we humans had moved past bigotry, racism, prejudice, and other ills that plague our world. Human trafficking is a world-wide disgrace. Racial tensions, religious intolerance, the ever widening gap between the have's and the have not's, barbaric violence, and injustice are just a few of the insufferable factors in a darkening world. Even so, come quickly Lord Jesus!

What did you pray for this morning? We all have personal concerns and issues that concern us. I know that God cares about each of us, but I also know that God cares for all of us. His heart must break as the world He created descend into chaos.

Today I am trying to take a longer view. I don't want to take for granted the grace extended me. I know that true freedom comes through Jesus Christ. This world is still bound in shackles. Jesus said, "You shall know the truth, and the truth will set you free" (John 8:32). Our statue of liberty is an old rugged cross.

I cannot fix all that is wrong in my own life, much less all that is wrong in the world. But I can pray. I can beseech God to work out His will in His world. I know the end of the story. Christ will return and I hope it is soon. Until then, I can pray. I can ask God to use you and me as we seek to be faithful. Until then, I can listen and obey the promptings of His Holy Spirit. I can pray.

I Pledge Allegiance

Most commonly, we attach those three words to the US flag and "the republic for which it stands" – but we pledge allegiance to other things in life. New citizens make a pledge. Newlyweds make a pledge. Scouts make a pledge. When you accept a job, you pledge to abide by company policies. When you join a civic club, you agree to their terms. When you join a church, you make commitments to the fellowship. When you become a Christian, you enter into a covenant relationship with God.

Under certain circumstances, a pledge might be required, but most often the pledge that matters is volunteered. It isn't the recitation of words; it is the dedication of the will. Webster's Dictionary defines allegiance as loyalty or devotion.

What's worth your allegiance? Your faith? Your church? Your marriage? Your family? Your friendships? Your school? Your work? Your community? Your country? We make decisions and take actions every day that illustrate the allegiance we have pledged.

What does allegiance require? There are a few things that come to mind – commitment, discipline, faithfulness, determination ...

November 11 is Veterans Day. In 1921, an unknown World War I American soldier was buried in Arlington National Cemetery. Similar ceremonies were conducted in England and France, each taking place at the highest place of honor in that country. For England, it was Westminster Abbey. For France, it was the Arc de Triomphe. November 11 was chosen because it was the day that recognized the ending of World War I – the 11th hour of the 11th day of the 11th month. The day became known as Armistice Day. In 1954, President Eisenhower signed a proclamation to name the day to honor and remember all veterans who have served their country.

We do not glorify war, nor do we attempt to wrap God in the American flag, but we do honor allegiance and sacrifice. We acknowledge that men and women have given much to serve. Thank a veteran even as you pray for peace.

Vacation Bible School

When you are in the ministry, you get to do some very different things. Some are fun, like having to dress in weird costumes. Some are gross, like participating in a pudding drenching contest. Some are necessary, like cleaning up after a big church family event. Some are choices, like driving the church bus around the neighborhood to pick up kids.

All of the above and many others have occurred during Vacation Bible School weeks. I remember the last one with fondness. My dad drove the bus through the neighborhoods behind Second Ponce de Leon Baptist Church in Atlanta so that children would have a safe way to VBS. Not too long ago, I met an old friend who told me that he used to ride that bus. During those days, we had two weeks of VBS. I think our volunteers might revolt if we did two weeks these days. They put in a great deal of work and invest a tremendous amount of energy and creativity so that VBS will provide an environment of fun activity and learning.

Good things happen at VBS. God things happen at VBS.

We want to help our boys and girls to learn how much God loves them. We desire to partner with parents as they go about the most important job an adult can have – raising a child. Many of our kids have wonderful insights about God, about the Bible, and about the church.

Some need a little help. Check out these answers:

Why did God create Eve after Adam? "God had to wait for her because He hadn't invented make-up yet."

How did David prepare to fight Goliath? "David probably carried a spare slingshot. You can never tell when you might get in an accident and sit on your good one.

Well, that's better than the adults who answered a Bible survey question with this interesting choice: Who was Joan of Arc? "Noah's wife."

What Will They Say Next?

Most of us went to Vacation Bible School when we were children. Some parents spend the summer taking their kids to one VBS after another – good solution to childcare when school is out. By August, those children could run their own VBS.

I am always amazed at children's insights and ideas. While talking about Elijah and his dealings with evil King Ahab, I asked "What is a prophet?" One girl was quick to answer: "A prophet is like an alarm clock. He's supposed to wake people up." You couldn't get a better answer in seminary, from a student or a professor.

Someone shared these gems with me:

- A Sunday School teacher was telling her class the story of the Good Samaritan. She asked her students, "If you saw a person lying by the road, all wounded and bleeding, what would you do?" One young lady broke the hushed silence: "I think I'd throw up."

- The class of youngsters was challenged to memorize Psalm 23. When the time came to see how the kids were doing, one young man named Rick was called upon. He had had a really hard time memorizing those six verses and was very nervous when his name was chosen. Stifling his fear, he spoke with conviction: "The Lord is my shepherd, and that's all I need to know."

- The pastor's five year-old daughter had noticed that her dad always bowed his head for a few moments before beginning his sermon. Curious, she asked him why. "Well, honey," he explained, "I'm asking the Lord to help me preach a good sermon." She took that in and then said, "How come He doesn't answer it?"

- Johnny and his family were having Sunday dinner at his grandmother's home. When everyone was seated and the food was being passed, little Johnny began eating his food. His mother spoke up quickly, "Johnny, we haven't said a prayer yet." He responded, "I don't need to say a prayer." His mother wasn't happy: "Of course we need to pray. We always say a prayer before we eat at our house." Johnny didn't skip a beat, "That's at our house. But this is Grandma's house and she knows how to cook." No word if Johnny survived to adulthood.

Yes, they can be brutally honest. But they can also open our eyes and hearts to the world they see and are trying to understand. Do they need to listen to us? Of course, we are wise and worldly. We know most, if not all, the answers, right? Perhaps we need to hang around kids more and listen to them. We just might learn something.

You Gotta Go

His first day had gone really well. New shoes, new shirt, new everything ... he looked really good, his mom told him. School wasn't so hard. Being in kindergarten was actually fun. He liked his teacher and he had met some new friends. Now, it was early on the second day and his mom was calling to him to get up. He didn't want to get up, but she kept at. Finally, he sat up and asked, "Why do I have to get up?" Mom responded, "It's almost time." "Time for what?" Mom was patient: "Time to go to school." He didn't like the sound of that. "School! You mean I gotta go back?!!"

There are things you want to do and there are things you have to do. It's a part of growing up. Seasons of life offer both. We are most often measured by how we address the "have-to's" of life.

Fall is a busy time for our families. We are praying that this will be a great school year. Thank you, teachers and administrators, for your investment in our children and youth. I pray for boldness and courage in these challenging days for students and faculty alike ... live your faith, share His love, show His grace!

Growing Up

I have seen many pictures of "First Day at School" – happy, excited (for the most part) kids and tearful moms and dads. I even saw one picture titled "Last first day" about one young man starting high school. I hate to be the one to break it to you, bud, but there will be more first days ahead.

Skyping with our grandson on "First Day at School" eve, we heard a recital about the new backpack, the carefully-selected clothes, the already-packed lunch, and the new teacher. It was great.

It reminds of two stories about kids and first days at school:

- Mom walked into her six year-old's bedroom to find him crying. "What's the matter, honey?" she asked. He sobbed, "I just figured out how to tie my shoes." She tried to buck him up, "That's great. That means you're growing up, dear!" He wailed, "No, it means I'll have to do it each day for the rest of my life!"

- The build-up for the first day was enormous. There was the trip to the school to find the classroom, the cafeteria, and other important places. They met the teacher. They went shopping – new duds, new backpack, new shoes. He got his hair cut. They had his favorite meal the night before. He went to be early. He had a good breakfast and helped pack his lunch. Pictures were taken. He was escorted to school. More pictures were taken. The first day was great! The next morning, mom woke him up: "It's time to get ready for school." He turned over and looked at his mom with shock on his face, "You mean I have to go back again?"

Growing up. I hope I get to do that one day. Paul wrote to the Philippians: "He who began a good work in you will complete it" (1:6). We're all under construction. We can be confident that God knows how much growth and development each of us needs. He will do His part. It's up to us to do ours "each day for the rest of my life!"

Through the Eyes of a Child

Have you ever noticed how often Jesus had children around Him? They wanted to touch Him, be near Him, and listen to Him. Even when His well-meaning disciples tried to keep them away, Jesus rebuked the adults and welcomed the kids.

Children should feel safe like Nora did when she wrote: "Dear God, I don't feel alone since I found out about You."

Children should feel hopeful and be honest like Frank who wrote: "Dear God, I'm doing the best I can.

Even at my advanced age, I still remember the men and women who cared for me, taught me, and served as role models for me at church.

I can still recall the names of those who worked in the nursery or taught me Sunday School, Missions, or Training Union.

I even remember the woman who would sit behind us in worship and pop us on the ear if we moved or spoke at the wrong time.

You'll learn a lot hanging around kids. One of my favorite stories: 3rd grade Sunday School teacher leaning over Johnny's shoulder while he is intently working on a drawing, "What are you drawing, Johnny?" Too busy to look up, he responds: "I'm drawing a picture of God." Wise teacher gently remarks, "But no one knows what God looks like." Still working too hard to look up, he says, "They will when I finish this picture."

All You Need is Love

Ah, the season of love! This will make you feel better: Total spending for Valentine's Day is expected to top $18.2 billion, according to the National Retail Federation. That's an average of $136.57 per person. Flowers, candy, cards, jewelry, fancy meals, and much more will be purchased on this fabricated, I mean, meaningful holiday.

After extensive research, I have found that the average male spends from 15 to 30 seconds while purchasing an appropriate card. If we're in trouble or have done something stupid, we could spend a whole minute searching for the right one. There we stand looking at acres of possibilities. Do I go sappy or do I go witty? Did the author of these verses fully capture the depth of my swirling emotions? Do I actually read what is written inside or do I just believe that I've picked the right look, the right verse, and, yes, the right gender. Do I buy a blank card and take a chance my own words will cause my true love's heart to flutter? Decisions, decisions.

We might need help, but who do we ask? Two young ladies were determined to help their spinster aunt find romance. They knew that a prominent judge in their small town had been widowed in the last few years. They began to plot. They handcrafted a Valentine's Day card and labored over just the right words to include in the card they would send to the judge on behalf of their unsuspecting aunt. They poured over the dictionary, searched through a Thesaurus, even looked in the Bible. One of the young women finally raised her head in triumph. "I finally found a word that rhymes with 'Valentine'" she exclaimed. "If it's in the Bible, it must be okay." So they put the finishing touches on their project and put the card in the mail. Several days later, the judge opened the envelope and read: "If you will be my Valentine, I will be your concubine." They meant well.

The Silly Season

Love can do strange things to you. It can make you say things like:

"Do you have a band aid? I scraped my knee falling for you."

"In the morning I can't eat; I'm thinking of you. In the evening I still can't eat; I'm thinking of you. In the night I can't sleep; I'm so hungry."

"You're my favorite. Oh, I forgot about chocolate. Next to chocolate, you're my favorite."

And this romantic line: "I love you with all my butt. I would have said all my heart, but my butt is bigger."

Do you remember your first love? Did your skin feel tingly? Did your face flush? Did you have trouble knowing what to say? No, you were cool, right? Not me. I was clueless.

I have learned some things about love.

- Love is easy. You meet someone. You are attracted by looks, similar interests, shared fun, hopes, dreams, obvious strengths and passion. You spend time learning each other's stories. You feel a pull to grow closer. You want to grow closer. You wake up thinking about them; you go to sleep thinking about them. Your world gets rocked.
- Love is hard. You get to know someone. You learn about idiosyncrasies, weaknesses, and faults. You disagree about

little things, then more important things. The shine is not so bright. You may feel ambivalence or question your judgment. You revaluate your desire for commitment. You realize there are two imperfect people in the relationship. You have the capacity to hurt each other deeply.

- Love is worth it. Your life is better because of this friend or lover. Your ragged edges fit into his or hers. You learn more about forgiveness, understanding, second chances, and grace. You learn how to say "I am sorry. I was wrong." You know that breaking down walls is much better than building them. You need that person in your life; that person needs you. You have created that place in your heart where the one you love fits so well. You keep working at it.

I'm no expert. I still wonder at the mystery of love. I am still amazed that I get to share my life with the love of my life. She lights up any room she enters. I am a better man because she said "Yes." I don't tell her enough what she means to me. I am blessed and I know it.

Hidden Treasures

Our mother never met a stranger. You can imagine how often three boys would complain when they saw mom on mission She would drag us to the grocery store ... or at least to the parking lot near the grocery store, where we were warned not to destroy either the car or each other. "I'll be back soon." We were certain that you could time her visits to the local grocery with a calendar. It took forever. After an agonizing day or so, one of us would be appointed to go into the store to "see what was taking so long." That always ended well.

When found, she would be in deep conversation with someone. Sometimes it was someone she knew from church or school or a ball team. Most often, it was someone she didn't know ... yet.

While it may have irritated three impatient and moody sons, our mother demonstrated an amazing gift to care for others, to show interest in other people's lives.

As the years passed, mom and dad would spend more time in the North Carolina mountains at their modest cabin near Jonas Ridge. Mom didn't change her approach. Neighbors, local craftsmen, shop keepers, church folks where dad was the interim preacher ... they all became friends.

One story to illustrate: The local handyman we hired was often at the cabin for projects. Mom got to know his wife. She was a war bride, a young German woman that an American GI met and married. After the war, they made their home in the NC mountains. The young wife was almost overwhelmed by the culture shock. Mom took her under wing and helped her with English and local customs.

One day, the younger woman invited mom to go upstairs. As they stood in the bedroom, she told my mom in almost a whisper, "I want to show you my pretties." Bending down, she began to lift dusty boxes from under the bed. Inside the numerous boxes was exquisite, hand-painted blue china. She had received the dishes from her grandmother in Germany as a wedding gift. They had never been out of their boxes. She had been told by her husband that to display or use them would have been considered "uppity" around their small community. They stayed in the boxes.

When mom told us that story, there were always tears in her eyes. Her empathy for that young German woman was such that she wanted to confront the husband. He never knew how close he came to serious injury, but his wife had made my mom promise she wouldn't talk to him.

What's the point beyond my admiration for my mother? I wonder what some of us have hidden away that has never been on display or utilized. Perhaps someone has convinced us to keep those things tucked away ... or perhaps we don't have the self-confidence to show the world who we really are and what we can really do. I know what our mother would say. She always made it an object lesson for us to reach and risk, even if it took all day at the grocery store.

A Gift for Mom

What's the perfect gift for mother?

You can get her flowers, buy her a card, take her out to eat, write her a letter of appreciation, give a donation to her favorite charity ... or you could ask her. She might not need more stuff; she might want something that doesn't cost a thing. I can hear some moms now:

- "Bring on the stuff"
- "Surprise me."

Perhaps we ought to consider:

- If you are tempted to wear the t-shirt that says "My mother is the travel agent for guilt trips," don't yield.
- If you are tempted to buy her the latest new and improved household appliance for Mother's Day, keep looking.
- If your mother says, "Do you want a piece of advice?" saying yes or no is irrelevant; get ready to accept it.

- If you decide to take your mom out for dinner, try a place that doesn't wrap the food.
- If you ask "what's for dinner?" be prepared for two items on the menu: "Take it or leave it." (Buddy Hackett)

Thank you, moms, for putting up with us. Thank you for loving us no matter what. Thanks for the sacrifices and extra effort you make. Thanks for the life lessons you teach and model.

Don't Forget Thanksgiving

Have you noticed? We seem to have rushed from Halloween to Christmas, right past Thanksgiving. Turn on the television and you'll see snow-covered landscapes with brand new cars that-you-have-to-buy-if-you're cool and people wearing clothes-you-have-to-have-if-you-go-out-in-public. Lots of money will help, too.

I love Christmas, but it's not time yet. For the people who have already finished their Christmas shopping, I think you are missing the point.

Thanksgiving means different things to different folks. Even with Black Friday looming, perhaps we should slow down and think about it. We should take the time to count blessings that we often take for granted. This may be the only time in months that you will be able to spend with family and friends without having to rush to the next appointment.

Giving thanks means expressing love and gratitude. Giving thanks flows from a grateful heart. It doesn't take a great deal of effort to be thankful. Think about it the next time you let someone in to your lane in heavy traffic and you don't even get a wave!

Giving thanks is very practical. Being able to get up in the morning. Taking a breath. Opening your eyes. Having a job. Loving and being loved by people. These and many others are gifts to be celebrated.

I hope you sit down to a table of fellowship during Thanksgiving. Whether you have a more traditional meal or something less grandiose, I pray you will be thankful for the people in your lives.

Most Thanksgiving meals come with rules. One six year-old boy was asked if there were rules he had to follow at such special occasions. He answered, "Yep, don't throw rolls at your sister." Makes perfect sense. If you start throwing rolls, what's next? He had an answer for that, too. "If you can't throw rolls, throw peas – they're harder to see and there's a lot more of 'em."

Silence

It was time to load up the car and head to grandma's for Thanksgiving. The annual trek was anticipated by most, dreaded by some ... well, one. Dad was not looking forward to the ten hour drive. He wasn't crazy about having to play referee with his five kids either. They could argue and fuss over anything. The inevitable barking would begin soon after they pulled out of the driveway.

"Mom, she's touching me!!"

"Dad, please lower the windows. Jimmy did it again!"

"That's my seat! I always sit there."

"I don't want your germs; don't breathe on me. In fact, don't breathe!"

What's not to like about the close family space, the intimate claustrophobia in the 10 year-old van? Mom tried reason, she tried compromise, she tried threats. You've heard it all, right?

"At our next stop, you can get a window seat."

"Can't we all just get along?"

"If you don't quit this racket, we're going to turn this car around!'

"If you don't stop that crying, I'll come back there and give you all something to really cry about!"

Then there was the whole issue of music. Everybody brought their own. Each one had his or her earphones or plugs but the volume was so loud, you could hear every sound from every device.

Before this trip, Dad had laid down the law. Everybody could bring a CD that could be played through the car sound system. You could choose 45 minutes of your music, and then it would be someone else's turn. They would draw straws to see who would go first. Dad thought it was a brilliant plan and congratulated himself for his ingenuity. Everyone has to be respectful of the various choices or they would lose their turn. Mom would provide volume control so nobody's ears would bleed.

The trip began in relative calm. Before they were out of the driveway, the first CD blared away. Dad's turn was fifth in order. When #4 was blessedly over, Dad inserted his CD. At first, there was concern that something was wrong with the CD player. Then Dad explained. For his 45-minute choice of music, he had selected silence. No music, no singing, no instruments, no nothing ... and the kids had to sit there and listen. This trip was not going to be so bad after all. Happy Thanksgiving!

Give Thanks

Two days before Thanksgiving, I sit down to write words of gratitude. In the rush of the season, it is difficult to hit 'pause' – to think, to reflect, to contemplate, to pray, and to give thanks. It really should not be so hard to consider and count blessings. I have tried to begin with things and people I too often take for granted. I think of people for whom Thanksgiving will be different this year – some with joy, some with grief.

Some have added to their families. Some face an empty chair this year at their table. Some have experienced success in business, sports, academics, and relationships. Some who have had a tough year of disappointment and discouragement.

Regardless, it seems so right to offer gratitude. I know you cannot force it or pretend, but somewhere in our souls we know we are loved by the infinite God. He created us out of that love. He sustains us with that love. He redeemed us because of that love.

In our broken world, we need to remember to say thanks. On September 28, 1863, Sarah Josepha Hale, a 74-year-old magazine editor, wrote a letter to President Abraham Lincoln to request that a day be set aside for a national day of thanksgiving. Lincoln honored that request in establishing the last Thursday of November as a national observance. Seventy-four years (October 3, 1789) to the day when George Washington declared a day of thanksgiving, Lincoln's proclamation directed that the nation pause for this recognition.

Fall of 1863. The still-young United States was suffering through the divisive and destructive Civil War. It did not seem like an appropriate time to express gratitude, but life rarely provides an easy path forward.

A part of the proclamation reads: "I therefore invite my fellow citizens ... to set apart and observe the last Thursday of November next, as a day of Thanksgiving and Praise to our beneficent Father who dwelleth in the heavens. And I recommend to them that while offering up the ascriptions just due to Him for such singular deliverances and blessings, they do also with humble penitence for our national perverseness and disobedience ... implore the interposition of the Almighty Hand to heal the wounds of the nation ..."

In our broken world, we also need to pray and work for peace for the sake of the Prince of Peace. Our many blessings afford us opportunity and inspiration to impact our world for Him. I am grateful that He would count us worthy to labor for Him.

Extra! Extra! Read All About It!

Most of the time headlines are teasers to get us to pay attention to a story. Sometimes headlines show that either the copy editor was asleep or not very bright. To wit:

- "Forecasters call for weather on Monday" *(Pittsburgh Post-Gazette)*
- "Amphibious pitcher makes debut" *(Boston Herald)*
- "Cows lose their jobs as milk prices drop" *(Baltimore Sun)*
- "State population to double; babies to blame" *(Clatchy News Service – Sacramento)*
- "Missippi's literacy program shows improvement" *(Associated Press)*
- "Breathing oxygen linked to staying alive" *(Mason County News)*

Wow, how can you not read such stories? An informed citizen is an enlightened citizen, right? Often, headlines can be misleading or confusing. Consider these possible biblical headlines:

- "Local farmer turn ship-builder warns of bad weather ahead"
- "Heavy favorite to face shepherd boy in mismatch"
- "Rumors spread as village girl is found pregnant"
- "Wild prophet draws huge crowds at River Jordan"
- "Itinerant preacher leads a parade at festival"
- "Roman governor orders execution of local troublemaker"
- "City in uproar over unconfirmed reports of mysterious appearances"

We read and hear a great deal of bad news these days. The world could certainly use some good news. I think I know where to find some. Let's see:

- "Followers of Galillean rabbi proclaim, 'He's alive! He's alive!'"

Sounds like Gospel to me, which actually means "Good News!"

Give Thanks

Thanksgiving was a special time for my mom. It was Christmas for dad, but mom loved having the family around her at Thanksgiving. The meal was great but the time together was what made it special. I hope this weekend has been that for you. Our families are often configured much differently these days, but relationships are still meant to be cherished.

So in honor of families, and particularly moms, here goes:

- The little girl had a note pinned to her multi-colored array of clothing. Her teacher bent over to read the hastily-scrawled writing that had to come from an embarrassed but defeated mother: "I hope you don't think I picked out this outfit."

- A neighbor looked across the fence and saw the young mother of three preschoolers sprawled on the backyard lawn. Alarmed and concerned, she rushed over to see if the young woman was alright. Looking up from the ground, the mom replied, "I'm fine. They wanted to play Avengers and I'm supposed to be the bad guy that got zapped. I'm lying here because it's the first chance I've had to rest all day."

- The teacher had called for a parents' conference. You remember those, or perhaps you have had one lately ... from either side. On this particular day, the teacher began the conference with these wise words: "I won't believe half of what he says about you if you pledge not to believe half of what he says about me."

- One more: "Mom," said the recently returned college student on fall break, "Now that I've been at school, I realize that I really need a car. I need you to talk to dad." Mom reflected on that for a moment as she gazed up at her son, whose hair had grown long and bushy. He saw her look and said, "Looks a lot like Jesus, huh? He had long hair, right?" She didn't hesitate in her response. "Yes, He had long hair and He walked everywhere He went."

I Want, I Want

According to the seasonal marketing that is bombarding us, everybody you know is getting a new car for Christmas. They must be – just look at the unending ads featuring people who look exactly like you and me ... if you are attractive 20-30 somethings with perfect teeth.

I'm not getting a new car. I missed that list. As I age, I realize I don't want much of anything. I certainly don't need much of anything. I am blessed, not by bigger piles of stuff, but by richer relationships with family and friends. I am learning to appreciate more and more living in the moment. Paul wrote to his friends in Philippi that he had reached contentment, regardless of circumstance. He lived in peace, the well-being that comes from trusting God with his life.

Christmas is still fun because of the peripheral excitement when a gift lights up little eyes, when a loved one is thrilled by generosity and thoughtfulness, when the sounds and sights of the season lift spirits. I don't want to be Scrooge. I want to laugh and sing and rejoice when friends and family get together.

I just don't want to get the message lost in all the noise that comes with the holidays. The birth of the Bethlehem babe changed the world, changed my life ... and I pray changed yours as well.

I'm So Busy!

The pastor met them at the door at the end of the service. "Hi Harold and Jane. It's really good to see you. I'd love to see you here more often." Harold and Jane were a bit sheepish at first. With their busy lives, they only made it to services a few times a year. Harold decided to present a defense for their inactivity. "You see, Pastor, our schedules are so hectic that our weekends require we take care of things we never get around to during the week." Then he paused, "But at least we keep the Ten Commandments." The pastor congratulated them, "I'm glad to hear that you abide by the Commandments." With pride in his voice, Harold responded, "Yes, we do. Jane keeps six of them, and I keep the other four."

I don't think it works that way, does it? Yes, we are busy people. It is not easy to get everything done on the list. It makes you wonder if perhaps the list is too long or perhaps the items on the list are not nearly as important as we once thought.

Do you remember Mister Rogers? He was once asked to address the National Press Club. As he began his remarks, he pulled a pocket watch out. He told the assembled media members and other guests that he was going to keep two minutes of silence. He urged them to use the time of quiet to remember people from their past who had encouraged them, mentored them, given them opportunities, served as role models, honed their skills, challenged their abilities, even made sacrifices for them.

A lot of the 'stuff' of life can be found on the list ... things to do, items to check off. Most of the substance of life doesn't appear on the list. When it's all said and done, what matters most are the relationships of our lives – the people who have reached us, and the people we have reached.

If you think about it, the Ten Commandments are really about relationships, too. The first part deals with our relationship with God. The second addresses our relationships with each other. Perhaps it would help if each of us took a few minutes to reflect about the people in our lives who have made a difference for us ... and give thanks.

Thank Him

Sallie Mathis has served on the custodial staff for over twenty years. I could always find her by listening. Most often, she was singing. She hasn't had an easy life and she gets down sometimes. But she chooses to sing. A few weeks before Christmas, she asked me if I was getting excited about Christmas. The look on her face told me that she was. She reminded me that she was thankful, that we all should be thankful for what we have.

I know sometimes it is easy to dwell on what we don't have. The holidays can be hard to get through for many people. At the same time, even when it is painful there are reasons to give thanks, to count our blessings.

Most of us will never fully understand the circumstances of the birth of Christ. Mary had to endure an assault on her reputation. Joseph had to withstand the temptation to avoid the embarrassment that his pending marriage might bring.

The journey to Bethlehem could not have been easy. The crowded village offered little accommodation to the expectant mother. Women often died in childbirth in those days and in those conditions. The King of kings was laid in a feeding trough.

The first witnesses to the birth were a gang of disreputable shepherds. When King Herod learned of the birth, he ordered a horrific campaign of infanticide. The young couple had to flee for their lives to Egypt.

It was hard. We want to paint haloes on the donkey and make the story whimsical, but the story almost ended before it began. God chose a hard-to-believe narrative to reveal His desire to rescue us from ourselves. He must have felt we were worth all the trouble.

Don't forget to be thankful this Christmas. Don't let the rush of the season ruin the magic and mystery. If you could have seen the joy in Sallie's face, you would know what I mean.

What's It Worth to You?

The pastor faced his congregation on the first Sunday of the year to preach his annual New Year's message. In his church, the sermon preceded the offering. His first words: "Now before I start, I wanted to give you an option this year. We want to begin in the right way so I have three sermons to offer. The first one lasts only five minutes but will cost you $100. The second one goes for 30 minutes but will cost you $50. The last one will take one hour but will cost you $10. We're going to receive the offering after I preach. Which sermon would you choose?"

One guy stood up and was called on by the preacher. "Is there a fourth option? I'd like the five minute version for $10." Tough crowd.

Doug Marlette was a Pulitzer Prize-winning editorial cartoonist whose work was featured in major newspapers for years. My favorite Marlette character was Reverend Will B. Dunn. Marlette described him this way: "He attends the sick, the divorced, and the bereaved – on his soaps. He keeps goldfish in the baptismal pool, feeds the hungry, visits the orphans, and never misses his aerobic dance class at noon. He is the lovable, laughable, local spiritual giant of Bypass, North Carolina – and human relations is his business."

Rev. Dunn was a master of preaching. Well, 'master' might be a little strong. In one strip, he is greeting his congregation: "Brothers and Sisters … Friends and Neighbors … Heathens and Hypocrites …

Have I left anyone out?" Then we see him looking out over his people and thinking, "To win an audience over, some ministers start off their sermons with a little joke. Of course, it depends on the congregation. I usually just toss 'em some red meat." [23]

Proclamation of the Word is not an easy task. Next time, you are in a service make sure you lift a prayer for the messenger. He or she needs all the help available!

[23] Doug Marlette, *"The Wit and Wisdom of Reverend Will B. Dunn"* Thomas B. Nelson, 1984

Look What I Found!

The car was built in May 1937 and originally owned by the first president of the British Racing Drivers' Club, a winner of the 24 hour Le Mans race. Its second owner was an English orthopedic surgeon who bought it in 1955. He kept the rare vehicle parked in his garage since the early 1960's. The automobile had not been driven in five decades. The doctor died in 2007. While settling his estate, the car was discovered in the garage – a 1937 Bugatti Type 57S Atalante Coupe – on January 2, 2009. A month later, the car sold at a Paris auction for $4.4 million.

Makes you want to take another look in your garage, right? How about the attic of your grandparents? Look under your bed and in your closets. Surely there is something really valuable tucked away just waiting to be discovered.

Some of us have undiscovered treasure in our lives. It might be a relationship we have never pursued or a talent we haven't developed. It might be a passion that is yet to be lit. It might be a calling we haven't followed.

I'm not going to find a rare, pricy car in my garage. I've looked. However, I can find moments and opportunities and challenges where God can reveal what really matters. I can discover true treasure that has eternal value.

Open my eyes, my heart, my spirit, Lord!

Time and Eternity

The old man stumbles from the scene. The past year has gone swiftly. 12 months we won't see again. The little one bounces in. The new year awaits. What we might have done, what we might have said yesterday cannot be recovered. We start anew.

Time and eternity come to my mind. Over the holidays, we are reminded how precious time really is. All that anticipation, all the rush, rushed by. Christmas will be a memory and a new year looms. Time marches on.

Heaven has been on my mind this time of year. Someone asked me what heaven is really like. The only way I can answer that question is to seek the glimpses that God affords us. I think of heaven as a place of no regrets, a place of perfect relationships, a place of unremitting joy, a place prepared by the Master Carpenter. It is a place where there is no more night, no more evil, no more death, no more tears, no more sorrow, no more pain. It is a place we were meant to be.

Ray Boltz sang a song about heaven that includes these phrases:

> "Thank you for giving to the Lord. I am a life that was changed.
> "Thank you for giving to the Lord. I am so glad that you gave."

You might be the kind of person who makes New Year's resolutions. You might have tried before and given up. You might think the whole thing silly. I know that the fitness centers around town will be full in January and not-so-much by mid-February.

I don't know how much time any of us have. I do know none of us is guaranteed anything beyond the present. I also know we don't have time to waste. It's just too precious. Isn't it worth considering how we influence and impact the lives around us? When we get to heaven, will we look around and see faces of those who heard about heaven from us? Will we see those we pointed in that direction?

We cannot save others – that's the work of the Holy Spirit – but God can use people like you and me to let others know about His love. He is the One who gathers the harvest, but He has entrusted the planting to us.

Love on another. Love someone into the fellowship of the church. Every study I have ever seen tells me that the number one reason why people attend church is that a friend invites them. Love someone into the Kingdom of God. No, you cannot make that happen, but you can introduce your friend to Jesus. You can pray. You can be present. Time is precious. Eternity matters.

Show Up

On December 26, 2004, the Indian Ocean tsunami and earthquake devastated parts of Indonesia Sri Lanka, India and Thailand. The disaster was the world's deadliest tsunami, with over 230,000 people killed and half a million injured by the waves that battered the low-lying coast. It struck with immense, destructive power that equaled 23,000 Hiroshima-type bombs.

Five months after the tragedy, I traveled with a group of Cooperative Baptist Fellowship pastors to visit mission posts in Thailand. We heard stories about and viewed areas where the gigantic wall of water caused such overwhelming damage. Whole villages just ceased to exist. Large ships lay rusting far inland. People were still searching for missing loved ones.

Many of the stories were heartbreaking, but some were inspiring. Indonesia is a part of the world where you cannot use the "m" word. Instead of saying "missionary" you have to say field personnel. Christians are such a small minority that they have to endure constant political pressure and oppression.

We traveled to a number of aid stations still operating near devastated sections of the country. Banners flew bearing the name of Christian relief organizations that were hard at work and would be for many months to come. They had been the first to respond to the crisis. They were the presence of Christ in a very dark time. They showed up.

We now live in a post-Christian world. You don't have to look far to realize that religion is losing its impact and relevance in a time when many think religion is a part of the problem, not the solution. We can moan and complain while we wring our hands or we can show up.

We have a story to tell to the nations. We have daily opportunities to live out our Christian witness. We have God-moments when we need to represent Him in word and deed. We can show up.

Sunday begins Advent, you know the season when we prepare and celebrate for the coming of the Christ Child … the season when God appeared in the flesh to give us life and hope. He showed up. We need to show up, too.

The Word Became Flesh

In Charles Swindoll's book *Jesus, The Greatest Life of all*, the author tells the story of Thomas Mott Osborne. [23] Having been appointed to the New York State Commission on Prison Reform Osborne decided to attempt something drastic. In October 1914, he entered Auburn Prison as an inmate. Like the other 1329 men incarcerated there, he was photographed, fingerprinted, stripped of his possessions, issued a suit of prison grays, and led to a cell – four feet wide, seven and a half feet long, and seven and a half feet tall. The only difference was that, unlike his fellow prisoners, Osborne could leave anytime he wanted. He wrote: "I am a voluntary prisoner, it is true; nevertheless, even a voluntary prisoner can't unlock the door to his cell."

It is difficult to grasp the transaction described in Scripture when the Word became flesh. According to Paul (Philippians 2:5-8), Jesus volunteered to be imprisoned in flesh, limited by time and space, restricted by human fatigue and need after laying down His rightful entitlement. The ultimate tale of the Prince becoming the Pauper unfolded in the life of Jesus of Nazareth.

In a sense, Christmas opens the story. The King of kings and Lord of lords chooses the helplessness and vulnerability of an infant to enter the world. The first gift of Christmas wasn't gold or frankincense or myrrh. It was the newborn son of Mary, wrapped in swaddling clothes. God with us ... a declaration that prisoners could find freedom from sin, evil, and death through One who chose to be one of us. Joy to the world!

[23] Charles Swindoll, *"Jesus: The Greatest Life of All,"* Thomas Nelson Publisher, 2002

A Story Worth Telling

He's got the whole world in His hands ...

> "In the beginning, God created the heavens and the earth ... And God created man in His own image ... And God saw all that He had made, and behold, it was very good."

The Garden perfect. The image clear. It was good!

The image was marred. Sin entered the world. Relationship, fellowship broken. Separation, alienation, pride. Humans breaking the law and the heart of God. Punishment. Banishment.

God is never taken by surprise. He had a plan. He reached, He gave, He loved.

He's got the whole world in His heart ...

> "But when the fullness of time came, God sent His Son ...For God so loved the world that He gave His Son so that those who believe in Him should not perish, but have eternal life."

Christmas is coming, full of tales of angels, shepherds, wise men ... but so much more. The story of Baby Jesus is neither the beginning nor the end. It is but a part of a wonderful rescue and reclamation story, an unfolding of God's effort to bring us to safety, to save us from ourselves and from our sin. It's a story worth telling. Who has heard the story from you?

Hope For the Bad Guys

Christmas movies. You probably have a favorite or two. Have you noticed that almost all of them have villains? There's the Grinch

(Boris Karloff was his voice in 1966), Harry and Marv from Home Alone, the prosecuting attorney in Miracle on 34th Street, Ebenezer Scrooge, the bully in Christmas Story, Clark Griswold's boss, the Bumble from Rudolph, Jack Frost in the third Santa movie, and of course, Mr. Potter from It's a Wonderful life. I'm certain you could think of others.

Most of them get rehabilitated to some degree ... except Old Man Potter. Never liked that guy. He still has George's money that Uncle Billy left at the bank.

I like the stories where the bad guys turn from their wicked ways. If we admit it, we all have a little villain in us. Would you talk to your mother like Kevin did to his before being banished to the attic? If you didn't say it, you probably thought it.

A part of the wonder of Christmas is grace. God demonstrated it best when He sent His Son into a sinful world. In John 3, Jesus said He came to save the world, not to condemn it. The Christ Child, innocent and pure, would become sin for humanity and pay an awful price for our redemption.

Grace suggests an undeserved gift. During this season of the year, we have opportunity to heal broken relationships, to start on a new path of spiritual growth, to focus on others instead of ourselves, and to model the attitude of Christ.

One of the reasons we like Christmas movies is that they contain whimsical, fantastic characters and storylines. They stir our imaginations and lighten our moods. They offer hope that good things will happen.

When you look at your Christmas list this year, who needs more than a present? Who needs the ministry of grace from you?

Who knows what Christmas miracle awaits when we treat others as Christ has treated us? There is hope for all of us…except Old Man Potter.

Almost Forgotten

The familiar characters of the Christmas story are easy to recall – Mary, Joseph, the Child, shepherds, angels, Herod, the magi, even the innkeeper – even though one is never mentioned in Scripture. If you have ever participated in a Christmas play or pageant, chances are you have played one of these parts. One Christmas, I was asked to play the donkey.

When we were growing up, we were required to fill one of these roles for the annual reading of Luke 2 by our mother. It seemed like it was the only time we ever wore robes – our costumes complete with dish towels and broom sticks. There were seven boys and one girl at grandmother's house. Guess who got to play Mary. The rest of us took turns with the plum job going to the oldest guys – Joseph. Last year's doll got placed in the manger. We had to stand still, make no noise, and act appropriately reverent … or else.

The stories we find in Matthew and Luke recount the wonder and mystery of that first Christmas. We can argue over how many wise men there were or whether Jesus was born in a stable or a cave, but the truth of God's grace and love leap from the pages of the Gospel. The Word became flesh and came to dwell with us!

Sometimes overlooked is the account of the birth of John the Baptist and the essential connection to the Christ story. Luke recorded the amazing events surrounding the child born to an elderly couple unable to bear children. Zechariah and Elizabeth are not insignificant actors in the unfolding drama of divine revelation. Their son would become the promised herald of the coming of the Lamb of God. Zechariah was told by the angel of the Lord: "He will be a man with the spirit and power of Elijah. He will prepare the people for the coming of the Lord." (Luke 1:17)

Zechariah was not the first person to doubt that God would do the unexpected. Abraham's wife, Sarah, laughed when she heard that she would bear a son in her advanced years.

This is the season of miracles. God bursts into our lives to remind us of His love for us and His hope for the world.

CHRISTmas ...

From a friend:

> "If you look for Me at Christmas,
> You won't need a special star
> I'm no longer just in Bethlehem.
> I'm right there where you are.
> You may not be aware of Me
> Amid the celebrations,
> But if you take a moment
> From your list of things to do
> And listen to your heart, you'll find
> I'm waiting there for you.
> You're the one I want to be with.
> You're the reason I came,
> And you'll find Me in the stillness
> As I'm whispering your name.
> Love, Jesus."

He loves each of us like He loves all of us. His gift of love and grace has your name on it. May the blessings of the One who came lift our spirits, encourage our hearts, and touch our lives be your wondrous experience this Christmas.

A Man of Many Names

Stephen Prothero is a professor of Religion at Boston University and has authored a number of books that deal with religion in America. Just after the release of his best-seller, *Religious Literacy*, he published *American Jesus – How the Son of God Became a National Icon*. [24] His research reaches a conclusion that "Jesus is a man nobody hates." He cites the number of Americans who claim to believe in and have some relationship with Jesus. Even people who do not adhere to such beliefs seem to have a positive opinion of Him.

He goes farther. "Here in America atheists and Buddhists are active producers and consumers of images of Jesus, who in many respects functions as a cultural icon." The question he wrestles with is: Which Jesus are we talking about?

Prothero believes we Americans have a history of continually remaking Jesus to resemble our current hero-types. He identified four cultural images of Jesus that have emerged:

- Enlightened Sage – Thomas Jefferson was the major proponent of Jesus as a great ethical teacher. In his book *The Philosophy of Jesus of Nazareth*, Jefferson reduced the Jesus of Scripture by removing any references to His miracles or divinity

- Sweet Savior – This image was primarily promoted during the evangelistic fervor of the 19th and early 20th centuries. Jesus was portrayed through story rather than doctrine; He became a friend with whom one must draw close.

- Manly Redeemer – Positioned as a reaction to what some seemed as a girly-man, effeminate wimp, Jesus became a testosterone-powered action hero. He stood tall and strong, courageous and bold to take on the enemies of good.

- Superstar – Jesus became the ultimate revolutionary, taking on the evils of the culture. As the rock star who defied convention, this hip Jesus rejected the trappings of tradition and institution in favor of a more personal experience with deity

So, who is Jesus to you? The Christ Child didn't come to fulfill our perceptions and preferences. He came to save sinners. He came to trade His life for ours. He came to become like us so we could become like Him. He didn't come to please or impress any of us. He came to honor and obey His Father. He never trusted the whims of fickle humanity.

When Joseph and Mary brought the Child to the Temple for His dedication, they were approached by an elderly man named Simeon (Luke 2:25-32). Simeon took the little one in his arms and spoke prophetic words that define Jesus: "I have seen Your salvation, which You have prepared for all people. He is a light to reveal God to the nations, and He is the glory of Your people Israel." He is salvation. He is hope. He is Emmanuel – God with us. We don't need a cultural reshaping of Jesus. We need Jesus.

[24] Stephen Prothero, *"American Jesus: How the Son of God Became a National Icon,"* Farrar, Straus, and Giroux Publishers, 2004.

A Tribute to the Grieving

We take so much for granted we think time stands still for us. Then life takes a painful turn and there's one less this Christmas.

We think of words left unsaid, there are things we could have done. The empty ache deep inside, hard to hide from everyone.

'Round us the pace rushes by, folks too busy to pay heed, But there are those who can know how great our loss and our need.

They have walked where we now walk, they know the depth of our grief. Their strength and understanding offers much needed relief.

Their love holds us 'cause they know, it won't be the same this year. No matter how hard we try, the one we miss won't be here.

One day heaven will be home, the pain of our parting o'er. We'll see the one gone ahead, our delight worth waiting for.

Now we must go on living until that great day arrives. Our dear one safe in God's hands, hope and faith brightens our lives.

The Journey that Changed the World

In the April 7, 2015 newsletter from the Center for Healthy Churches, Bill Wilson wrote a column entitled: "Vision and Venture at Advent." He began with: "It was Vaclav Havel who described the dilemma every leader has with the issue of vision – 'Vision is not enough; it must be combined with venture. It is not enough to stare up the steps; we must step up the stairs.'"

The story of Jesus offers compelling evidence that the two – vision and venture – should be inseparable. Joseph, who sometimes appears as a bit player in the drama, received a vision from God. Amidst his concerns about what he should do with a suddenly pregnant fiancée, he struggles with how to make the problem go away. Through a heavenly messenger, he is given a vision of his future: "Joseph, son of David, do not be afraid to go ahead with your marriage to Mary. For the child within her has been conceived by the Holy Spirit. And she will have a son, and you are to name him Jesus, for he will save his people from their sins" (Matthew 1:18-25).

Mary, understandably confused and frightened, receives her own vision and submits to Gabriel's message: "I am the Lord's servant, and I am willing to accept whatever He wants. May everything you have said come true" (Luke 1:38).

Their journey to Bethlehem is set in the framework of an imperial decree. Caesar Augustus has ordered a census of his empire. The tax rolls need to be updated. People must return to their ancestral homes to obey the decree. While the males are targeted, it is interesting that both Joseph and Mary are descendants of David, Israel's greatest king. The lineage is an important verification of messianic prophecy.

According to Havel's word picture, Joseph and Mary did indeed stare up the steps and then stepped up the stairs. They were willing to take the journey, not just to Bethlehem, but also to obedience.

Jesus embodied vision and venture in His life and ministry. He was laser-focused on accomplishing His mission. He refused to allow anything or anyone to deter Him. He lived the life His Father sent Him to live.

Can that be said of us? Are we living the life we were created to live? Is our heart set on those things that have eternal significance? What better time than Christmas to renew our commitment to both vision and venture.

Merry Christmas. Let's celebrate together and let's penetrate the world with our witness. There are stairs that need steppin'.

Almost Made It

I had it all figured out. If I sat on the stairs and was quiet enough, my parents wouldn't even know that I was there. I was determined to stay awake until Santa came. Almost made it. I woke up on Christmas morning in my bed. My attempts at stealth had not worked. I fell asleep on the stairs, and then dad picked me up and deposited me in the bed. That was hard since I was 16 at the time.

Kids don't wait well. Do you remember thinking Christmas would never get here? As children, we knew something was up. Whispers when they thought we weren't close enough to hear… mysterious rustling near closets…vague answers to pointed questions.

Some of us were pretty good at snooping. Some could open a package and reseal it, believing that no one could detect the damage to the wrapping. Charles Swindoll told the story of his childhood when he was checking out the gifts under the tree. He had given repeated hints that he wanted a basketball for Christmas. Seeing a round package with his name on it assured him that his wishes were about to come true. He didn't bother to examine the present any closer. To his chagrin, when he opened the package he discovered a brand new globe. Almost made it.

Our impatience spills over when we consider the condition of our world. Closer to home, few of us like to wait for anything. We look for the shortest line, move toward it believing we get through faster. Almost made it. The person at the register decides to go on break or the person in front of you pulls out a folder full of coupons. We (as in me) are in a hurry too much of the time. It affects us (as in me) when we drive so we lean on the horn or have conversations with people in cars ahead of us who cannot possibly hear us.

If I could give us all a gift this Christmas, it would be one of shalom. It is a wish for well-being, for contentment, for confidence that we can rest in the amazing love of God. After all, Christmas is really all about His gift, not ours.

A Love Story

NEWS FLASH!! It's not your birthday, it's His. With apologies to those who actually have birthdays around Christmas, too often we can forget Whose birthday we celebrate this time of year. Can you imagine a birthday party where everyone but the guest of honor gets a present? Mike Slaughter, lead pastor of Ginghamsburg Methodist Church in Ohio, has written an interesting book entitled *Christmas is not your Birthday*. [25] In the flyleaf, these words are written: "This Christmas, cut through the hype that leaves you exhausted and broke at the end of the year. Instead, experience the joy of giving sacrificially, and the love of a Savior who gave everything He had for us."

We have dressed up the story more than a little bit. Haloes on the donkey, a baby that doesn't cry, throngs of shepherds and angels ... we have sanitized the account of a desperate father, an anxious teenage mother, primitive and unsanitary conditions, and a death threat from a tyrant.

Christmas is truly a story of love and generosity. What was the first Christmas gift? Was it the message of blessing received by a young girl named Mary? Was it the concert of hope the shepherds heard from the heavenly choir? Most of us think of the first gift, wrapped in swaddling clothes and lying in a manger.

The gift of God's Son gave us all value, established once and for all that we humans were worth redeeming. Our Creator was determined to be our Savior.

[25] Michael Slaughter, *"Christmas is Not Your Birthday,"* Abingdon Press, 2011

The Best Christmas Ever

It's Christmas week. For some, it took forever. For others, it arrived in the blink of an eye. Your positioning in the two groups probably has something to do with your age.

We can list all the reasons we might not enjoy Christmas. We can complain about the increased traffic or the mob mentality at the mall or the overdose of Christmas movies or music. We overspend, overeat, and overschedule. We can worry about what to get for people who don't really need anything. Erma Bombeck found a solution after wondering:

"Wouldn't it be wonderful to find the one gift that you didn't have to dust, that had to be used right away, that was practical, that fit everyone, that was personal, and that would be remembered for a long time?" Then she answered her own question: "I made a gift certificate for a flu shot."

The sights and sounds of the season are awe-inspiring until about December 26th. For some, their favorite Christmas lights are the tail lights of their relatives. Christmas can bring out the Scrooge in us, but I'd rather contemplate what makes the season so meaningful. It would certainly be helpful if we were better at remembering whose birthday we are celebrating.

Mike Slaughter pastors Ginghamsburg United Methodist Church in Ohio. He wrote a book, *Christmas Is Not Your Birthday*, where he challenged readers to experience the joy of living and giving like Jesus.

I think of how Jesus laid down the glory of heaven to pick up the grime of earth. All the glitter and lights in the world cannot cover up the desperate need in the human heart. In humility and obedience, the Son would follow the Father's plan while it leads to a manger, a cross, and a tomb.

I think of a frightened young woman, still in her teens, carrying a child in her womb. She is far from home. She finds herself in unfamiliar surroundings. The only place available to place her newborn son is a feeding trough for farm animals. Perhaps a local midwife has been summoned to assist in the birth.

I think of a man entrusted with a daunting task. He has been asked to provide for and protect his young wife and the child. He has been told of the child's identity, which has added overwhelming responsibility to the stewardship of the lives under his care.

It seems to me that the best Christmas ever is any Christmas when I choose to remember what matters most ... who matters most

Light Out of Darkness

A young German soldier was shipped to the front in the last days of World War II. Aware that his army was in desperate straits and the outcome was certain, he surrendered to the first British soldier he met. He was sent to a POW camp for the duration of the war.

While in the camp, he came to know some fellow soldiers as well as some Allied personnel who were Christians. Far from home, discouraged by his circumstances, and horrified as he learned of the ghastly horrors of concentration camps much different than the one where he was held, he began to consider matters of the spirit for the first time in his life. An American chaplain gave him a New Testament that he read with great interest. His life changed.

That young man was Jürgen Moltmann. He became one of the foremost theologians of our time. One of his greatest contributions was his classic work, Theology of Hope. He spoke of the transformation he experienced: "Many of us then, and I was one, glimpsed the light that radiates from the divine child. This light did not allow me to perish. This hope kept us alive."

He knew the power of darkness, but he also knew that light was stronger still: "Today I see before me the millions of the imprisoned, the exiled, the deported, the tortured, and the silenced everywhere in the world where people are pushed into darkness. For it is on them that the divine light now shines."

More than ever, the world needs the light, the life, the hope of Jesus Christ. Jesus, who proclaimed Himself the Light of the world, called His followers to be light and salt in the world He died to save. The season of Christmas gives us many opportunities to push back the darkness!

Reflections on Christmas

Some of my favorite stories/thoughts on the season:

- The carol reads: "O come let us adore Him" not "O come let us ignore Him."

- The pastor and his wife had bundled their kids into the car for the trip to church for the annual Christmas Eve candlelight service. The youngest of the bunch piped up from the back seat: "Hey, Dad, are you going to let us enjoy this Christmas or are you going to try to explain it to everybody?"

- From a song recorded by Point of Grace: "We're alive, we can breathe, but do we really care for this world in need? So close your eyes and share the dream. Let everyone on earth believe. The Child was born, the stars shone bright, and love came down at Christmas time. So let your voices fill the air. Everyone, watch and pray that the sun will shine on a brighter day. Join your hands, lift them high for this gift of life; for love came down at Christmas time."

- Willa Cather's "The Burglar's Christmas" is a story about a young man who left home much like the prodigal son in Luke 15. Leaving his family behind back east, he winds up in Chicago without a job or friends. Things go from bad to worse as he finally resorts to breaking into a house to find some food on Christmas Eve. He is caught in the act by the homeowners, his parents. They had moved to Chicago when they lost all trace of him. His mother weeps as he begins to confess the mess he has made of his life. Turning to flee the house, his parents beg him to stay so he can start over. He pauses and looks at them, "I wonder if you know how much you have to pardon." His mother responds, "O son, much or little, what does it matter? Have you wandered so far and paid such a bitter price for knowledge and not yet learned that love has nothing to do with pardon and forgiveness, that it only loves, and loves, and loves?"

- December seems to be the busiest month for plastic surgeons. A report in plasticsurgeryportal.com mentions December as the busiest month for many plastic surgeons, with some of them performing almost double the number of procedures on any given day during December. Some suggest that plastic surgery makes the perfect Christmas gift. Try that out on a loved one: "You need to get a lift or a tuck. Merry Christmas!"

Your night may not be silent. Hoping for calm may be a pipe dream. But I hope you will experience the joy and wonder of God's gift. Open your Bible and find a quiet place, if but just for a few minutes. Read Luke or Matthew or John or Isaiah and give thanks for your Savior. Merry Christ-mas!

Roses for Mom

Christmas is a time for magic and mystery. It is also a time of generosity and grace ...

It was Christmas Eve. The florist shop stayed open late and was doing a brisk business. A line waited at the counter. In that line was a 7 year-old boy. His clothes looked worn out and his shoes had more than a few holes in them. When it was finally his turn, he placed a wadded up dollar bill on the counter and spoke boldly,

"Mister, do you have any roses for my mom? I'm willing to pay a buck for 'em."

Roses for $1? The other customers couldn't help but snicker and whisper some comments of incredulity. The shopkeeper looked down at the boy and said, "Let me see what I can do for you." The man headed for the back of the shop. After a few minutes he returned with a dozen long-stemmed red roses, picked up the dollar bill, and placed the roses in the boy's arms. "You're in luck, son. On Christmas Eve, we have a special on roses for young men who want to do something nice for their mothers. Merry Christmas!"

With a big smile on his face, the boy gathered his roses and walked proudly out of the store with his head held high. "Wait til mom sees these!"

May you find opportunity to bring joy this Christmas to someone who really needs it!

Whaddya Get?

I remember my favorite Christmas present. It was Christmas of 1990. We were planning to spend it with Kim's parents, brothers, and families in Tallahassee. I drove to Jacksonville to help lead the Christmas Eve service at our church. When I left early that afternoon, I saw the grandsons busily and happily engaged swinging from a T-bar between two big trees in grandpa's back yard. It was cold and the boys were wrapped up with coats, stocking caps, and gloves. I remember thinking to myself that those gloves might make it difficult to hang on to the bar while swinging.

When I finally returned late that evening, my headlights picked up a sight I hope I never see again. My father-in-law was pacing in the driveway. I knew something was wrong. I had never seen him so shaken.

The story spilled out. Our youngest son had taken his turn on the swing. While heading down the line, his grip had slipped. He fell twelve feet and landed on his neck. His grandfather raced over to him and found him not breathing. After a few moments, his chest began to rise and fall. An ambulance was summoned to take him to the hospital. He suffered a concussion and some bumps and bruises, but he was released with the proper cautionary instructions. All that had happened while I was away.

Christmas 1990 could have been a tragic memory for our family. We could have lost him. Our story had a happy ending. He was wearing a heavy coat and he fell on to a covering of leaves. His angle of impact was such that he didn't break his neck. That was a long night with him sleeping between us, both of us too concerned and frightened to close our eyes. When he got up for Christmas morning, he walked like Tim Conway playing an old man. He was sore, but he was alive.

What did I get? More than I deserve. I never take Christmas for granted. I wish all stories had happy endings. My heart breaks for those whose stories have turned out in different ways. This Christmas appreciate what and who you have.

Now What?

Now what? The week between Christmas and New Year's Day is a little strange. It's not that time stands still, but we do find ourselves somewhat stuck between the past and the future. The build-up to Christmas has dissolved. The presents have been opened (some already returned or exchanged). The bills are not due yet, for the most part. Only a few days remain to close accounts, make one last sale, ask for one more donation, take care of one last obligation before the calendar turns. School won't open for a few more days. So, now what do we do? How do we bring in a new year?

The end of any year should cause us to reflect. What surprised us last year? What broke our hearts? What have we learned about ourselves? Do we look forward to a new year with anticipation? Dread? Hope? Fear?

The end of any year should cause us to dream, to plan, to resolve. We know what happens to most New Year's resolutions. All you have to do is visit your local fitness center in January and then return 4-5 weeks later. How do we turn good intentions into reality, into action?

Jesus spoke to His followers about a plan that has a lot of merit: "Seek first the Kingdom of God and His righteousness and all these things will be added to you" (Matthew 6:33). With God the only audience that ever truly matters, let's plan to find ways to please and honor Him. "These things" refer to what we need to live full and meaningful lives.

Because of God's love for us and His interest in us, we can trust Him, Jesus said, to provide. Why not build our resolutions on the truth of God's Word? It's worth a try, don't you think?

Have You Got the Time?

Perhaps it was the wrong way to ask. A man approached a woman and asked, "Have you got the time?" The woman, evidently in a rush and not very polite, responded, "Yes," and kept walking. I guess he should have asked, "Would you give me the time?"

Both questions have interesting implications:

- Have you got the time? Time for what? We all know that time is the one thing that cannot be recovered. Once we have spent it, it's gone. Have you got the time to look at me, listen to me, share with me, endure with me, suffer with me, pray with me, rejoice with me, worship with me?

- Would you give me the time? Are you willing to invest in me? Can you allow me into your life? Is my presence in your life an interruption or an opportunity? Would you notice me, pay attention to me?

Okay, we have people who can be time thieves. They rob us, monopolizing our time for selfish reasons. We've all been guilty of that from time to time ourselves.

Time is precious, but can't we better stewards of it? Ask yourself: "Who gets my time?" "Who should get my time that doesn't?" If you measure how you distribute your time by how important you think you are, you may need a new measuring stick.

The Gospels are full of stories about Jesus dealing with interruptions. Seekers, ill people, children, outcasts, undesirables - all seemed to get the attention of Jesus when He could have spent His time some other way.

Dear God, don't let us miss the moment. Please don't allow us to abuse the gift of time.

You're kidding, right?

Apprentice angel to supervisor: "Hey, boss, I just heard the strangest rumor."

"What are you talking about?"

"Some of the other angels were whispering and I wonder what's going on."

"What did you hear?"

"I heard that there was a baby to be born soon."

"Did you miss orientation or what? That's how it's done down there. Babies are born every day."

"Yes sir, but this is supposed to be really unusual, and get this, the word is that the King is personally involved."

"The King is always involved when it comes to what happens on earth."

"Yes sir, but the story is that He is going to be that baby! How does that work?"

"Well, this is way above your pay grade but I'll give it try. When the Father gave humans the gift of free will, He made it possible for them to accept it or reject it. He knew that humanity would fall so He put His plan in place. Someone would have to take the penalty of their disobedience and rebellion. The King volunteered to be that someone."

"So He had to become one of them? Why couldn't He just send some of us to straighten out the mess that humans made?"

"It's not easy to understand but when you love someone like the Father loves those creatures, you are willing to make sacrifices. In this case, the greatest sacrifice anyone could imagine."

"Let me get this straight. The King becomes a baby, lives like a regular human, tries to show people how God feels about them, then is willing to lay down His life to save them?"

"Well, there's more to it, but that is really what is about to happen."

"You're kidding, right?"

Things I Learned from My Dad

As I got older, it seemed by Dad got smarter. Now at my advanced age I realize he was pretty smart all along. I just didn't get it at the time when I thought I knew everything. The truth has hit – the older I get the more I need to know.

Dads should be important in our lives as mentors and models. I was blessed to have one who did both well. I learned a few things.

- Anybody can complain; try to see the good in a situation and make it better.
- Keep smiling and singing; folks will think you're up to something.
- Give your kids the gift of showing love, honor, and respect to your wife.
- Time is precious; do the good, the fun, the meaningful now.
- When you're talking to a child, try listening more than you speak.
- When you're talking to a child, look him/her in the eye even if it means you do it on one knee.

- If it is important to your child, it should be important to you.
- If someone offers you a choice of 2 desserts, always say yes … to both.
- Never quit playing, even if your wife tells you to grow up.
- Sometimes the best response to what your wife says is just "yes, ma'am."
- Be proud of who you are, but don't be satisfied.
- You're human; you're going to mess it up sometimes. Admitting you made a mistake and asking for forgiveness teaches a powerful lesson.
- Read. Read. Read. Read for inspiration, knowledge, insight, and enjoyment.
- At some point you will be an embarrassment to your kids no matter how cool you think you are.
- Never let the important people in your life wonder about your love for them.
- Love the church; it's full of imperfect people, just like you.
- Love God knowing you can never match the love He has for you.
- Follow your call. Do what you were created to do.
- Spend your life well.
- Laugh, then laugh some more.

There were times when I took my father for granted, but I always considered him my hero. I wish I had told him more often. Happy Father's Day.

Respect Dads

Yeah, I know. Compared to Mother's Day, Father's Day is a single to a home run. Mother's Day ranks just below Christmas and Easter, in 2015 totaling 133 million cards (to 90 million for dads). People spent over $11 billion for moms, a little over $8 billion for dads. The president of the National Retail Federation said, "Dads tend to be more low-maintenance than mom. While moms love to receive luxury items such as jewelry or a trip to the spa, dads are happy with an afternoon barbecue or watching the ball game without distraction."

What about it guys? If that's not enough, check out these texts:

Teen: "What time are you picking me up?"

Dad: "Who is this?"

Teen: "Your son."

Dad: "How did you get this number?"

Teen: "I programmed your phone, remember?"

Dad: "How do I delete people?"

Mom: "Your father is driving me crazy. When are you coming home?"

Teen: "I'm out with friends so not til late."

Mom: "It's OK. I put Ambien in his tea. He won't be annoying me much longer."

Teen: "Hey!"

Dad: "Aren't you supposed to be at school?"

Teen: "Aren't you supposed to be at work?"

Dad: "Touché."

Teen: "Happy 49th, Dad! I love you so much!"

Dad: "It's 48! You ruined my day."

Mom: "Come downstairs and talk to me please."

Teen: "Isn't Dad there?"

Mom: "Yes, but I like you more."

Makes you feel all warm and fuzzy inside, right? Reminds me of Rodney Dangerfield: "I get no respect." Truth is, it's an honor to be a dad. While there are no perfect dads around, I can look around and see a great number of men who take their roles as fathers very seriously. My brothers and I were privileged to have a godly dad who provided a great example of how a husband should love his wife and a father should love his children. He's been gone twenty years and we still miss him. I'd love to pick up the phone and seek his counsel and wisdom. He was always there for me.

Father's Day might not be a big deal to everyone, but I hope that if you still have your dad, give him some respect, show him your love. If you are a dad, turn to your Father for wisdom. Love your kids, lead your kids, bless your kids. Happy Father's Day!

The Perfect Father

Like many of our people, I have been blessed by a rich heritage in my family. I've been fortunate to have godly men as grandfathers, father, and father-in-law. Now one of our sons is a dad. He's doing it right, as a man and as a husband. One of the best gifts he can give his kids is a godly marriage.

I don't know any perfect dads ... except one. When God chose to reveal Himself to us, He used the image of a father. When Jesus came, one of the most important invitations He offered was to encourage us to seek His Father; to address Him as Abba ... which is like the word some of us use when we talk to our dads. I never called mine 'Father' – it just didn't fit!

Father's Day is not an easy day for all of us. We've lost our dads or there is a strain in relationships or there is distance we can't seem to close. Perhaps this day is about grace or forgiveness or recommitment.

One little guy prayed, "I pray that my dad will be happily ever after." Another one said, "Sometimes I pray he'd be just like my mom when he grows up." One more: "When my dad goes to the flea market, I pray he wouldn't bring home fleas." I pray it's a time when we draw close to the only perfect Father you and I will ever know. Happy Father's Day.

A Reason for Honor

Father's Day, contrary to popular misconception, was not established as a holiday in order to help greeting card manufacturers sell more cards. In fact, when a "Father's Day" was first proposed, there were no Father's Day cards!

Mrs. John B. Dodd, of Washington, first proposed the idea of a "Father's Day" in 1909. Mrs. Dodd wanted a special day to honor her father, William Smart. William Smart, a Civil War veteran, was widowed when his wife (Mrs. Dodd's mother) died in childbirth with their sixth child. Mr. Smart was left to raise the newborn and his other five children by himself on a rural farm in eastern Washington state. It was after Mrs. Dodd became an adult that she realized the strength and selflessness her father had shown in raising his children as a single parent.

The first Father's Day was observed on June 19, 1910, in Spokane, Washington. At about the same time in various towns and cities across America, other people were beginning to celebrate a "Father's Day." In 1924 President Calvin Coolidge supported the idea of a national Father's Day. Finally, in 1966 President Lyndon Johnson signed a presidential proclamation declaring the third Sunday of June as Father's Day

Father's Day has become a day to not only honor your father, but all men who act as a father figure. Stepfathers, uncles, grandfathers and adult male friends are all to be honored on Father's Day.

In our broken world, we need strong fathers, solid male figures in our lives. As I reached adulthood, I was amazed that so many of my peers lacked that presence in their lives. It made me even more grateful for a legacy of men of faith and courage in my life. None were perfect, but they knew that. They also knew where to turn when their wisdom and strength fell short.

One of the "good guys" in Hollywood, actor James Stewart was a huge fan favorite. He came from a small town in Pennsylvania where his dad ran a hardware store. When storm clouds gathered over the US, Stewart answered the call to serve his country. Just before he left to pilot bombers and command a squadron, his father slipped a note in his son's pocket: "My dear Jim boy, soon after you read this letter you will be on your way to the worst sort of danger. I am banking on the enclosed copy of the 91st Psalm. The thing that takes the place of fear and worry is the promise of these words. I can say no more. I love you more that I can tell you. Dad."

Imagine that ... a father who relies on the Father. That's the way it I supposed to be. Open a Bible and read the psalmist's words.

Before Jimmy Stewart left to fight overseas with his bomber squadron, his father, an Indiana, Pennsylvania, hardware store owner and staunch Presbyterian, slipped a note into his son's pocket. The note read: "My dear Jim boy, Soon after you read this letter, you will be on your way to the worst sort of danger.... I am banking on the enclosed copy of the 91st Psalm. The thing that takes the place of fear and worry is the promise of these words.... I can say no more.... I love you more than I can tell you. Dad."

The 91st Psalm? Here are a few of the promises to which Jimmy Stewart's father referred:

Those who love me, I will deliver;
I will protect those who know my name.
When they call to me, I will answer them;
I will be with them in trouble,
I will rescue them and honor them.
With long life I will satisfy them
and show them my salvation.

Father's Day

Did it start in Grafton, West Virginia in 1908 or Spokane, Washington in 1910? Was it inspired by Anna Jarvis' crusade to honor mothers or dedicated to celebrate Civil War vet William Jackson Stuart's noble efforts to raise his six children as a single parent? You can find those who will suggest other origins. Does it really matter? The third Sunday in June was set aside to recognize the role of fathers. It took a while to catch on and some will say it never has.

In popular culture, it seems that a typical image of dad is the stumbling, bumbling, comic figure who is never quite on top of things. Fathers can be easy targets. Even in the 50's sit com, Father Knows Best, Robert Young's father figure need plenty of help solving the family problems in less than 30 minutes each week.

Parenting today is far from easy. With the pace of life, economic pressures, complexities of changing schedules, families have a difficult time finding respite, much less balance. One little boy was asked what he would give his dad for Father's Day. He responded, "I would give him his very own bike ... and the time to ride it." Or this youngster who said his Father's Day gift for dad would be a new watch "so he wouldn't come home so late."

Being a dad, being a parent is a sacred stewardship. None of us get it right all the time, but there are things we have to remember, priorities we have to live by. On my desk is the picture of a solitary boy standing on the beach, gazing over the water. Underneath the picture are these words: "A hundred years from now it will not matter what my bank account was, the sort of house I lived in, or the kind of car I drove ... but the world may be different because I was important in the life of a child."

Notes and Reflections

Printed in the USA
CPSIA information can be obtained
at www.ICGtesting.com
JSHW011550031024
70793JS00003B/4